FV.

St. Louis Community College

Forest Park
Florissant Valley
Meramec

Instructional Resources
St. Louis, Missouri

Call Me
Lesbian

Call Me Lesbian

Lesbian Lives, Lesbian Theory

■

Julia Penelope

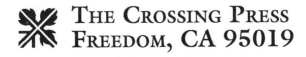

THE CROSSING PRESS
FREEDOM, CA 95019

Cover design and illustration by AnneMarie Arnold

Printed in the U.S.A.

Library of Congress Cataloging-in-Publication Data

Penelope, Julia, 1941-
    Call Me Lesbian: lesbian lives, lesbian theory /Julia Penelope.
        p. cm.
    Includes bibliographical references
    ISBN 0-89594-497-9 (cloth). - - ISBN 0-89594-496-0 (paper)
    1. Lesbianism- -United States. 2. Gays--United States- -Identity.
    I. Title.
HQ75.6.U5P46 1992
305.48'9664--dc20   91-37914
                                                                CIP

ACKNOWLEDGMENTS

The ideas and analyses developed in this sampling of my essays owes much to the thinking of many other Lesbians, some published, some not, but too many for me to name here individually. At the risk of omitting someone whose name should be here, I want to thank Debbie Alicen, Alix Dobkin, Maxine Feldman, Marilyn Frye, Anne Leighton, Kate Moran, Kathy Munzer, Marilyn Murphy, Merril Mushroom, Sarah Valentine, and Irene Weiss for good talks and good times; the members of my incest survivors' groups in Lincoln, Nebraska and St. Louis, Missouri; the Schlesinger Library at Radcliffe College for having me as an Honorary Visiting Scholar in 1990-91, where I did much of the research for "Does It Take One to Know One?," and to the helpful and knowledgeable librarians at the Schlesinger and other Harvard Libraries; the collective and volunteers of the Lesbian Herstory Archives, especially Judith Schwarz and Joan Nestle; and all my Lesbian audiences for their thoughtful questions. I also want to thank Mary Stockton of Crones' Harvest in Jamaica Plain, Massachusetts and the collective that produces the annual W.I.T.C.H. Series for creating and maintaining spaces where I could present the original versions of unpublished essays.

Every essay has been extensively revised, including those previously published, and the versions published here owe much of their improvement to the comments and suggestions of Sarah Lucia Hoagland and Melinda Storch, my editor at The Crossing Press, both of whom spent hours with me on the telephone. I'm especially grateful to Melinda for her patience and caring when I faltered, and to Elaine Goldman Gill of The Crossing Press for her support and encouragement of this and other projects. In spite of all the help I've received at every stage in the preparation of these essays, all errors of commission and omission are mine alone.

"Whose Past are We Reclaiming?" is a revised version of an article that first appeared in *Common Lives/Lesbian Lives* 13 (Autumn 1984), 16-35.

Different versions of "Does it Take One to Know One?" were delivered at the Lesbian and Gay Conference at Beloit College in April, 1991, and as part of the Visiting Scholar Colloquium Series at the Schlesinger Library, May 2, 1991.

"The Lesbian Perspective" was originally published in *Lesbian Philosophies and Cultures*, edited by Jeffner Allen (Albany: SUNY Press, 1990). The published version benefited from the helpful comments of Lesbians in audiences at the University of Illinois-Champaign/Urbana, Southern Illinois University-Edwardsville, Washington University, the Building Community Conference held in Portland, Oregon (November, 1986), and in Cleveland, Ohio. I want to thank those Lesbians for their valuable suggestions, and Joyce Trebilcot for urging me to talk about Lesbian consensus reality.

"Wimmin- and Lesbian-Only Spaces: Thought into Action" first appeared in *off our backs* XX, 5 (May, 1990), 14-16.

"Do We Mean What We Say? Horizontal Hostility and the World We Would

Create" was first read at Crones' Harvest in Jamaica Plain, Massachusetts; the version published here owes much to the audience's questions and comments during the discussion that followed.

"Heteropatriarchal Semantics and Lesbian Identity: The Ways a Lesbian Can Be" was originally published In *Lesbian Ethics* 2, 2 (Fall, 1986), 58-80, as an effort to sort out responses to Linda Strega's article and the responses to it of Paula Mariedaughter and Mary Crane. I'm grateful to Jeanette Silveira for creating a journal where that discussion could take place, to Linda Strega and Bev Jo for their support, encouragement, and critical comments on an early version of this essay. I've revised it, deleting most of my references to Linda Strega's initiating article and the responses to Strega by Paula Mariedaughter and Mary Crane, in order to focus more clearly on my analysis of language and behavior.

"The Lesbian New-Rotics: Bogus or Breakthrough?" was first read as part of the 1991 W.I.T.C.H. Lecture Series at Crone's Harvest in Jamaica Plain, Massachusetts, February 26, 1991.

"Controlling Interests, Consuming Passions: Sexual Metaphors" was first read at the conference on "Feminism Sexuality and Power" at Mt. Holyoke College, Oct. 25-30, 1986. Although I've thought about the questions I raise here for several years, the development of my own ideas about Lesbian sexuality owes much to discussions with many friends over the years, among them: Sarah Valentine, Kate Moran, Debbie Alicen, Beth Binhammer, Ellenora Ward, and the members of my incest survivors' groups in Lincoln, Nebraska and St. Louis, Missouri. A portion of this essay appeared in *Lesbian Ethics* 2, 3 (Summer, 1987), 84-94, with the title, "The Illusion of Control: Sado-masochism and the Sexual Metaphors of Childhood."

"Killing Us Softly: A Murder Mystery" was originally read at a meeting of the Midwest Women's Studies Association held in St. Louis, Missouri, April, 1987.

This book is dedicated to all my Lesbian friends—
near, far, and in-between—
who keep me moving.

Table of Contents

Introduction

Lesbian identities, lesbian perspective, lesbian issues, lesbian oppression, oppressiveness, lesbian sexuality, lesbian herstory, language, lesbian space, lesbian politics... do you have a minute? How about a lifetime? With *Call Me Lesbian* Julia Penelope offers us nine provocative essays reflecting on many u.s. lesbian practices. This is a passionately engaged work, full of complexity and challenges.

Is there a lesbian consensus reality? Well, yes and no. Can we trust our feelings? Well, yes and no. Can we reclaim words from a heteropatriarchal context? Well, yes and no. Is feminism useful to us? Well, yes and no. Can we claim lesbian identities and identify a lesbian perspective? Well, yes.

The questions Julia raises are located in experience, her experience. And the answers she offers resist neat categories. They involve ambiguity, even contradiction when approached from a linear framework (a veritable postmodernist delight); but from a deeply engaged framework, one receptive to the contexts of the questions themselves, her answers direct themselves to lived lesbian lives.

Are there features of perceiving the world which simply *are* part of lesbian existence? Yes, says Julia. For one thing, our perceptions of women. Women, or lesbians, become our focus in a way not conceived in heteropatriarchy. A second feature involves our sense of difference ("There was something I sensed, even as a child."). To conceive of ourselves we must challenge conventional knowledge at some level, particularly knowledge that renders us non-existent. A third feature is our "bad attitude," the means by which we cross a boundary between the known, that is safe-because-familiar, and the dangerous, that is unknown.

In other words, the lesbian perspective originates through denial and resistance, through a sense of difference. It expresses itself by way of saying "No" to perceived coercion. Thus, argues Julia, the lesbian perspective is born of, encourages, and even demands deviant and unpopular thinking. There are no givens for us beyond being deviant.

Nevertheless the process of identifying ourselves as lesbians allows us to reinterpret many events. Things appear differently from a lesbian perspective than they do from a heterosexual perspective. As a result, the lesbian perspective holds the possibility of "furious self-creation." These essays examine many of our efforts toward self-creation and are themselves charts of known-but-dangerous waters. In fact they challenge us about what we think safe and what dangerous, mostly by considering structures of heteropatriarchy through the strictures of its language.

Does the fact that there is a lesbian perspective mean there is a lesbian consensus reality? Yes and no. Yes in that there is a perspective, a starting point of denial and resistance. But no, in that beyond this we are not in agreement about the values we adopt, as Julia discusses throughout these essays. What is the point of a lesbian consensus reality? In a word, our survival.

In coming out we negate the reality that negates us. But here begins the complexity. How do we choose to deal with the defining categories of male cultures. Do we work to place ourselves within these boundaries, do we remain at the periphery, do we work to create our own context? Do we try to fit ourselves into heteropatriarchal values, accept heteropatriarchal meaning because known and hence familiar and safe—that is, predictable? Or do we reject them, denying the essentialism of heterosexual dualism (which is really a monism) and the value that woman is for man, but also risking the total loss of meaning for lack of a language that does not reflect that essentialism? This is no idle fear—it finds its way even into the hearts of separatists.

Because of the different ways we place ourselves and are placed in relation to heteropatriarchal values, argues Julia, while there is a lesbian perspective, there is no lesbian consensus reality. Now if this is so, is there a definition of 'lesbian', and are there lesbian identities? No, and of course.

In discussing her own coming out, Julia tells us of her pain and confusion. She knew she loved women, but because of what society said about *who* loves women, she thought as a child that she must be a man. For my own part, as a child I always had one best girlfriend about whom I was passionately jealous. I also hated adult women (my mother's friends), from at least 6, because they behaved so stupidly around men, and then tried to tell me what to do, especially with their stupid manners. I didn't believe I was a man, but I knew I wasn't a woman. Yet Julia knew she was a lesbian from childhood. I came out as a result of the possibilities of female connection created by the women's liberation movement.

Who is lesbian? And when is she a lesbian? In fact, is a single definition of what it means to be a lesbian possible? A good portion of the differences in coming out between Julia and me are class related. A single definition will provide no basis for an understanding of that.

One common definition is a sexual one. But Julia points out, for example, some lesbians are celibate and some were once married and bore children. Some are still hidden in marriages. On the other hand, some straight women have lesbian attractions, even affairs. This does not make them lesbians. A sexual definition is reductionist.

While there certainly are lesbian identities, Julia argues, no single definition of what it means to be a lesbian is possible. Our lesbian identities emerge from the particular experiences we face, from our backgrounds and from when and how we finally come out; so a definition of what it means to be a lesbian will serve only academic classifiers and heteropatriarchy, but not us. Such a definition will rob us of what we need: the particular information about each others' lives (gossip)—how we survive, what we compromise, how we emerge, what we lose of our selves, our successes—all matters that are quite different for each lesbian's life.

If there is complexity in the questions of perspective, consensus reality and definition, there is ambiguity, even contradiction, in the question of trusting our feelings. Can we trust them? Well, it's our feelings that tell us we love lesbians. But as Julia illustrates over and over, we must constantly ask where our feelings come from. For even our deepest feelings don't exist in a vacuum: we have internalized patriarchal descriptions of who and what we are. And our internal responses are often located in our herstories. Some feelings simply are patriarchal scripts and some are out of context: everything we know and feel safe with needs questioning. On the other hand, heteropatriarchy makes it easy to disbelieve in the integrity of our feelings. Too often our desires for each other and our memories of violence done us are gaslighted.

Questioning our feelings involves risks. Acknowledging our lesbian identity also involves risks. And here is the contradiction: we are having to question the very sources (our feelings) of our ability to come out as lesbians (we both must and cannot trust our feelings). Yet this contradiction resolves itself into complexity when we think of contexts. For coming out as a lesbian and acknowledging the lesbian perspective allows us to evaluate our feelings and experiences and take the risks of change. What does it mean, asks Julia, to think not as a lesbian in a heteropatriarchal context but as a lesbian in a lesbian context? The flip phrase, "politically incorrect," served to relieve some of the pressures we were putting on ourselves and each other, but it has also done our efforts toward trying to develop non-oppressive values a disservice.

The question of context raises the question of language which involves even greater complexity and ambiguity, particularly concerning the matter of claiming words. Language is not neutral, argues Julia, is not a simple "conductor" of ideas and information from one mind to another. Language constructs a reality, and words gain their life within social context. Now if one is operating from a lesbian perspective, a perspective of denial and resistance, the question of which words we can claim from a heteropatriarchal context is significant.

Which words can we claim as lesbians? Lesbian? Dyke? Feminine? Erotic? Sadomasochism? Virgin? Cunt? Witch? Hag? Woman? The attempt to claim words is the attempt to change the dominant shape of reality. For example, claiming 'hag' involves changing the valuation of old women: going back to middle and old english meanings and revaluing them, reclaiming, actually, an old meaning from a time when old women (particularly old peasant women) were respected in their communities in europe.

The effort to claim 'erotic' is an attempt to claim a sexuality for ourselves, outside the heteropatriarchal framework. And yet Julia challenges this particular effort. She argues that words which have a positive valuation in heteropatriarchy are not going to successfully transfer to a lesbian context. On the other hand, some words which may have a surface appearance of negative valuation in heteropatriarchy such as 'sadomasochism' may still not successfully transfer, in this case because 'sadomasochism' requires the importation of a heteropatriarchal context to get its charge. Other words may limit our imaginations. What would it be like to identify ourselves beyond the category 'woman'? What would it be like to instead regard the basic human female category as 'lesbian'?

Context is the key. And it is central to the question of consensus reality. As lesbians, are we trying to make meaning inside or outside a heteropatriarchal context? As we discuss our use of words like 'cunt' or 'virgin' are we invoking heteropatriarchy or a lesbian-centered reality?

The question of language has occupied Julia's entire career, is her most precious gift to us. She argues that our early experiences with language encourage us to believe there is a single reality (which keeps us from believing we can develop other contexts and so other meanings). She challenges the idea that words exist in a simple one-to-one correspondence to reality. She suggests that our experiences become meaningful only when we gather them within the limits of language. She shows us how language reflects values and determines the limits of our thinking at times. She challenges us to examine the context of the words we use. She shows us how certain tricks in language such as name-calling contribute to our horizontal hostility, and how others, such as the use of psych-predicates, perpetuate our feelings of victimization. And she raises questions of class. In fact, far from the early '70s challenge that attention to language is classist, Julia makes connections between classism and language use. She thus challenges the lesbian temptation to dismiss questions of language as "just" a problem of semantics. She shows us that sticks and stones may break our bones, but words can kill our spirits.

Perhaps the issue with the most ambiguity and contradictions for Julia is the question of feminism. She, like many lesbians, rejected feminism during the '80s. But let a heterosexual woman go too far—defining feminism in terms of heteropatriarchal values, declaring it dead, and blaming her disappointment on radical feminism—and Julia is right back in the ring, snarling and snapping and generally reclaiming feminism.

What is the value/need/use of feminism for lesbians? The prior question, of course, is what does feminism mean? So much of it has to do with heterosexual women trying to get a better deal with men. That is, when we participate in events named "feminist," including women's studies, what we all too often find is a focus on how heterosexual women can get on better with men, rather than a focus on women's oppression as well as women's strength and resistance. Lived and practiced feminism has been a constant source of pain for so many lesbians because of heterosexual women's continued loyalty to men and because of feminism's failed promise of friendship among women—even among those of similar backgrounds, not to mention across class and race.

And yet, Julia argues, we lesbians need analysis for our lives. While early feminist analysis may have trivialized significant aspects of lesbian existence, Julia notes, the kernels of truth embedded in radical feminist analysis can give us ways of deeply examining our lives and the values we carry in them. We lesbians have internalized heteropatriarchal values and so keep bringing them into lesbian space— "the pig in the head," we used to call it—and we need an analysis that helps us sort them out. That a particular thing feels good, that it feels familiar and so secure, that it has meaning for us, that we do it, is not enough. How we think and frame our understanding of ourselves and others makes a big difference. How we understand our herstories is important. And whether we believe change is possible (and desirable!) matters. The close-in, microscopic perspective contains important information for us. But we also need the macroscopic, distant view that radical feminism (of the going-to-the-root variety) offers. It is in the interplay between the two (through which surface all the ambiguity, complexity and even contradiction of our lives) that we gain perspective.

And here is the value of Julia's writing. The ideas develop out of her particular experience and reflect back on it. Those who remain outside (objective) are in no better position than those who remain immersed in the particular (subjective). It is in the play, the movement—out to theory and back to practice and out to theory again—that ambiguity and contradiction become first apparent and then resolve themselves into complexity and richness.

And so, Julia argues, a lesbian movement outside the framework of radical feminism (of the going-to-the-root variety) cannot succeed. This is a significant claim for a life-long lesbian who did not come out because of the possibilities of the women's liberation movement, but emerged on the streets of Miami long before. Julia urges us to celebrate ourselves, but also challenges us to change. After all, coming out is about risk, and as a result, change. Radical feminism is about change, and as a result, risk.

Lesbianism is a political category because of what 'woman' means (at least in american-anglo-european industrialized society) but (at least so far) it is not a political analysis. And this brings us to the complexity, even contradiction, of the lesbian perspective. After all, if the lesbian perspective is, at its heart, being deviant, then at first we're deviant from patriarchy, but then we turn right around and are deviant from that deviancy and wind up cutting off our noses, not to mention our stomachs, hips, hearts, even brains, to spite ourselves. If being deviant is central to the lesbian perspective in heteropatriarchy, then the possibility of putting our hearts into truly creating new value can seem a threat—it goes against what we have relied upon to survive. (Again, we must question everything.) It's so much safer (more predictable) to remain on the periphery of anything than to take the risk of constructing something new and then to stick with it, developing it as we challenge, argue with, and disagree with each other.

We need the lesbian perspective to initiate the creation of new value but we need the feminist analysis to guide the rejection of patriarchal structures. Lesbianism may not be a political analysis. It is, however, an identity we can choose to claim, an identity with profound possibilities (particularly the possibility of challenging american-anglo-european ideas of difference as a threat together with heterosexual dualism).

Questions of change are crucial for us, for our survival in a world that wishes us disappeared, because our existence calls into question their comfortableness with their own coerced framework. Questions of hope are even more crucial. With the failure (to date) of feminism to succeed in promoting loyalty and love among women and with the grip on patriarchal values so many lesbians have for fear of loss of meaning, are there grounds for hope or is the heteropatriarchy simply too capable?

Well, two avenues we are pursuing as lesbians challenge heteropatriarchal hegemony: breaking the silence and breaking the isolation. In speaking out about incest, about sexual harassment, about rape, about battering, about ritual abuse, about what men have done and about ways we carry the violence into ourselves, in Julia's case about incest and about the effects of claiming a "butch" identity, we are breaking the silence heteropatriarchy needs to pass its values on to the next generation as normal and without a glitch.[1] Breaking the silence means we undergo deep and significant changes: claiming our past, learning to touch, changing our sense of safety, working to understand each other, and perhaps, most important, being willing to persist through all the errors and failures.

Breaking isolation means remembering our work is about loving each other. It involves focusing on each other and giving sustenance to the lesbian perspective. Even with our bitter arguments we keep breaking the isolation. It is when we withdraw permanently from lesbian community-building that we declare patriarchy supreme. Through our arguments and disagreements, we focus on each other and thereby call lesbian community into existence. Thus, breaking the isolation means being present to each other. When we fail to be present to each other, Julia argues, we invalidate lesbianism.

In other words, breaking the isolation involves changing our idea of community. Certainly Julia has changed her idea of community.[2] If we think community is something we come to to be "safe," we will leave it when we find it is not, thereby contributing to its apparent unsafety.[3] If we think it is something that exists all set, requiring no constructive work from us, we will read its structures and institutions from an assumed position of powerlessness. If we think it is a place in which we have common values, we will fail to engage with each other beyond initial identification and will treat difference as a threat. If we think it is a place of rules and definitions, we will cast differences in terms of hierarchy. If we think community is a place where we can find respect, we need to think carefully about what respect means. Respect does not mean agreement, necessarily: respect means taking each other seriously. And in focusing on each other, we are doing just that. We come to community as lesbians to create lesbian values with other lesbians who are quite different. Community is our possibilities. (And this indicates the seriousness of the hypocrisy of those who use lesbian-only or women-only space to try to undermine it: such use denies our possibilities, denies they even exist.

In breaking the silence and breaking the isolation, we participate in our own creation. Julia's passionate challenges to lesbian signs and practices is fueled by her life long commitment to lesbians. Do we have a minute? Do we have a lesbian lifetime? Yes, as a matter of fact, we do.

Sarah Lucia Hoagland
August, 1991, Chicago, Illinois

Footnotes

1. In her current concert, Alix Dobkin makes this point, and it gave me pause because I realized how cynical (de-moralized) I had become about our lesbian moving and I remembered that despite the increase of right-wing thinking, we have been doing a tremendous amount of important work.

2. In "Lesbian Relationships and the Vision of Community," (*Feminary* 9, no. 1 (Spring 1978) Julia distinguished between community and subculture in part by identifying community as something one joins because of a commitment to common ideals. And she suggested that while we have a subculture, we do not yet have community.

3. One of the concerns we express in dealing with various oppressions in community is that those with privilege can simply withdraw, leaving the rest more exposed and hence less safe than before the collective effort began.

<u>Whose</u> Past
Are We Reclaiming?

O ver the past two decades, those of us involved in women's, Lesbian, or gay liberation have grown accustomed to hearing about words like *Dyke* being "reclaimed" from the heteropatriarchal context, and equally accustomed to the rhetoric that argues for such "reclamations." Since the late 1970s, Lesbians have heard much about the desirability of "reclaiming" the labels *butch* and *femme* and the role behaviors associated with them.[1] However, unlike the word *Dyke*, which was an intense pejorative for Lesbians in the 1950s and '60s, those labels bring in their wake specific modes of relating among Lesbians and ways of identifying and comporting ourselves in the world that some of us have abandoned (with relief). The relationships signified by the labels *butch* and *femme* are now being romanticized, especially those of "femmes." I hope that Lesbians thinking about identifying themselves as "butch" or "femme" will take into consideration what I have to say about how I understood the labels when I was first coming out and how my adoption of the "butch" role and its behaviors affected me. When other Lesbians say they're "reclaiming" *butch* and *femme*, they're "reclaiming" attitudes and behaviors whose effects I am still struggling with. I cannot remain silent about my own experience as a "butch" and the damage that role caused.

Much of the current rhetoric about role-playing among Lesbians reveals confusion about the labels *butch* and *femme*, how they should be applied and to whom, and the nature of the roles themselves. It may help to know, for instance, that the desirability of declaring oneself "butch" or "femme" back in the '50s and '60s was not a simple, noncontroversial issue. I remember Lesbians with whom I associated who looked down on those of us who relied on roles to define ourselves and our relationships, and I knew that there were Lesbians who wouldn't consider having a relationship with me because I identified as a "butch." More than one Lesbian told me, to my face: "If I wanted a man, I'd go out and get a *real* one. Who wants a bad imitation? I like women." As far as I know, there have always been Lesbians who attacked roles and disapproved of other Lesbians who were "into" them; there were those who felt comfortable with roles and defended them; and there were those who didn't care one way or another.

Even within the framework of the roles there was a lot of variation, and many Lesbians switched back and forth (for example, the descriptions published by Merril Mushroom[2]) depending on who they were lovers with at the time. If they were attracted to a Lesbian who was a femme, they were butch; if they were sleeping with a butch, they were femme. Then, as now, the sexual behavior of individual Lesbians depended on who they were attracted to and who they were sleeping with. We referred to such Lesbians as *ki-ki*, *bluffs* (a blend of *butch + fluff*), or *switch-hitters* (also used then, as now, to refer to bisexuals). The label *butch* covered a spectrum of social and sexual behaviors (not always both) and several different terms specified the type of "butch."

Along a continuum of "masculinity," one could find a suitable term for herself, ranging from *femmy butch*, just plain *butch, dyke, bull-dyke/bull-dagger, diesel dyke, truck driver, Mack truck driver*, to the *stompin' diesel dyke* and the *rompin', stompin' diesel dyke*, with whom nobody wanted to mess. (Although these terms were all in use in the '50s, hardly anyone that I knew would've called herself by any name other than *butch*. The rest of the terms were usually used of someone else in a pejorative sense, and most of us were insulted if anyone called us a "dyke" or a "bull-dyke." Few of us wanted to be perceived as "too masculine.") If there were similar variations among femmes, and terms to name them, I was unaware of them (with the exception of *butchy femme*).

I realize as I say this that my lack of information about femmes in those days was caused by my adherence to the social behaviors the roles proscribed. We were separated from each other; our "community" was fragmented by the assumptions we learned with the roles we adopted. I didn't have any femme friends that I can remember, and I know that I had a lot of butch friends. We hung out together, protected and defended each other, consoled each other over failed relationships, and complained about the femmes, who were only of interest to us if we wanted to sleep with them. If I weren't sexually attracted to a femme, there didn't seem to be any reason why I should bother getting to know her. Of course, if anyone'd asked me back then if I were only interested in femmes for sexual reasons, I'd've loudly denied the accusation. (Does any of this sound familiar?)

I say all of this because there's nothing really new in the current wave of justification for reverting to the roles. None of the issues have changed, none of the problems have disappeared; we're just going around and around with the same old stuff. The boundaries weren't clear then and they aren't clear now. I don't think they ever will be. Each Lesbian seems to have her own understanding of what a role is and how it "fits" or doesn't "fit" her behavior, and I see no reason for expecting agreement on this. In fact, I think it's a pseudo-issue, like "monogamy"/ "nonmonogamy"—one that diverts our attention from important issues (like the prejudices we practice based on weight, height, race, age, ethnic and class backgrounds, none of which we've dealt with adequately). As nearly as I can tell, each Lesbian does what she wants to do or is capable of doing sexually, and the rest be damned. From my experiences, the range of sexuality was so diverse then as to make the terms *butch* and *femme* virtually meaningless; it still is.

The impulse to revive the labels *butch* and *femme* and inject some political respectability into their usage (however belatedly) by talking about "gut feelings," "intuitions," and "power" is the Lesbian manifestation of the contemporary rightwing backlash, further encouraged by '50s nostalgia ("Happy Days"), and the illusion of security we get by going back to what some imagine to have been "better days," (usually because they didn't have to live through them), and talking about "reclaiming our heritage." Honoring our past, however, doesn't necessitate elaborate justifications or incorporation into our present lives.

There's a difference between writing history and rewriting it, between documenting and romanticizing, and I don't think we know the difference yet. We call our present our "heritage," as though it were behind us; we say we're going "back" to our past to reclaim what we want to preserve for our future, and end up with no clear sense of our present. Let's admit, for starters, that there are millions of Lesbians still alive who never once considered abandoning role-playing. Most of them never heard that roles were declared "politically incorrect" in the early '70s, and those who did hear the noise went right on doing what they were doing. The only Lesbians who considered role-playing an "issue" were Lesbian-Feminists, a more visible minority of the mostly invisible Lesbian minority. But here we are, glibly talking about "reclaiming our past" when many of us aren't even dead yet! *Whose* past are we "reclaiming"?

When I began to hear in the late 1970s that other Lesbians were starting to call themselves "butch" and "femme" again, I was surprised. But after I thought about it, the reversion made its own kind of sense. I, too, have sometimes thought about how nice it'd be just to put aside everything I've believed since 1972 and go back to calling myself "butch." Those were the times when I was really confused, discouraged, or tired of being alone, when I felt I couldn't live another day without a label (an "identity," if you will). Something that would make my attempted relationships with other Lesbians more structured and less murky, less scary. At least, I would think to myself, as a butch I knew where I stood and what was expected of me; I knew how to act and what to do in specific situations. When I was a butch, I didn't feel at a loss about how to approach a Lesbian I was attracted to; I knew how to go about getting to know other Lesbians. I've imagined more than once how easy it'd be to go to a bar as a butch once again and pick up another Lesbian. (This was all yearning on my part, you understand, for a simpler way of relating to other Lesbians, because I was never very good at "picking up" other Lesbians even when I was a butch! So "going back" was a fantasy constructed out of exhaustion.)

Yes, the roles provided me with a structure for relating to other Lesbians and helped me through some of the initial awkwardness of meeting Lesbians, because I could identify my personal desires and preferred ways of relating sexually. But I recognize that the very easiness of slipping into those roles is a trap for me, and it's one I need to remain wary of. I think Lesbians must continue to question where our "gut feelings" come from, what needs they serve, and the political significance of our willingness to act on such feelings. I don't think we can pick and choose as we will from the heteropatriarchy's myths about Lesbian sexuality without a coherent ideological framework and the values and ethics such a framework suggests. I think each of us must take responsibility for what she chooses to claim or "reclaim" for herself; choices made without critical examination are, I believe, suspect, because every choice we make, every label we use to identify ourselves, carries with it its own limitations for our behavior and reflects the values we've committed ourselves to. To assert that our choices don't have limitations is ridiculous, and to believe that we make choices without value judgments is absurd. Going around saying that we shouldn't be making value judgments is a value judgment itself. We were smart enough to see through the heterosexual sham. Surely we can stop deluding ourselves.

Just because a Lesbian happens to be doing whatever it is, whether it's being a "butch" or a "femme," or being "into" sado-masochism, or being "monogamous" or "nonmonogamous," doesn't mean that it's OK, or that all the rest of us have to validate it or support it. It's past time, I think, for us to admit that we don't share a common framework for making our most important decisions—those having to do with our sexual and emotional relationships—and to face the fact that we're going to disagree about our basic values. Trying to "explain" our choices to each other, or constructing justifications for our preferred behaviors really isn't necessary. Lesbians who think that other Lesbians should condone their choices, or even copy them, once we've been told "how it really is," assume that the rest of us are stupid, that somehow we haven't seen "the way and the true light." They assume that if we disapprove of their decision to call themselves "butch" or "femme" it's because we don't understand about roles and, furthermore, that we don't know what we're talking about. Well, I do. I was there in the '50s and '60s. I was a butch, but I'm not now, and I have no intention of going back to that framework as a way of defining myself and who I am in my relationships.

These days, many Lesbians seem to want to quit, or to back up, or to retire from the processes of change, to stop asking themselves questions about why they feel the way they do and where those feelings come from. I think many of us are just tired. I understand the desire to stop changing; I often feel that way. I know from my own experience that change isn't just "hard"; it's frustrating, frightening, and, too often, not even particularly rewarding—immediately. It's an uncertain process, especially when I don't have a clear idea of how to go about it or what my goals are, if there are any. Sometimes I'm not aware that I'm changing until I'm well into it, and then I look forward to those short-lived resting places I call "plateaus," the times between the unsettling anxiety of changes, when I think, "Ah-ha, maybe this is who I've been becoming. Now I know who I am—at last!" But those serene, self-confident times never seem to last long enough, and I find myself asking new questions about what I want, who I am, why I do some things but not others, and I'm changing once more. I do know that, for me, there's no such thing as no change, and I believe that, as Lesbians, instead of using our energies trying to transform what we've learned from heteropatriarchal cultures, trying to squeeze ourselves into their framework or bending it until it feels comfortable for us, we should be actively unlearning what we've been taught by heterosexuals, and busy transforming ourselves. It's simply presumptuous for any of us to assume that any knowledge we have is untainted or that we can haphazardly pick and choose what we want from the heteropatriarchy's menu without severe repercussions in our lives. Everything we believe, we've learned from the heteropatriarchy—every single bit of it. We have no experience to call our "own," because, from the day we're born, our experiences were described for us by heterosexuals, starting with our parents. It's not enough to assert, "this is how I feel," as though that explains everything. Sure, we all have our feelings, but if we stop asking where those feelings are coming from, we'll continue to recycle issues that aren't our issues, in which case we should concede that Lesbianism is a "bedroom issue."[3]

If there's one thing most Lesbians have in common, it's the ability to say "no" to coercion. Tell one of us *not* to do something, and she'll turn right around and do it. That's the essence of the Lesbian. Our first "no" was to the privileges and rewards of heterosexuality, and we took it from there. Even those of us who do want to feel as if we belong or fit somewhere want to have it on our own terms or not at all.

I've called myself a lot of things in my life, for example. I'm not equally proud of all the labels I've chosen, but I won't deny them, either. I was raised a Republican in the Democratic South because my family hated racism and the corruption of southern Democrats; at sixteen I fancied myself a beatnik and an existentialist; at seventeen I called myself a Leninist, in the conservative 1950s; at eighteen I decided I was an Ayn Randian objectivist[4]; by the time I was twenty-four and living in New York City in the early 1960s, I was registered as a Libertarian Conservative, in spite of the ridicule of my closest friends, all socialists or Communists. (Or, maybe, because of their ridicule.) Radicalized by the fervor of my students at the University of Georgia in 1969, I became active in gay liberation and then became a Feminist in 1972.[5] In December, 1973, I began to identify myself as a separatist and, although I've also called myself a radical Feminist or a Lesbian-Feminist since then, I've remained steadfastly committed to separatism and the political analysis the term specifies.[6] In 1982, I stopped calling myself a "Feminist" of any sort.[7]

Through all of the political shifts marked by my adoption of one label and the rejection of another, right up until I began to grasp the significance of early [second wave] Feminism for me, I was, and called myself, a "stone butch." Unlike terms such as *diesel dyke*, *bull-dyke*, and *truck driver*, names connected with one's height, weight, width, and manner of dress (i.e., looks), *stone butch* was a term that did clearly designate the range of a Lesbian's sexual activities. A "stone butch" did not allow her lovers to touch her, whether it was a one-night stand or a three-year relationship (and, if she did, she never admitted it!). I was a stone butch from the age of sixteen until I was thirty-one. For fifteen years of my life as a Lesbian, I refused to let another Lesbian make love to me, with the exception of one lover who threatened to end our relationship if I didn't allow her to make love to me. I wasn't always content with remaining a stone butch, but I had what seemed to me then to be excellent reasons for not allowing other Lesbians to make love to me; it is those reasons I want to talk about, because it is my understanding of what I protected by calling myself a stone butch that underlies my opposition to Lesbians who wish to "reclaim" roles for themselves.

After mooning around after countless other adolescent girls, whose mothers always forbade them to associate with me, I managed, with the help of a gay teacher, to become sexually involved with another woman. We were lovers for almost three years, from tenth grade through the spring of our senior year. In all that time, I never let her make love to me. In fact, I almost always contrived to keep my clothes on because I was ashamed of my body. I thought I was fat and ugly, hence, undesirable and unattractive. Now, I have no way of explaining how I convinced myself that she (and other women) weren't perfectly aware of what my body looked like, but I believed that clothes somehow hid my body or made it not so hideous to someone else's eyes. I felt "safe" as long as my body was covered.

During this time, I constructed various theories to explain my desire for women in a world that clearly told me that only men loved women, that only men could have sex with women, that only men could marry women. The theory I regarded as the most satisfying combined my belief in reincarnation with the recently announced sex-change operation of Christine Jorgenson (which I'd read about in *Confidential*, a slick 1950s magazine similar in tone and content to *The National Enquirer*). I decided that something I'd done in a past life (my karma) had dictated that I would spend my life as a male soul "trapped" in a female body, as punishment for some transgression. This theory helped to explain my feelings in early childhood when I believed that some mistake had been made along the way, that I'd certainly been meant to be a boy and someone had slipped up when the bodies were being passed out. I believed I was "really" a man. Like Rachel Brody (*Common Lives/Lesbian Lives* 12 [Spring 1984]), I was uncomfortable with my femaleness (at least what I was told I was supposed to be as a "female") because I couldn't accept the weakness, passivity, and powerlessness that such "femaleness" required.

Since I refused to be "female," as I understood it, I concluded that I had to be "male." As a result of this belief, my fantasies about my life with my adolescent lover focused on both of us moving to a large city (usually Greenwich Village, where many of the Lesbian novels I read were set) where no one knew either of us, and I would wear men's clothes and pass as a man. In that way, I reasoned, we could be married and "live happily ever after." But I also knew, from reading those early Lesbian novels, that there was such a thing as a Lesbian, a woman who loved other women, that I was a Lesbian, and that there were other Lesbians "out there" if only I could find them. Somehow, I held this information comfortably (I think) alongside my belief that I was a man "inside." However I looked at my situation or tried to explain it, I did love women; I was sexually and emotionally attracted to women, and only to women. (My "heterosexual phase" lasted maybe three seconds, no more.)

So I went about finding other Lesbians. There was, for example, a handsome woman who drove a lunch truck out to the factories every day at 2:00 p.m., and I'd sit on the fence by the street and wave to her as she went by, and she'd wave back to me, although she never stopped. From her friendly gesture, I drew strength in the midst of my isolation from my heterosexual peers. At fourteen, I ventured into a working-class Lesbian bar called Googie's; it was so notorious in Miami that I'd heard about it at school, where its existence was a subject much talked about and tittered over. It was, they said, a place where women went who thought they were men. My kind of place, I thought, and off I went.

I waited for a weekend when my mother and stepfather had gone fishing, put on my best jeans, borrowed a shirt and socks from his wardrobe and slicked my hair back with butch wax. (Yep, that's what it was called back then.) I took a bus to the bar on 17th Avenue, and paced outside for hours. Next to the bar was a place that sold hubcaps, and I must've memorized every hubcap hanging on the chain-link fence as I walked up and down. That first time, I never did get up the nerve to walk in.

When I did make it inside, the second time, it was a terrifying, stark experience that remains vivid in my memory. I walked in and stood off to the side near the door I'd come in. I didn't dare approach the bar; they'd ask for ID. I stood there sweating and trying to look like I knew what I was doing. Finally, a very drunk woman stumbled over to me, waving her beer bottle in the air, and asked me if she could buy me a drink. I looked at her, and I was repelled. I thought to myself, she's ugly. Her face was already heavily lined; her teeth were black and rotten; her laughter was harsh and desperate to my ears. It seemed as though I stood looking at her for a long time, but I know it could only have been a few seconds before I turned and fled.

Now I understand much more about what her life must've been like, but the reality at the time was so unlike the fantasies I'd built on the information I'd gotten from the novels I'd read, in which Lesbians were almost always independently wealthy, superb horsewomen, and artists, besides. The reality clearly lacked glamour, and not a single one of the Lesbians I'd seen had been wearing jodhpurs. What was hardest for me to bear were their faces, the tension in their jaws, the hardness in their eyes. They looked like everything I detested in men, and I vowed that I'd never become "that way," hardened and embittered. Instead, I promised myself, I would be for my lovers what no man could or would be: soft, tender, and gentle. Remembering, too, the rotted teeth of the woman who'd approached me, for years I carefully brushed my teeth after making love because a faggot told me that going down on women rotted out Dykes' front teeth. (Really!)

Finally, a guy I'd been "dating" for cover asked me if I was gay; after thinking a couple of weeks about the possible motivations for his question, I told him I was. Through him I came out into the "gay community" of Miami/Miami Beach in the mid-'50s. Because we were underage, we hung out downtown, on Flagler Street (Miami's main street at the time) and at the bus station, and on Sundays we went to the gay beach at 21st Street and Collins Avenue on Miami Beach. Older gaymen[8] who picked up my male friends took me along, and through them I began to meet a few other Lesbians. When we were sixteen, we obtained fake ID's and started hanging out in the bars. Most of us were working class or lower middle-class, especially those who spent a lot of time in the bars, and by the time I graduated from high school I knew a lot about the night life of Miami and Miami Beach. I knew innumerable con games I'd learned on Flagler Street and Collins Avenue, and I counted among my closest friends hookers, prostitutes, call-girls, B-girls, bar-maids, and strippers, some of whom made good money on the side from making porno flicks. I could roll a drunk, elude the Mafia in the back alleys of Miami Beach (some of my friends weren't so lucky), and cadge drinks in the bars from hopeful "straights" trying to pick up a Dyke for a ménage à trois, without committing myself to fulfilling their fantasies. Out in the beer and wine bars on West 79th Street, I hung out with the Dykes who worked in the factories of Hialeah and Opa-Locka, drove diaper or lunch trucks, and played pool with a vengeance. Any way you look at it, I knew the score for a lot of games.

At first, though, I wasn't "into" roles. In fact, I can't remember really thinking about roles for a couple of years. Certainly I didn't call myself either "butch" or "femme," although, looking back, it's likely that the other gays around me assumed that I identified as a butch. At sixteen, I was hot after Stefanie, an "older" woman of twenty-one or so, who kept me at arm's length because, she said, I was "too young" for her. I'd met her at a seedy Miami apartment house which we called "Sex Manor," for obvious reasons, and it was in her apartment there that she finally relented and let me make love to her. Then she wanted to know if I minded if she made love to me. Surprised, I said, "Of course not." But it was near dawn; I was exhausted and drunk. The last thing I remember is her beginning to make love to me. Then I must've passed out. It was afternoon by the time I made it down to the gay beach. One friend after another came up to me and asked me if I'd gone "femme." At first, I was puzzled, but after I'd been asked the same question a few times, I finally asked someone why they wanted to know. The reply is still accurate in my mind: "Stefanie is going up and down the beach telling everyone that you flipped for her." "*Flipped* for her? What does that mean?" "She's saying you've turned femme for her."

I remember, from those moments, a confusion of emotions, none of them pleasant. Humiliation, puzzlement, embarrassment, anger, and a sense of being somehow insulted, degraded, used, ridiculed. "No," I said, "No. I fell asleep." From that truthful assertion, I regained some of the esteem I vaguely knew I'd lost as a result of her boasting. In those moments, I learned everything important I needed to know about the roles "butch" and "femme," and the relative power associated with each of them. I knew, as surely as I felt humiliated, that Stefanie was, by her claims, asserting that she had taken a large measure of power from me, and it was a "loss" I vowed never to repeat. From that day until 1972, when I attended a workshop on the political mistrust between "old" and "new" dykes, I called myself a stone butch, and, by and large, lived it, too.

For fifteen years, no matter how badly I might have wanted to let another woman touch me, no matter how badly I craved sexual release, I remained untouched and untouchable. By refusing to allow another Lesbian to give me any measure of pleasure, I felt in my guts that I thereby retained my power and my autonomy. In that way, power and sexual pleasure became equated in my mind. What if, after all, I did let someone make love to me and I "lost control"? I believed that my "loss of control" would give her "power over" me. If I "submitted," I would no longer "belong" to myself. With every year that passed, I became more and more protective of my "autonomy," my independence, which I associated with being "butch," and it became harder and harder for me to think about shedding the butch role that had become so essential to my sense of self, my sense of being powerful.

The flip side of this self-protectiveness was that, just as I based my own sense of power on making love to other women, I perceived their willingness to let me make love to them as a "giving up" of power. When they "yielded" to me, "surrendered" themselves to me passionately, made themselves "vulnerable" to me, I became powerful. I was absorbed by the anticipatory thrills of the "chase," and my sexuality was dependent on the sexual charge I experienced when I made a new "conquest." By identifying my own sexuality with power, and making satisfaction dependent on controlling another Lesbian's body, I'd bound myself to the constant need to rekindle that "charge" over and over again. Because I saw sex as a way of empowering myself, I saw the women I made love to as giving up their power to me, and it was never long before I had to find another "conquest." If I were "getting" power, then my lover of the moment must be "losing" power, and I would begin to disengage myself from a Lesbian I'd begun to despise because I perceived her as "powerless" and "weak." The very "femininity," the softness, that had first drawn me to her would now repulse me, and I would refuse to make love to her.[9] My refusal, like my previous love-making, became an assertion of my "power over" her.

I was not a lovable Lesbian, but I was safe. As long as I didn't manifest any of those behaviors I associated with weakness, I was strong, I was "powerful." But all of my emotional energy went into maintaining my façade, into protecting myself from the strength of my sexual desire, into pretending that an occasional indulgence in tribadism was sufficient for my sexual release. And I maintained all the lies necessary to my role until I was twenty-six, when I could no longer sustain my pretense. Then, I discovered I was trapped in the role and couldn't just put it aside or shrug it off like an outgrown skin. It was my skin. It was my being. Who was I if I wasn't a stone butch?

It was the radical analysis of early Feminism that gave me a "way out," a context that explained why I was unhappy with my identity as a butch, and that not only permitted me to step out of my role but also gave me good reasons for abandoning it. The Radical Feminism that supported Lesbianism and celibacy rather than heterosexuality, that named men as the oppressors of all women, that declared that the "personal is political," was the Feminism that freed me. (It is not to be confused with the diluted pap currently being called "feminism.") Because Radical Feminist analysis said that the butch/femme roles were models, imitations, of heterosexual relationships, I could begin to think of myself and my sexuality in ways that had been impossible for twenty years of my life. More importantly, Radical Feminism also offered me alternatives for structuring my relationships with other Lesbians—different ways of perceiving myself and identifying my needs in a relationship. The consistency and accuracy of that early, radical analysis taught me that power and sex weren't necessarily connected, thereby enabling me to dissociate sexual relationships from power by debunking the idea that my own power was somehow a result of being a butch. Once I understood that power did not inhere in the roles, and that the roles delimited spheres of power in a relationship, I could begin to seek new ways of defining myself. I have to say here that the emotional and sexual damage I experienced from living within the limitations of my butch role has taken me years to identify, comprehend, and disengage myself from, and I know that I haven't yet worked through every bit of it. But I've changed a lot, and knowing that makes me feel good—for a lot of reasons.

For one thing, I'm more confident of my ability to change, and I've become less resistant to looking inside myself and making deep emotional changes as I've discovered the benefits that previous changes have brought into my life. By ceasing to label myself "butch," I took the first step toward giving myself permission to explore my sexuality, which had remained an unknown, even scary, quality; to identify what I was feeling, something I'd not been able to do before; to take risks in relationships; and to accept my own need for pleasure. The results of my efforts have only gradually begun to be visible to me because I've had so much to unlearn, and I've made a lot of mistakes, some of them repeatedly. Although I can now look back and see the kinds of things I learned from living and relating as a stone butch, I have come to understand that adopting that label for myself was a defensive survival tactic that, perhaps, served me positively in some ways, but severely damaged me in others. I responded to a specific event within the social and political environment in which I happened to be; I seized what I saw as available to me without any way of foreseeing the sexual and emotional consequences in my own life. I cannot deny my past or go back and undo the pain I know I caused other Lesbians, but I wish I'd listened to the Lesbians who tried to warn me.

I cannot pretend that I was entirely happy during those years, nor can I romanticize my experiences as justifiable or inevitable. I made my choices amid situational variables I didn't fully comprehend and in accord with my best understanding at the time. I can look back, though, and say, "I thought this," "I did this," "I acted thus and so," and share that information with other Lesbians.

Whatever definitions or explanations are now offered as reasons for going back to playing roles, it is necessary to understand that those of us who chose them and lived by them manifested our choice in every sphere of our life. I wasn't a butch only in bed. I was a butch in the bar, on the street, on the dance floor, and during those solitary moments when I examined myself in the mirror. As I've learned new responses and behaviors, I've discarded the shell I inhabited as a butch. Working from the outside in, the first behaviors I dropped were the very obvious and trivial, but symbolic, external gestures: lighting another woman's cigarette, opening doors and holding them for femmes (butches frequently had awkward stand-offs in this situation), leading when I danced (although I still don't follow very well), and maintaining that I didn't know how to cook. I strutted, swaggered, blustered, and swore, mostly to hide my insecurities, self-doubts, and lack of confidence. And, sometimes, I had to put my body on the line and fight when men or other butches called my bluff.

Less obvious, but more significant remnants of my days as a butch that I've been unlearning include: my inability to cry, even when I want to very badly; my refusal to give or accept affection, even hugs; my assumption that touch is, inherently, a sexual overture; my cool, even cold, façade that keeps everyone at arm's length. These, and other butch traits are still with me, but I'm working on getting rid of them. I'm still not good at crying when I feel like it, for example; that automatic reflex in my throat that blocks emotional responses sometimes shuts my tears down. I still have trouble being touched, especially by strange women, but I'm trying to accept touch without pulling back. I no longer feel as though I'm living inside a glass bubble. When I felt safe inside the bubble, it was because I thought no one could reach me, which was fairly accurate. As I started to feel increasingly uncomfortable inside that bubble, a therapist pointed out to me that the bubble worked in two ways: not only did it keep other women out, it also kept me in. I was prisoner of my own defenses; what I intended as protection was also entrapment. Maybe that sounds simple and obvious to other Dykes, but it was a revelation for me.

At another level, most important for me has been the expansion of my sexual feelings: learning to respond to sexual touch, unfreezing my senses, and realizing how my emotional responses increase as I become more confident of my ability to be sexual. It wasn't until the fall of 1977, for example, that I consciously thought to myself that I *deserved* sexual pleasure from a lover, and, furthermore, that another Lesbian might, in fact, derive pleasure for herself from giving me pleasure. *That* was a new concept to me! Just as sex had become for me an obligation, an act I performed on demand (after the first flush of "victory" had passed) I'd assumed other Lesbians would likewise feel that making love to me was an obligation. It had never occurred to me that withholding myself might be seen as denial. Absorbing that idea enabled me to begin to ask for affection as well as sexual satisfaction. It was hard, and I faked a lot of orgasms along the way, but I was learning how to feel after years of living without physical or emotional responses.

More recently, my participation in an incest survivors' group opened up deeper areas of my sexual dysfunction that I'm still working on, and I discover new information in my body and my mind about every two weeks now. Coming to terms with the ways in which my incest experience distorted and atrophied my sexual and emotional responses has made it possible for me to go through changes much more quickly and with less resistance because I found out, by talking and sharing my fears with other Lesbian incest survivors,[10] that I wasn't "the only one." I know, for example, that my three worst tickle places are the spots on my body where my stepfather held me down when he tried to rape me. I know that my prior inability to sleep if a lover were touching me, in any way, is due to the fact that I often awakened in the dark to find my stepfather crouching by my bed, fondling my breast. I know that my dislike of any kind of physical contact, but especially touches that I interpret as sexual, can be traced back to the sexual demands my stepfather made as expressions of my "love" for him. The equation of fulfilling someone else's sexual needs as "proof" of love is something I've dismantled only in the last year. Making love because I want to is a new discovery for me.

I've learned the exquisite pleasure of allowing another Lesbian to touch me, letting my feelings move through my body and being aware of what I'm feeling. Before, I was absent during love-making; I went away out of my body. I would lie there, without making a sound, without saying anything about what I liked or didn't like. It probably wasn't much fun to make love to me. Now, I've found out that I can be noisy and that I can say what pleases me and what doesn't. Finally, after being a Lesbian for twenty-nine years [in 1984], I enjoy it.

Having learned, by trial and error, how to let another Lesbian touch me, and giving myself permission to enjoy it, I'm no longer terrified of intimacy or of emotional demands that might be made on me. My definition of safety has changed radically. Whereas I used to need to feel removed and uninvolved in order to perceive myself as strong, I now feel safe only if I can be honest about my emotions and take the risk of talking about what I'm feeling. As I've become more certain of my ability to be close and intimate with another Lesbian, I've learned to let go of my tremendous need to *control*—not only my own emotional and sexual responses, but those of my lover as well. And I know that Lesbian sexuality isn't about "power and trust."

A few years ago I'd've said it was. Now I wouldn't. Those are words borrowed from heteropatriarchal psychobabble. When I was a stone butch, I reveled in what I perceived as my "power" to turn another woman on, my "power" to make her respond to my touch, to get her to relinquish her "control" over her body. I knew all the tricks to get a woman to "trust" me, but they were only tricks, nothing more, and I am ashamed to admit this. I certainly didn't "trust" anyone, especially myself. I have learned that when I believed myself to be most "in control" of my mind, my body, my life, I was *least* "in control." When I would have declared, and believed, that I was "on top" of relationships and events in my life, I was most the victim of my past and the consequences of my experiences. Realizing this in my own life, I have come to believe that the most damaging idea we've learned from our culture is the equation of power with control, and its corollary, the identification of control with autonomy and independence. I don't think we understand any of those abstract words, although we like to hear ourselves talk about them, and, unless we methodically undertake to dismantle the cognitive linkages among them in our minds, we will continue to incorporate their results in our lives and re-enact their destructive scenarios in the most vital and sensitive area of our existence: our sexual relationships with other Lesbians. I finally had to start with the unpopular and unflattering premise that I couldn't trust my feelings and perceptions at the times when I should have been surest and most confident of their accuracy—when I was being sexually intimate, being a "Lesbian." The turning point for me came when I grasped the essential deception promoted by the idea that "control is power": that when I was most "controlled," i.e., unable and unwilling to respond spontaneously and deeply, I was least "in control," i.e., able to respond physically and emotionally in the ways that I *wanted* to. I had to realize that my inability to "let go" resulted from my need to be "in control" at every moment; that if I wanted to "let go," but couldn't convince my body to do it, then my "control" was illusory and destructive.

I began there, with the idea that being able to let myself respond sexually was powerful; that when I felt "out of control," I was most "in control." The false descriptions of my sexuality that I'd learned from the heteropatriarchy had set me at war with myself. There were years when I had to make do with no descriptions, no words to talk about what I was feeling, because there were no words I could trust. There are still words and phrases I cannot trust, not when I use them and not when other Lesbians use them. The result is a new understanding of my feelings and perceptions, a new respect for and confidence in them.

I have learned that my intense feelings when I make love—that combination of heat, strength, elation, and euphoria that wells up in me and fills my body—is *joy*. What I'm experiencing is joy, not "power." Likewise, when my lover makes love to me, I now know myself to be really centered when I am most present to her, when I am able to let go of my need to control and experience fully the ways she pleasures me. When I was a stone butch, I believed that I was "in control"; now I know that I was *being controlled* by my past. I had so internalized *external* descriptions of my feelings that it's taken me twelve years to get to a point where the links between the labels, descriptions, and my ways of thinking about myself are beginning to dissolve. And I don't believe that there are any "short cuts" that we can trust to unlearn all the damaging ideas that distort our perceptions and disease our sexual relationships. I don't think we can delude ourselves by claiming that we can "transform" labels and behaviors created and given their meaning by the heteropatriarchy, or that *our* reliance on them in our lives is somehow "different" because we're Lesbians. I think we must leave behind everything that we "know" and feel "safe" with, and begin to confront the risks and terror of becoming Lesbians, of creating a category that doesn't yet exist; we don't know what it would mean to be a Lesbian in any terms other than those defined for us by society.

It may seem, at this point, that my sexual and emotional failures were as much due to my incest experience as to identifying myself and living as a stone butch. While that is partly true, I have also realized that adopting the facade of a butch protected me from having to deal with the consequences of my incest experience. Naming myself butch enabled me to misdescribe the reasons for my emotional and sexual coldness, and to ignore, even trivialize, my utter inability to be intimate (indeed, my fear of intimacy). In that way, my inability to cry, my aloofness, my need to control everything around me, my refusal to allow a Lesbian to touch me could be "explained" as my "butchness." Whatever my perceived inadequacies as a lover, they were to be understood as part of my role, and, therefore, characteristics that weren't open for discussion, and certainly not aspects of my behavior or thinking that I was willing to change.

Yes, early second-wave Lesbian-Feminists trivialized role-playing in Lesbian relationships and, yes, they didn't really understand what they were attacking. But the kernel of truth that I perceived in their analysis started me on a decade of growth and change that I cannot deny and that I will not repudiate. I was unhappy with who I was, and Feminist analysis explained to me why I was unhappy. For that essential insight, I will always be grateful. If they hadn't challenged my identification as a "butch," I might never have started trying to change the way I thought and acted, and I might never have learned to love. Having come so far, I won't go back. My new-found joy and confidence in my sexuality and my ability to cherish my desire is too precious to entrust to labels that have trapped me before, and I can't imagine what I would gain, positively, by resorting to old words and phrases to describe myself. Too often, I think, we fail to recognize the very real power that words exert in our minds. We seem to believe the chant we used as children to ward off taunters and bullies: "Sticks and stones may break my bones, but words and names can never hurt me." Well, they do hurt us, much more than we realize. They frame our perceptions, limit our actions, and perpetuate only some behaviors as though they had a validity of their own, independent of the culture which finds them so useful to its purposes. There isn't enough room in old language for the Lesbian I'm still discovering.

Endnotes

1. For one of the most quoted *and* eloquent essays representing this position, I recommend Joan Nestle's "Butch/Fem Relationships: Sexual Courage in the 1950s," *Heresies: The Sex Issue* 12, 3 (1981), 21-24; reprinted in *A Restricted Country* by Joan Nestle (Ithaca, N.Y.: Firebrand Books, 1987). Readers might find the following essays interesting as well: Karla Jay, "The Spirit is Liberationist but the Flesh Is. . ., Or, You Can't Always Get Into Bed With Your Dogma," in *After You're Out*, eds. Karla Jay and Allen Young (New York: Links Books, 1975), 211-214; Cherríe Moraga and Amber Hollibaugh, "What We're Rollin Around in Bed With: Sexual Silences in Feminism," in *Powers of Desire: The Politics of Sexuality*, eds. Ann Snitow, Christine Stansell, and Sharon Thompson (Boston: Monthly Review Press, 1983); Donna Allegra, "Butch on the Streets," in *Fight Back!: Feminist Resistance to Male Violence*, eds. Fréderique Delacoste and Felice Newman (Minneapolis, MN: Cleis Press, 1981), 44-45; Linda Strega, "The Big Sell-Out: Lesbian Femininity," *Lesbian Ethics* 1, 3 (Fall, 1985), 73-84 (reprinted as Part 2 of Chapter Four in *Dykes-Loving-Dykes* by Bev Jo, Linda Strega, and Ruston [Oakland, CA: published by the authors, 1990], 155-166); Paula Mariedaughter's response to Linda Strega, "Too Butch for Straights, Too Femme for Dykes," *Lesbian Ethics* 2, 1 (Spring, 1986), 96-100; also in that issue of *Lesbian Ethics*, Mary Crane's response to Linda Strega, in "Letters," pp. 102-103.

2. In "Confessions of a Butch Dyke," *Common Lives/Lesbian Lives* 9 (Fall 1983), 39-45.

3. Those who wish to trivialize Lesbianism as a *political* issue call it a "bedroom issue," implying that our sexuality doesn't have "important" consequences in our lives beyond what we do in our bedrooms (and living rooms, cars, and bathtubs). I use the phrase here in that demeaning sense to indicate my belief that Lesbianism will, indeed, cease to have significant political ramifications if we refuse to engage ourselves in personal change. I lived through the political oppressions of the 1950s and '60s, the witch hunts and the purges. I was kicked out of two universities for being a Lesbian; I lived out the oppressive constraints of the butch role because I thought it was part of being a Lesbian. To willingly return to to those conditions is, for me, the same as admitting that we've been kidding ourselves for fifteen years, that being a Lesbian really isn't a *political* issue, and I know too well that it is. External structures of oppression have direct and immediate emotional and economic consequences in the lives of the oppressed, and role-playing is one of the ways in which Lesbians internalize our oppression and bring it into our relationships with each other.

4. Ayn Rand wrote *The Fountainhead*, *Atlas Shrugged*, and *The Virtue of Selfishness* to illustrate her philosophy, which she called Objectivism. It's essentially an elaborate justification for laissez-faire capitalism that extols the virtues of individualism and acting out of self-interest.

5. By *Feminist*, I'm not referring to reformist organizations like the National Organization for Women or the National Women's Political Caucus, which don't question the social structure and seek merely superficial legal reforms *within* the terms of the patriarchy. Fortunately for me, I became acquainted with radical, grass-roots Feminism, which insisted upon the consciousness-raising group as a necessary first step toward radical social change. My first Feminist literature was *The Furies* and *Amazon Quarterly*, not *Ms.*, and that has made a difference in what I regard as "Feminist politics." I have no use for a politics that is only interested in replacing men with women without thorough-going changes in the social system itself, and I'm not convinced by what I've seen that electing women to Congress will make my

life any better.

6. When Separatism is being judged, it seems that different rules apply from those used to judge the validity of other political self-namings. Thus, a lot of Lesbians call themselves socialists or Communists in spite of the fact that they're living in a capitalist state, but no one questions their integrity or good sense. But, as soon as a Lesbian names herself a separatist, she's asked to justify her politics because she lives in a patriarchy, as though the political stance itself is somehow invalid if claimed in the very context it is intended to defy.

7. During the times when I'm frustrated by politics and despair that I will not live to see any significant changes made by Lesbians and Feminists in the U.S., I sometimes decide to change my political label—drop *Feminist*, drop *Separatist*—as though that will make me feel better!

8. In this revision, I've adopted Marilyn Murphy's use of the compound *gaymen* in her collected essays, *Are You Girls Traveling Alone?: Adventures in Lesbianic Logic* (Los Angeles: Clothespin Fever Press, 1991).

9. For an honest and unapologetic description of what butches think about other women, femmes in particular, read Jan Brown's "Sex, Lies, and Penetration: A Butch Finally 'Fesses Up," *OutLook* 7 (Winter 1990), 30-34. What she has to say may be hard to read, but she told the truth!

10. Incest survivors aren't the only Lesbians who have sexual and emotional hang-ups. In spite of the temptation to generalize the dysfunctions of incest survivors, I've chosen here to name specifically the sexual abuse I experienced: incest. I know from talking with a lot of other Lesbians that many who are not incest survivors are afraid of emotional and physical intimacy, cannot be "present" with their lovers when they make love, cannot stay in a relationship and feel good about it for more than two weeks, cannot have orgasms, and really don't like being touched. More than one Lesbian has told me she "envies" me (her word) because being an incest survivor has given me a "safe" way of beginning to talk about my sexual and emotional problems. I don't think Lesbians will feel "safe" talking about our problems with sex and relationships until we're willing to reject the destructive myths about our sexuality, such as the statement in *The Joy of Lesbian Sex* (Dr. Emily L. Sisley and Bertha Harris, 1977) that "there are no frigid Lesbians," and unless we can talk about sexual issues without someone telling us that sado-masochism and its "scenes" will "cure" us.

Does It Take One
To Know One?

I n this postmodern, post-structuralist era (some would add "post-Feminist"),
when identity is a troublesome issue, I'm going to talk about Lesbian identity,
who has it, who doesn't, and how we know. First, I want to remind my
readers that asking "*who* is a Lesbian" is a new question, one barely twenty years
old, if that, and largely discussed, until recently, only among ourselves, when we
wonder out loud if so-and-so "is" or "isn't." If anything, raising the question and
debating possible resolutions signify the relative luxury we enjoy today. The
uncertainty of our present situation derives from the late nineteenth century, when
the sexologists, reacting to the first wave of women's liberation, needed to label
women's "romantic friendships" in order to stigmatize them. Up to that point, there
were no words to name love between women and so, as some would have it, there
were no "Lesbians" like us. Because the sexologists assumed the naturalness and
goodness of heterosexuality and the unnaturalness, the pervertedness of Lesbianism, they asked "*What* is a Lesbian?" and "*Why* is a Lesbian?" The *who* of a
Lesbian, however, was irrelevant for their purposes and so remained implicit in
their questions, leaving that task, thankfully, to us.

There are three aspects of identity that should be considered in any attempt to
define who is a Lesbian. First, Lesbians must somehow be taken out from under the
two "umbrella" categories that have hidden us in the past, and continue to do so
today: the categories 'woman' and 'homosexual' (or 'gay'). The process of
extrication has to be performed without obscuring or erasing the ways Lesbians
have lived and functioned within either category. Second, there is the academic
debate between the "essentialists," those who maintain that our identities are
innate, and the "social constructionists," those who claim that our identities are the
result of social forces peculiar to the time and place we are born into. Third, there
is the growing body of testimonies—interviews, biographies, autobiographies,
letters, diaries, and personal narratives—about our lives from Lesbians ourselves,
and the facts, interpretations, and impressions we have about "who" we are. It is
our real-life stories, finally, that provide both the proof and the challenge to
defining *who* is or is not a "Lesbian."

17

Because being a Lesbian has been a personal, not an intellectual, focus of my life, I want to approach defining Lesbians by starting with my own story. I haven't always known that there could be any question about who is or is not a Lesbian. For me, there was no question. It was something I knew as soon as I became aware of myself in the world and began to compare what I felt with what I was being told I *should* feel. At first, I had no word to describe who I was. So I made up theories to explain to my own satisfaction why what I felt conflicted with what I kept hearing. I was four or five when I heard the song, "The Girl That I Marry." Along with "Don't Fence Me In" and "Would You Rather Be a Mule?," it was one of my favorites. I pondered what the girl *I* would marry would be like. One afternoon, when the song was playing on the radio, I informed my mother, solemnly, that the girl I married would be just like her.

She was not flattered. In fact, she seemed disturbed. She said: "Girls can't marry girls. Only boys can marry girls." I was puzzled. *I* was disturbed. "Why can't girls marry girls?" I asked, expecting a reasonable answer. Instead, I was told: "That's the way it is." A most unsatisfactory answer!

Well, if girls couldn't marry girls, if only boys could marry girls, I figured I must be a boy. I'd been offered no alternatives, so I had to be one or the other. Of course, my genitals certainly identified me as a girl, so I figured that god had made a mistake in my construction and I must be a boy *inside*. My insides just didn't match up with my outsides. Such logic is the fruit of rampant heterosexualism. In an either/or framework, one's mind must seek some way out of a conceptual impossibility. Because I knew I desired women, because I knew I was female, I arrived at what seemed to me at the time the most logical conclusion. I must've been very convincing about this "mistake" because my mother rushed me off to the doctor for an examination. He confirmed that I was indeed female. He told my mother reassuringly: "It's all in her head." *Really*! That much, at least, was true.

My story so far is a story commonly told by lifelong Lesbians. Radclyffe Hall offered it as one of Stephen Gordon's explanations of her "inversion" in *The Well of Loneliness* (1928), and New Orleans native Doris Lunden, born five years before me, has told her version (Bulkin, 1980a: 26-44).[1] Like countless fictional and true-to-life Lesbians, I've never, not once, been heterosexual, thought I was heterosexual or, for that matter, tried to imitate heterosexual women.[2] For me, however, not being one thing did not immediately translate into being something else. During all the years I loved women, in all the years I lived as a Lesbian, I didn't call myself *Lesbian* until I forced the word through clenched teeth in 1972.

At nine, I called myself *homosexual*. I found the word in a library book, probably by a sexologist, although I no longer remember. At eleven, I learned from an "advice" column (written about me) that the word for me was *queer*, and then lay awake at night waiting for someone to cart me off to an asylum for "the cure." At fifteen, I began calling myself *gay*, because that's what my new-found friends on Miami Beach called themselves. I described myself as "gay" until I became a

Feminist.

I tell you these things about my life to illustrate several points about identity. First, the label *Lesbian* wasn't part of my idea of myself until I was thirty-one. I not only referred to my identity with several different labels, I explained my identity to myself in various ways. I needed explanations because I clearly didn't fit in with the version of life presented to me and I wanted to know why. At the very least, I wanted to find a way that I fit into the world as I was being told it was, and I used the information that came to hand. Changing the world hadn't yet occurred to me.

Second, each label I used to describe myself changed how I thought about my identity. When I thought I was a *homosexual* at nine, I knew from what I'd read that this was not a good thing to be. Yet, the descriptions fit me perfectly: tomboy, likes to wear pants, has short hair, hates to sew. I was a happy invert! The word *queer*, and the disapproval and hostility with which it was used, changed that. I grasped for the first time that my difference was really a very bad thing and that I was a very bad person: I was a girl who liked other girls. Somehow, the unanimous disapproval adults demonstrated made my situation clear: I was expected—no, not just expected, I was being ordered—to like boys, or else. . . The prospects were terrifying, and I spent my high school years being depressed, suicidal, and carving on my arms with knives. Fortunately, no one noticed. I didn't end up institutionalized. It was the 1950s. All my mother and stepfather cared about was "what the neighbors thought." They were upwardly mobile, and locking me away would've been too embarrassing to contemplate. What *would* the neighbors have thought?

You can imagine my relief when, at fourteen, I found other "queers" and learned to call myself *gay*. I was no longer alone, and being "gay" was a great improvement. I felt I belonged somewhere. But I still hadn't found other women who loved women. All I knew were gaymen. They were good friends and fun companions—at least I had a social life and a reason to go out at night—but they weren't Lesbians. In spite of these changes in labels and the ways I thought of my identity, one thing didn't change. At the core of my identity was the fact that I was a female who wanted to be emotionally and sexually intimate *only* with women.

When I finally called myself *Lesbian* in 1972, I had no idea how drastically my life would change. Being a Lesbian was very different from being "gay." For one thing, I was no longer a member of a group that consisted primarily of men, their concerns, their language. *Circle jerk*, *rough trade*, and *drag queen* had no relevance for me except when I listened to my gay male friends talking about their lives. The word *Lesbian* gave me an identity, separate from men, as a woman who loved women. It validated my desire to know women, to be with women, to touch women—not as an invert, homosexual or "gay girl," but as a woman. And it was the label *Lesbian* that ignited my desire for a community of women like myself.

Given my brief history and the fact that I'm quite sure I have always been a Lesbian, it should be clear that I'm among those cast in the "essentialist" role in "post-modern" debates. I do believe that my own Lesbianism is innate; I was *born* a Lesbian. I don't understand why so many of the popular theorists of our day describe essentialism and social constructionism as necessarily opposing accounts of sexual identity. What Lillian Faderman (1991) had to say with respect to these accounts is typical.

> As will be revealed in the pages of this book, in the debate between the 'essentialists' (who believe that one is born a lesbian and that there have always been lesbians in the past just as there are lesbians today) and the 'social constructionists' (who believe that certain social conditions were necessary before 'the lesbian' could emerge as a social entity) my own research has caused me to align myself on the side of the social constructionists. (p. 8)

Judging from my own experience, both accounts of Lesbian identity are accurate. It's not an either/or situation. I was born a Lesbian in a specific social and historical context. For example, the information about Lesbians available to me influenced how I interpreted my feelings and experiences. The various labels I used to grasp the implications of my identity both limited and aided me as I tried to come to terms with being a Lesbian. I grew up poor in an urban environment. But because Miami was a city dependent on tourism for its economy, not industry or manufacturing, I think I had more access to and opportunities for exploring the then-burgeoning post-World War II gay sub-culture than, say, a Lesbian growing up in Dallas, Texas. I also enjoyed reading, and, because I was intellectually curious, I actively sought information about Lesbians. I'm suggesting that there's a complicated interplay of many different aspects and incidents of our personal, social, and historical experience that makes facile generalizations impossible. I believe there have been Lesbians "like" me (but also "not like" me) throughout history, even though they could not have called themselves "Lesbians," and even though their experience and interpretations of themselves were shaped by their own historical, economic, and cultural contexts.

Faderman, although rightly refusing to offer a single, encompassing definition of "the lesbian" (5), is nevertheless firm in asserting that there were no Lesbians prior to the twentieth century.

> Before women could live as lesbians the society in which they lived had to evolve to accommodate, however grudgingly, the possibility of lesbianism— the conception needed to be formulated; urbanization and its relative anonymity and population abundance were important; it was necessary that institutions be established where they could meet women with similar interests; it was helpful that the country [the U.S.] enjoyed sufficient population growth so that pressure to procreate was not overwhelming; it was also helpful that the issues of sexuality and sexual freedom became increasingly open; and it was most crucial that women have the opportunity for economic self-sufficiency that would free them from the constant surveillance of family. The possibility of life as a lesbian had to be socially constructed in order for women to be able to choose such a life. Thus it was not until our century that such a choice became widely viable for significant numbers of women. (pp. 8-9)

Faderman's account seems convincing until one looks closely at what she said. "Urbanization and its relative anonymity" provided women who wanted to love other women with large cities to escape to; in many cases, such women didn't wait around for someone else to establish "institutions" where they could meet—they created them for themselves; "population growth" is not causally related to the "pressure to procreate"—heterosexuals in countries with serious overpopulation continue to reproduce; and, while it has been easier in the twentieth century for women to find ways of living independently, others in the past also managed it, choosing to live as priestesses, nuns, prostitutes, or, having rejected such occupations, cross-dressed so that they could work as men and make a livable wage. However one looks at the issue, all of Faderman's contributing factors presuppose women who have already identified themselves as non-heterosexual, however they think of themselves. By Faderman's own terms, society did not "construct" their identity; it has merely provided, in the twentieth century, conditions that make it easier for us to act on that identity.

Faderman, having aligned herself with the social constructionists, is nevertheless willing to concede that "some women, statistically very few, may have been 'born different'," but the way she accounts for the likes of me is appalling. By "born different," she means "genetically or hormonally 'abnormal'. . ." (8). Well, so much for contemporary sexual enlightenment! In fact, according to Faderman's analysis, because at one point in my life I believed that I was a man "trapped in a woman's body," I should now be a transsexual as a result of "gender dysphoria" (4-5; 60; 304). In this way, Faderman utterly discounts the reports of Lesbians like myself, the "statistically few," and seems incapable of comprehending our reports as crude attempts to understand how we could desire other women in a culture that repeatedly asserted that only men could desire women. I'm so glad my mother refused to let me have a sex-change operation when I asked for one at fourteen! It would have been a terrible mistake.

It seems to me that the "debate" between essentialists and social constructionists is nothing more than an academic brouhaha contrived to advance the now academically respectable discipline of Lesbian and gay studies. The two points of view are not mutually exclusive, although they are presented that way, nor should it be necessary to dismiss Lesbians like myself as "abnormal" in order to preserve not only one's theory, but one's stake in such a fabricated dispute.

I'm still ambivalent about asking "who" is a Lesbian, not only because I know there are no simple answers, but also because the question implies the need to establish parameters for who we might "justifiably" claim as members of our historical continuity, and the implication that we must "justify" our claims is repellant. But some attempt to identify Lesbian selves is an essential part of establishing our historical continuity. Having a history presupposes some accessible answer or answers to that question. How else can we find those who went before us? Identifying Lesbians, however, is a complicated endeavor. As Bonnie

Zimmerman pointed out in *The Safe Sea of Women* (1990: 50), "There are no simple, 'common sense' answers to such a question."

Yet, the fact that historians persist in assuming that all women are and have been heterosexual since time began, without so much as a thoughtful pause, compels me to make the effort. As Judith Schwarz put it in her article on the Katharines Bates and Coman: "In effect, the standard of assuming all women to be heterosexual until positively proven otherwise is at least as biased and historically incorrect as declaring all [women who refused to marry or] enjoyed a close friendship with another woman to be lesbians" (1979: 60). Frances Doughty (1982) was blunter:

> For how many [assumed] heterosexual subjects is there specific evidence of what they actually did in bed? Why are there different standards of evidence in establishing heterosexuality as opposed to homosexuality? (p. 123)

Susan Cavin, writing in *Lesbian Origins* (1985), identified the assumption of heterosexuality as "a major problem" (21) that produces partial and distorted histories.

Because androcentric historians have not asked "who" explicitly, their histories are patrilineal chronologies in which women appear only if they were associated with a "great man." June Stephenson's history (1986), intended to correct women's invisibility in male histories, exemplifies heterosexualist attitudes with a vengeance: she dutifully undertakes a summary of "male/female relationships" for each historical era she discusses.

Because Lesbians are ignored in most histories, including histories of sexuality, at some point we have to explain how we identify those we include as members of the category 'Lesbian'—not, however, in order to placate skeptical critics, but to please ourselves.

Determining Lesbian identity is a task of historical proportions. Unlike other sorts of identity, Lesbians possess no readily apparent identifying characteristics of space or time, nor can we look to origins or particular circumstances. Someone born in Thailand, Norway, or Ghana can claim that national identity as a birthright unless she surrenders it or is exiled. Someone born in 600 B.C.E., 1848 or 1956 C.E. "belongs" to that time period, whether she embraced or rejected its customs and values.

Consequently, Lesbian history is a hidden history, a submerged history, lived between the lines of one's time and country. Our submersion is twofold. First, we are hidden in conventional histories, unnamed, unacknowledged, undescribed, or, even in biographies and autobiographies of our lives, misdescribed, suppressed, or simply denied. As Lillian Faderman angrily said of biographies of Margaret Anderson, Lady Mary Montagu, Anna Seward, and Carson McCullers: ". . .it is impossible to discover the [lesbian] record by reading what. . .their twentieth-century biographers have had to say about their lives" (1982: 115). Virginia Spencer Carr's biography of Carson McCullers, *The Lonely Hunter* (1975), exemplifies the extremes to which biographers will go in their efforts to deny Lesbian identity to their subjects.

But not all of the blame can be attributed to conventional historians and biographers. Lesbians have collaborated in their own erasure just as surely as they were, in fact, Lesbians. Few were as open about their Lesbian loving as was Katharine Lee Bates as she mourned her loss of Katharine Coman earlier in this century. One may, and should, excuse our predecessors for their reticence; knowing the probable consequences of disclosure in a hostile culture forces us to read, as Dickinson wrote, "aslant."

In this endeavor, the Lesbian historian learns quickly to read through the oblique and vague codings of Lesbian and non-Lesbian alike. Language, specifically the language of subversion and suggestion, is at the core of Lesbian identification. Frances Doughty, writing in 1982, urged us "to continue to expand and to discuss the concept of coding, already accepted in connection with Gertrude Stein's poetry" (124-125). More recently, Penelope Engelbrecht demonstrated with Stein's poem "Lifting Belly" that: ". . . after a few pages it becomes obvious that ["lifting belly"] signifies 'lesbian sexuality',," while the verb *say* "signifies the lesbian sex act" (1990: 98). Bonnie S. Anderson and Judith P. Zinsser, in the first chapter of their two-volume work, *A History of Their Own* (1988), wrote: ". . . from antiquity on, Sappho was criticized for being 'irregular' and a 'woman-lover'" because there were no words to describe woman-loving women until the last hundred years.

Women we might call Lesbians have existed throughout history, and various societies have devised a terminology for describing them. Prior to the late nineteenth century, Lesbians might be called *tribades* or *fricatrices*, but, more often, were simply described as indulging in "unnatural vice" or "unnatural lust" because their sexuality was nonreproductive. Louis Crompton has attributed the criminalization of Lesbian behaviors and the resulting descriptions to Christian moral theology's condemnation of "sexual pleasure without procreation" (1980/81: 13-14). JR Roberts' description of the case of Sarah Norman and Mary Hammond, two women ". . .charged with 'leude behauior each with other vpon a bed'" in Plymouth County in 1648 (1980: 57) illustrates the punitive results of the heterosexual imperative.

You may be familiar with some of the more frequent phrases for describing Lesbians, such as "devoted companions," "loving friends," or "lonely spinsters." Even after the sexologists' linguistic innovations, the word *Lesbian* continued to be shunned. In 1919, Florence Guy Woolston, in her anthropological spoof, ". . . Marriage Customs and Taboo among the Early Heterodities," described members of the Greenwich Village Heterodoxy Club who didn't "mate" as *Resistants*. Elisabeth Craigin's novel, *Either Is Love*, was described on its dust jacket as an "*interfeminine* romance" [my emphasis] when it was first published in 1937.

In the early nineteenth century, the word *invert*, which means, literally, 'to turn inside out or upside down', was extended to encompass what we now call homosexuality, but it wasn't until after 1850 that men coined the words *homosexual*, *sapphist* and *Lesbian*. Exactly which man can claim to have created the word *homosexual* remains the subject of debate. In *Myths and Mysteries of Same-Sex Love* (1991), Christine Downing, apparently following Havelock Ellis ([1897] 1936:2) or Manfred Herzer (1985), says that the word "was evidently coined in 1869 by a German physician, brought into more popular usage in Germany around 1880, and introduced into English in 1892" (3-4). (Karoly Maria Kertbeny's ancestry was Austrian and Hungarian, but he practiced medicine in Germany.)

The strangely late appearance of these labels in public discourse deserves some comment here. The *Oxford English Dictionary* (*OED*) offers no illustrative quotations for *invert* in its homosexual sense, and has failed for years to list the word *Lesbian*, except in its archaic senses in the supplement, even though Havelock Ellis, the German sexologist, introduced it in 1897. The *OED* does have an entry for *Sapphism*, for which the earliest citation is 1890. But the lack of a label doesn't mean that there were no women-loving women before the last decade of the nineteenth century, only that having a label became important when the sexologists wanted to drum up some business.

The *OED* defines a *Sapphist* as 'one addicted to Sapphism'; *Sapphism* is defined as 'unnatural sexual relations between women'. Interestingly, the word *heterosexual* postdates all the terms for same-sex love, a fact which points to a newly developed self-consciousness about sexuality in general, at least in western cultures. Prior to the end of the nineteenth century, sexualities were either "natural" or "unnatural," that is, reproductive or non-reproductive. *Heterosexual*, in fact, first appeared in 1901 and referred to an "abnormal or perverted appetite toward the opposite sex." Of this innovation Christine Downing says:

> What is most fascinating…is…how the definition of homosexuality as deviant sexuality comes to constitute the basis for the definition of normal sexuality—which helps explain why the term *homosexual* antedates the term *heterosexual*. Homosexuality, once defined, 'becomes the center of everyone's haunting nightmare,' the clue to the full truth about the sexuality of all of us. (p. 6)

In her interpretation, Downing is following the lead of Michel Foucault (1978). Consequently, she misses (or ignores) the opprobrium intended by the original definition. The term *heterosexual* didn't have the same long-lasting consequences for heterosexuals, however deviant, because heterosexuality is the "normal," the assumed, the implicit sexuality against which all others are tried. *Heterosexual*, although the newer term, shed its early stigma, with related labels *satyr* and *nymphomaniac* similarly losing currency, although to a lesser degree (the psycho-medical disease, "satyriasis," recently did resurface in the television show

"L.A. Law," as the "problem" of the divorce lawyer, Arnold Becker).

For several millenia, then, it suited patriarchal cultures and the men who governed them to ignore love between women. So unspeakable was the idea that women could and did love each other passionately that male scholars felt quite justified in changing Sappho's female references to their male counterparts (as though she might have made a mistake). The appearance of labels to explicitly denote same-sex love radically altered public discourse about sexuality. Perhaps the most quoted scholar on the subject of sexuality and its entry into public discourses is Michel Foucault, whose *History of Sexuality* (1978) has already had a significant, if implosive, effect on the issue of Lesbian identity, for he is the one who indicted the sexologists for making what had been "a temporary aberration," as he called it, into a species, the homosexual (43).

Foucault's reconstruction and description of the "history of sexuality" reflects an obtuse disingenuousness that borders on misrepresentation. Contrary to the claims of academic Feminists who have taken up Foucault's reorganization of the discourse on "sexuality," he didn't spend much time examining how women's sexuality was formulated by successive generations of male speakers, and he ignored Lesbianism altogether. Apparently, the idea that there are some females who find men repugnant, who never place male interests and whims at the centers of our lives, was too fantastical a notion to be taken seriously.

At the outset, Foucault claimed that he wanted to account for why sex is talked about and "to discover who does the speaking and the institutions that store and distribute what is said about sex" (11). In fact, however, Foucault's "history of sexuality" fails even to suggest *who* "does the speaking" or *how* sex "is put into discourse," and his readers are later enjoined *not* to ask such questions. Not only does he neglect to point out that the public discourse he examines was (and remains) the domain of white, male heterosexuals, and that it is *their* discourses he is talking about, he also doesn't bother to point out that his is simply one more European male's treatise on how the rest of us have "misunderstood" the significance of that discursive tradition in our own lives.

What Foucault went to great lengths to construct is a fortuitous history, one in which male domination is reduced to a happenstance intersection of "relationships of force" in which some discourses are privileged (men's) while others (women's) are silenced. Foucault himself is silent about the specific sexes of those who are "privileged" and those who are not. Power, we are to understand, is not something we need to address "in the order of sexuality."

> We must not look for who has the power in the order of sexuality (men, adults, parents, doctors) and who is deprived of it (women, adolescents, children, patients); nor for who has the right to know and who is forced to remain ignorant. We must seek rather the pattern of the modifications which the relationships of force imply by the very nature of their process. (p. 99)

As this quotation suggests, the abstract language of Foucault's treatise and what he tries to hide beneath the language are intended to charm us into acquiescence. (That Foucault was a homosexual pederast may partially explain his allusions to children's sexuality.)[3]

The case Foucault chose to exemplify his analysis is telling, and bears on the issue of Lesbian identity. In order to illustrate how discourses are the multiple outcomes of "various strategies," he chose the introduction and stigmatization of homosexuals by the sexologists.

> There is no question that the appearance in nineteenth-century psychiatry, jurisprudence, and literature of a whole series of discourses on the species and subspecies of homosexuality, inversion, pederasty, and 'psychic hermaphrodism' made possible a strong advance of social controls into this area of 'perversity'; but it also made possible the formation of a 'reverse' discourse: homosexuality began to speak in its own behalf, to demand that its legitimacy or 'naturality' be acknowledged, *often in the same vocabulary*, using the same categories by which it was medically disqualified. There is not, on the one side, a discourse of power, and opposite it, another discourse that runs counter to it. Discourses are tactical elements or blocks operating in the field of force relations; there can exist different and even contradictory discourses within *the same strategy*;. . . [my emphases] (pp. 101-102)

On the one hand, Foucault claimed that homosexuals could not begin to argue for their naturalness nor petition heterosexual societies for acceptance *until* the sexologists had named and identified them. That is what occurred, as far as I know, but the connection need not be construed as *causal*. On the other hand, there is clearly more to be said when specific individuals, all of them white, male, and heterosexual, take it upon themselves to describe and stigmatize a group, in this instance, homosexuals. What is it if *not* "a discourse of power"? This is not the result of "various discourse strategies" but a response from a group already deprived of the right to speak by the group empowered to name them in the first place.

By calling this situation a "reverse discourse," and saying that the sexologists and early homosexual rights activists used "the same strategy," Foucault failed to realize that this example would be better treated as an illustration of the power of naming. Those turn-of-the-century activists used what was, at the time, the only language available to them, a language not *theirs*. Because the early activists resorted to the vocabulary and categories of the sexologists, they, perhaps unknowingly, undermined their own arguments. It remained for activists of the mid-twentieth century to challenge the terms of those who named us.

My alternative description of the situation may also account for the fact that very few Lesbians joined the early homosexual rights groups. Perhaps those women who loved women recognized that using the sexologists' words and categories, and the assumptions that created them—even to argue for their right to exist unhindered by heterosexual society and its institutions—would be a futile endeavor. My analysis may also explain why hardly any women, well into the twentieth century, called themselves "Lesbians," (for example, Katharine Bates and Katharine Coman, and Molly Dewson and Polly Porter), however frank and open they were about living with and loving another woman.

Furthermore, there is disingenuousness in Foucault's choice of this illustration and the way he used it. As he presented it, the only "change" introduced by the sexologists was to transform the sodomite, "a temporary aberration," into a species, the homosexual (43). The label, we are to understand, fixed gaymen in a "phase." As his discussions make clear, Foucault focused on *male* homosexuality because it suited him to do so. But the sexologists themselves were as much, if not more, concerned with what they called the "female invert," with Lesbianism.

Foucault's account does more than make Lesbians invisible; it distorts, by omission, the actual effects on Lesbians, and on our understanding of ourselves, of the sexologists' pronouncements. While a few Lesbians did join with gaymen in the "reverse discourse" of the late nineteenth century (Steakley, 1975; Lauritsen and Thorstad, 1974; Faderman and Ericksson, 1980), their relation to the pronouncements of the sexologists and their role in the "reverse discourse" were problematic precisely *because* they were women. As Sheila Jeffreys pointed out in *The Spinster and Her Enemies* (1985), "Contemporary male gay historians have seen [Havelock Ellis, a major sexologist] as performing a service to male homosexuals by breaking down the stereotype that they were effeminate. For women the service he performed was quite different" (106).

At the same time that the sexologists were debunking the stereotype of gaymen as effeminate and creating the species 'homosexual', they were simultaneously making of the corresponding Lesbian stereotype a "scientific" fact. Jeffreys (1985:106) illustrates this from Havelock Ellis' *Sexual Inversion* ([1897] 1936):

> When they still retain female garments, these usually show some traits of masculine simplicity, and there is nearly always a disdain for the petty feminine articles of the toilet. Even when this is not obvious, there are all sorts of instinctive gestures and habits which may suggest to female acquaintances the remark that such a person 'ought to have been a man'. The brusque energetic movements, the attitude of the arms, the direct speech, the inflexions of the voice, the masculine straightforwardness and sense of honour, and especially the attitude towards men, free from any suggestion either of shyness or audacity, will often suggest the underlying psychic abnormality to a keen observer.
>
> In the habits not only is there frequently a pronounced taste for smoking cigarettes, often found in quite feminine women, but also a decided taste and tolerance for cigars. There is also a dislike and sometimes incapacity for needlework and other domestic occupations, while there is some capacity for athletics. (Ellis: 250)

In fact, hypotheses explaining the lateness of western patriarchies to name Lesbianism as a "sexuality" and the time during which the labels and their definitions appeared have been addressed by several Feminist scholars. Until the late nineteenth century, there was no such topic as "Lesbianism" in the public, political, male sphere of discourse. Jeffreys observed that "Historians could not fail to notice the expression of the sentiments Lillian Faderman calls 'romantic friendships.' Instead, they tried to ignore them or explain them away so that they could not be allowed to challenge their heterosexual account of history" (1985: 103). In fact, romantic friendships between women had been actively encouraged up to this time, and "Men tended to see these relationships as very good practice for their future wives in the habit of loving" (Jeffreys, 1989: 19).

This male beneficence abruptly stopped when women began to create other lives for themselves beyond the heterosexuality constructed for them. In *Surpassing the Love of Men* (1981), Lillian Faderman suggested that the increasing possibility that women could live independently of men, a turn of events traceable to the nineteenth-century women's liberation movement, threatened male hegemony and the institution of marriage which bound women to them in mandatory heterosexuality: "If they [women] gained all the freedom that feminists agitated for, what would attract them to marriage? Not sex drive, since women were not acknowledged to have one. . . .." (237). For the male psyches threatened by the spectre of economically independent and politically active women, "the sexologists' theories. . .came along at a most convenient time to bolster arguments that a woman's desire for independence meant she was not really a woman" (Faderman, 1981: 238). As Jeffreys (1989:20) described this period of transition, "Emotional relationships between women were harmless only when women had no choice to be independent of men, and became dangerous when the possibility of women avoiding heterosexuality became a reality."

In order to make credible this new threat to heterosexual domesticity, the sexologists created the "pseudo-homosexual," "a woman who did not necessarily fit the masculine stereotype, had been seduced by a 'real homosexual' and led away from a natural heterosexuality, to which it was hoped that she would return" (Jeffreys, 1985:108). "Real" Lesbians, according to the sexologists (like Krafft-Ebing and Havelock Ellis), were "born that way," whereas the "pseudo-homosexual" was a "natural" heterosexual temporarily seduced away from men by a "real Lesbian." By positing a transitory category between the innate sexualities of Lesbians and their heterosexual sisters, the sexologists were able to stigmatize not only the nineteenth-century Feminists who smoked and didn't like needlework, but the women who, till then, had freely enjoyed passionate romantic friendships free from male comment or censure.

Through the defining of any physical caresses between women as 'pseudo-homosexuality' by the sexologists, the isolation and stigmatising of lesbianism was accomplished, and women's friendships were impoverished by the suspicion cast upon any physical expression of emotion. (Jeffreys, 1985:109)

Historically, men have controlled what Foucault called "talk about sex" and its meaning, both in public and in private. With isolated exceptions (e.g., Sappho, and Lesbians mentioned by Martial, Lucian, and other ancient writers), all women had been assumed to be heterosexual until the end of the nineteenth century, when it suited men's purposes to codify and stigmatize any and all intense female relationships explicitly, and especially those in which the physical passion of like to like might be acted upon. Since then, Lesbians have lived under siege and in the closet.

Not surprisingly, the sexologists grounded their definitions of *Lesbian* and *homosexual* on the expression of genital sexuality, simultaneously locking several Lesbian generations into their discourse framework and erecting a physically intimidating barrier between those who do and those who don't, between Lesbians and "heterosexual women." In spite of some exceptions (like the Chinese sexual literature of the Ming dynasty [1368-1644 B.C.E.], where "sapphism among the womenfolk of a household was not only viewed tolerantly, but on occasion even encouraged," especially when "a man joins them, as in the posture of the Gobbling Fishes" [van Gulik, 1961: 274]), the male version of "the history of sexuality" has either ignored or disapproved of passionate intimacy among women. For more than a hundred years, women have hidden from themselves on one side of that protective wall: "Well, she and I didn't 'do it,' so I must be normal," "We may have 'done it,' but I was drunk," or "Yeah, 'it' was nice, but I still prefer men." Others, whether they called themselves "Lesbian" or not, vaulted the wall and blazed the paths many of us now follow. Imagine Charlotte Cushman and Harriet Hosmer,[4] dressed up in their tailored outfits, riding astride their horses through the streets of Rome in the nineteenth century!

There is a time in a Lesbian's life when she first becomes aware of the wall, the line between "them" and "us," and considers its height, its breadth, and the strength of her desire. She takes her own measure, and she says either "I must jump now" or "Perhaps this will pass." Whichever statement she acts on, her life becomes a battlefield on which she confronts the threats and lies of what men have said and continue to say about women, our sexualities, and what our actions "mean" in their world. Even if she marries and bears children, as many Lesbians did in the past and still do today (until they find out better), she knows in her mind what she will not reveal to anyone else.

Yet, in spite of the evidence of history, in spite of the evidence of our experience, we find self-identified Lesbian-Feminists, like Lillian Faderman, in 1991, who want to assert that there were no Lesbians prior to the late nineteenth century because they didn't, couldn't, call themselves "Lesbians." One such writer is Ann Ferguson (1982), whose description of "who" is a Lesbian rules out all but those of us who've lived in the twentieth century and then excludes what would be a majority of twentieth-century Lesbians:

> [A] Lesbian is a woman who has sexual and erotic-emotional ties primarily with women or who sees herself as centrally involved with a community of self-identified lesbians whose sexual and erotic-emotional ties are primarily with women; and who is herself a self-identified lesbian. (pp. 155)

Ferguson based her definition on three premises, each of which reflects the naive belief that there is, necessarily, a close correspondence between language and the experience we use words to describe, and, furthermore, assumes that, without a label, we are incapable of constructing an identity, as though we cannot imagine what men's language neglects to make speakable:

> 1) a person cannot be said to have a sexual identity that is not self-conscious;
> 2) it is not meaningful to conjecture that someone is a Lesbian who refuses to acknowledge herself as such;
> 3) a person cannot be anything unless others can identify her or him as such. (pp. 154-55)

In an attempt to "do justice" to some modern ideal of "what a lesbian is," at the expense of our historical continuity, Ferguson produced premises that are ahistorical, in the interest of "historical relevance" (Phelan 1989: 71), and that leave out the confusions Lesbians face when we sort our experiences and feelings and attempt to describe them. Some Lesbians, for example, as soon as they realize that they love other women, are so horrified and panicked that they go out and have sex with every man they can find. But, as they finally realize, that doesn't make them heterosexuals. Shane Phelan lauds Ferguson for making sex acts the defining characteristic of a "real" Lesbian, but it is hardly a "new definition" (Phelan, 71). Lesbianism is not a "modern phenomenon" as Ferguson believes (Phelan, 75); only the names and the particularities of environment have changed.

When we consider the varieties of Lesbian experience and the many ways we know ourselves in the world, Ferguson's premises, and the definition they buttress, leave us empty-handed. What, for example, does "self-conscious" mean? What about the "new" Lesbian who has acknowledged to herself that she's a Lesbian but hasn't yet had an opportunity to explore her possibilities for acting on her self-knowledge? What about women who unself-consciously love other women because no one has told them they "shouldn't"? What about the Ladies of Llangollen?[5] Is there any way of determining whether or not they were "self-conscious"?

Ferguson's first premise, except for the least ambiguous cases, is as unprovable as the question of sexual activity, and so functions to keep us from searching the past for our forerunners. Determining whether a dead woman was "self-conscious" about an identity is impossible. It is also true that most heterosexual women remain *unself-conscious* about their identity when they're alive.

In Ferguson's second premise, the verb *refuse* so narrows our ability to conjecture that we can only call "Lesbians" those who know other Lesbians exist. It isn't meaningful, for example, to say that Sappho or Aphra Behn "refused" to acknowledge their Lesbianism, and it ignores those Lesbians who reject labels. This premise applies only to those of us who are highly visible: it *is* meaningless to conjecture about which movie stars, writers, or politicians might be Lesbians because they are most likely to "refuse to acknowledge" their Lesbianism. Yet, such conjectures are necessary elements of Lesbian attempts to establish and maintain our historical continuity, which is always in danger of annihilation. Approvingly, Shane Phelan glosses this second premise as meaning that "we cannot simply enlist women from history and label them lesbian; not because it slurs their reputation, but because it is obfuscatory" (1989: 71). Phelan arrogantly dismisses more than forty years of painstaking Lesbian research as though the work of scholars like Jeannette Foster and Judith Schwarz were nothing more than fanciful and yearning imagination. Furthermore, accepting such dicta seals every Lesbian who has ever lived, including those of us still living, in the vacuum of our present, forbidden to look backward, unable to look forward. *That* is obfuscatory!

Finally, Ferguson's third premise suggests so many counter-examples and implies so many "what ifs" that it's vacuous. Who, for example, are the "others" who must be able to identify one as a Lesbian? If, for example, a Lesbian is passing as heterosexual for economic and/or social reasons and no one but her lover knows she's a Lesbian, is she a "real" Lesbian? What if a closeted Lesbian doesn't have a lover and *no one* else knows she's a Lesbian? Such tests ignore the social and economic conditions Lesbians face.

Given Ferguson's premises, it isn't surprising that her definition excludes women who are Lesbians but deny it and those who remain closeted all their lives and maintain secrecy about their identity, yet it includes bisexuals and women who claim to be Lesbians for some period of time. Phelan doesn't argue with this aspect of Ferguson's definition, but claiming Colette and Djuna Barnes, both bisexuals, seems to be what she objected to earlier: enlisting "women from history" (71). There is no good reason I can think of for including women known to be bisexuals in Lesbian history. And what about "hasbeans"? If they satisfied all of Ferguson's criteria for two years and then decided they loved a man, were they "real" Lesbians for just those years or only "passing through"? Was it "a phase"?

If we follow Ferguson's thinking to its logical conclusion, we are left with Natalie Barney's Paris salon,[6] maybe the Daughters of Bilitis (1957-1972),[7] and the post-Stonewall Lesbian groups that have come and gone since 1969. Ferguson's definition would probably exclude Sappho and Aphra Behn, and the many Lesbians still living in cultural and social isolation, some of whom have never heard the word *Lesbian* or, because of their circumstances, have been unable to find other Lesbians to whom they might relate. It would also exclude the women-loving women of Southeast Asia, for example, who are afraid that naming themselves *Lesbians* will give men an excuse to destroy the women-only spaces traditional to their culture. Their fear of what the label might result in doesn't mean they aren't "real" Lesbians. A definition of *Lesbian* that excludes so many who live and love *as* Lesbians, yet includes so many undeserving of the name, is no definition at all.

Making sexual activity the only, or primary, criterion of who is a Lesbian isn't as conclusive as it might seem and leads to false conclusions as well, a fact illustrated by the sociological and psychological studies of Lesbians that make identity contingent on specific sexual acts (Kitzinger, 1987: 67). As Faderman observes:

> Not even a sexual interest in other women is absolutely central to the evolving definition of lesbianism: a woman who has a sexual relationship with another woman is not necessarily a lesbian—she may simply be experimenting; her attraction to a particular woman may be an anomaly in a life that is otherwise exclusively heterosexual; sex with other women may be nothing more than part of a large sexual repertoire. On the other hand, women with little sexual interest in other females may nevertheless see themselves as lesbian as long as their energies are given to women's concerns and they are critical of the institution of heterosexuality. The criterion for identifying oneself as a lesbian has come to resemble the liberal criterion for identifying oneself as a Jew: you are one only if you consider yourself one. (1991: 5)

Did Vita Sackville-West "get it on" with Rosamund, Violet Trefusis, and Virginia Woolf? Did Sarah Ponsonby and Eleanor Butler (the Ladies of Llangollen) "do it" before or after Wordsworth came to visit?

Why not, then, simply say that a Lesbian is any woman who *says* she's a Lesbian, as Faderman finally does (1991: 5)? I think that's what I might have said at twenty, after the Daughters of Bilitis started publishing *The Ladder* in 1957, but before the Stonewall Riots in 1969. If a woman told me she was a Lesbian, I believed her, unless time and observation gave me reason to doubt it. Such simplicity is attractive if we consider only those Lesbians like myself who were born Lesbians, who have never felt any heterosexual inclination, and who live our entire lives loving only women.

For many reasons, such solutions are inadequate. All Sappho did was live and work on the island that gave us our name. Sarah Ponsonby and Eleanor Butler set up housekeeping years before the sexologists thought about "curing" their disposition. Vita Sackville-West, Violet Trefusis, and Virginia Woolf each had husbands waiting back home. Not all women who enter into sexual relationships with other women remain Lesbians. Colette and Bessie Smith were bisexuals, not Lesbians, and should be represented as such. My first lover was not a Lesbian, in spite of our three-year relationship, unless you interpret her unwillingness to "fight society" (her words) as evidence that she was both a Lesbian and a coward.

There is also the phenomenon of the "hasbean." Most of us have known not one but several "hasbeans," women who had one or more Lesbian relationships but, for a variety of reasons, later became heterosexuals. The Harlem songwriter and male impersonator Gladys Bentley documented her own change in an article published in *Ebony* in 1952, entitled "I Am a Woman Again," (Roberts, 1982: 104), but I wonder who picked the title. Some women say, "I'm not a Lesbian. I'm only attracted to one woman," in effect asserting that a particular Lesbian relationship is an anomaly and denying that the experience is repeatable. Sometimes it's true, sometimes it's not. Some women point to specific aspects of the Lesbian stereotype to deny that they're Lesbians: "I don't have a crewcut," "I don't wear overalls and flannel shirts," "I still like men." In a certain kind of Lesbian novel, at least one character can be expected to flee the scene when she sees Lesbians wearing pants and ties and opening the door for her on her first visit to a Lesbian bar; she always comforts herself by saying, "I can't be a Lesbian. I'm not ugly. I don't want to be a man. I love lipstick and high heels."

On the other hand, there are women who are clearly heterosexual who, while maintaining active sexual relationships with men, claim to be Lesbians. Their principle justification for calling themselves Lesbians has been that they're "broadening the definition" of what it means to be a Lesbian, as though its "narrowness" required correction. Recent examples I can mention here are Holly Near and Susun Weed, whose identities are being debated in 1991 issues of *Lesbian Connection*. There are women who live most of their lives as heterosexuals, marry, raise children, and then at forty, fifty, sixty, or seventy become Lesbians. Sometimes, they become lovers with a woman from their kaffee klatsch, dojo, daycare center, or bridge club.

Such examples indicate two things. First, Lesbian identity cannot be based solely on one or more sexual acts, because the experience of Lesbian sexual intimacies isn't limited to life-long Lesbians. Lots of women experience Lesbian attractions whether or not they act on them, and some Lesbians, for many different reasons, remain celibate all their lives. Second, there is no one kind of Lesbian. Instead, each of us comes to our Lesbianism at different times, in different circumstances, and with different backgrounds. There are many paths to a Lesbian identity. The most discussed experiential difference so far is that between born Lesbians and Lesbians who renounce heterosexuality later in their lives,[8] but it's certainly not the only one.

Lesbianism is an active identity. Once we jump the wall, we know that "being a Lesbian" means more than touching women and being touched by women. Living "as a Lesbian" involves more than sexual intimacies and orgasmic rushes. Yes, for many of us, the physical, the anatomical, the sexual is one significant aspect of the Lesbian act. Frances Doughty, noting that professional historians emphasize "a sexual/genital definition of lesbianism," cautions that using genital contact "as a criterion of 'real' lesbianism, imposes a male heterosexual imagery on

[our] sexuality" (1982: 123). An adequate definition must include our sexuality without making it the only deciding factor. We cannot forget that some Lesbians, like some heterosexual women, choose celibacy, choose not to act on their emotional and sexual feelings. Are they "real" Lesbians? I say "yes."

Certainly, Lesbian identity is partially a social construct. Whose isn't? We see and hear evidence every day that reveals how heterosexuality is socially constructed. But what the social constructionists leave out of their formulation is our individual capacity to act and to react. We are not simply passive objects caught up in and overwhelmed by the flow of events. We make events happen. Our actions affect historical processes whether we are noticed or not. Parents, teachers, and psychologists certainly did try to coerce me into heterosexuality, but I resisted, and so have a lot of other Lesbians.

Of course how we conceive of ourselves is a result of accumulated experiences, and the conception itself is structured by, among other things: the age at which we first think of ourselves as Lesbians; the information on which we base our identification; where we live; the autonomy we have; how mobile we are; and so on. Furthermore, "identity" and our experience of it are entwined. To make this point, consider the simplest contrast. A Lesbian who knew she was "different" while she was a nine-year-old living on a farm in western Idaho with her parents has a very different sense of what "being a Lesbian" means from someone who grew up in Pittsburgh, was heterosexually married, raised three children, and "became" a Lesbian at the age of fifty-four. When we factor in class, racial differences, and religious and ethnic backgrounds, the contrastive potentials multiply. There can be no doubt that Lesbians differ one from another in numerous ways: in how we perceive our Lesbianism, and how we choose to act or not act on our perceptions.

If our identities are socially constructed to some degree, there is one significant aspect of Lesbian identity that cannot be overlooked or discounted, and that is what others have called our "invisibility." Lesbian invisibility is assuredly "socially constructed," but it is not true, as Ann Ferguson has said, that "it is false that lesbians are invisible in our society." She maintains that the word *Lesbian* denotes "quite visible lesbians, e.g., working class butches, those who appear to act like men as well as to have sex with women" (1990: 74).

Even if one grants Ferguson's presentation, focusing on the negative use of the word *Lesbian* doesn't contradict the fact that most Lesbians spend some portion of our lives invisible to ourselves as well as to others. Because some of us hear the word *Lesbian* applied to "quite visible" Lesbians as we're growing up, many assume that we "can't be" Lesbians because we don't *look like* the individual to whom the label was applied. The stereotype has served to coerce some Lesbians into heterosexual relationships, just as some heterosexual women lived as Lesbians for part of their lives because they did fit the stereotype.

Invisibility is part of the social construction of a Lesbian identity because so many of us, especially if we were born before 1970, developed our identities in an informational vacuum. Imagine that you are nine years old, living in the U.S. in 1959. If your parents could afford a TV, you have grown up with "Leave It to Beaver" and "Father Knows Best," the "Ed Sullivan Show" and "I Love Lucy." You're a voracious reader, so you've read encyclopedias, all the Nancy Drew mysteries and *The Wizard of Oz*. On Saturdays, you go to the movies with your friends, and you've seen westerns, horror flicks, the usual fare. (Your parents probably didn't allow you to see *The Children's Hour* or *Compulsion*. Just as well.) You still go to church on Sundays, you attend school five days a week. . . yet, where in all these activities are you learning about being a Lesbian, living as a Lesbian? Nowhere.

How do you feel? What do you think? You feel, well, "different." All you know is that you don't feel the desires, have the aspirations, or seek the same activities that your parents, peers, teachers, and every television show, movie, book, and magazine tells you you're supposed to feel, have, and seek. You don't have a name for the "Lesbian inside you," the invisible Lesbian who is variously shocked, appalled, or disgusted by what is presented to her as a "life worth living."

If one wishes to understand the Lesbian experience, one must somehow imagine what it is like growing up into an identity that's unmentionable in any positive or helpful context. As the heterosexual agenda becomes clearer and clearer and its requirements and strictures become more and more insistently coercive, Lesbians have very few options, none of which are attractive. Of course, there's silence about what one is feeling. This is probably the most popular solution. We keep our dismay and discomfort to ourselves. Telling parents or other relatives can have results that range from the dismissive "It's just a phase" to painful rejection, the humiliation of psychotherapy and other "cures," and/or the destruction of institutionalization and shock treatments—all the tortures and torments this society reserves for the misfits, the recalcitrant and the uncooperative.

Telling one's friends usually, but not always, leads to their disapproval, discomfort, and eventual rejection. If one is unfortunate enough to tell a friend who has a big mouth, all of the painful events listed above may ensue: she may tell one or more of your other friends, one of them may tell her parents, then they call your school or church, etc., etc. As long as a Lesbian is a minor, she depends upon the compassion and goodwill of those who share and control her life, and she is all too often betrayed.

Worse, even our silence may only buy us time. A parent may find and read one's diary, journal, or that precious bundle of letters and notes you've hidden with your underwear. Or, you may succumb to the pressure and frustration of silence, finally get up your nerve to tell a girlfriend how you feel about her, and set some or all of the preceding consequences in motion. Worse, you may decide that your feelings are "wrong" or "wrong-headed," stifle every thought and feeling inside you, and embark on a life of faked heterosexuality. You suppress your identity and put your inner self in a state of suspended animation, perhaps to waken at some later point in your life, perhaps not. Without any external validation of who you are, who can you be?

This is "invisibility." It is real. It is the silence imposed on a self that instinctively rejects the identity displayed, coerced, imposed by everyone and everything in her life. It is a silence that smothers, deadens, sucks the life out of her. It is a virtually sealed vacuum. There is no air to breathe, no light to illumine what is obscured, hazy, nameless. It is intended to and does, more often than we would like, succeed in destruction of the self.

But some survive. Many of us survive to arrive at a destination, a resting place. Some of us have lived to tell our stories, to create Lesbian texts, to read Lesbian texts, even to write commentaries and criticisms of Lesbian texts. All of these activities must be pluralized, multiplied, complicated, and pluralized again, because there is no single, narrow, one-sentence definition of "The Lesbian." The sexologists may have been the ones to name us, but we can, and do, create ourselves. Out of a mishmash of disinformation, misinformation and outright lies, each Lesbian constructs some story about who she is and who she might someday be, and she approaches her literature, if she is lucky enough to stumble upon it, with that construction, looking for additional pieces of her story.

Lesbians have proposed numerous definitions for the term *Lesbian*, no one of them adequate without lengthy qualification. Marilyn Frye has described our problem as "a flirtation with meaninglessness—dancing about a region of cognitive gaps and negative semantic spaces." She argues that "the standard vocabulary of those whose [conceptual system] it is will not be adequate to the defining of a term which denotes it" (1983: 154). Teresa de Lauretis, following Frye's analysis, finds that "the term 'lesbian' proves to be extraordinarily resistant to standard procedures of semantic analysis. . .because lesbians are not countenanced by the dominant conceptual scheme" (1990: 143). Certainly, as Penelope Engelbrecht has said, "Lesbian Desire is not a Foucauldian function of power, or a Lacanian privilege of the subject, but a Brossardian enaction of mutual 'wanting'" (1990: 92).

Does it take one to know one? Usually, yes. Our guesses are right more often than they're wrong, but we do guess wrong every once in a while (and even our "wrong" guesses may be vindicated at a later date). Bonnie Zimmerman is right: there is no simple, "common sense" answer to the question, "Who is a Lesbian?" One definition of *Lesbian* will never be satisfactory or comprehensive. In fact, not even her three Lesbian types—"lesbian-from-birth, lesbian-by-choice, lesbian-through-love"—suffice to address the complexities of Lesbian identity I've only touched upon here. There's no reason to think that there's only one kind of Lesbian, just as there's no one kind of heterosexual. There are varieties of Lesbian identity that originate in our experiences and the ways we come to identify as Lesbians, and it is to all of our experiences, with our interpretations, our changes in course, and our contradictions that we must, in the final analysis, be faithful.

Endnotes

1. Lesbian journals such as *Sinister Wisdom* and *Common Lives/Lesbian Lives* often publish personal narratives of the sort I mention here, and Susan Wolfe and I collected more than thirty in *The Original Coming Out Stories* ([1980] 1989).

2. In her review of *The Coming Out Stories* (1980), Marilyn Frye, cautioning that "The temptation to disown our former selves can encourage us to falsify our histories," expressed her disbelief that a "majority of the coming out storytellers tell us they never had any interest in men, or that men repulsed, overwhelmed, or bored them, and I am not sure whether this presents a true picture of lesbians in general. I, for one, was very interested in men for quite a number of years, particularly in powerful, eccentric, intelligent men from whom I learned a lot about philosophy, music, wine, food, and drugs. Either I am a quite unusual lesbian, or the anthology represents a skewed selection of lesbians, or we are inventing a myth about ourselves..." (1980: 98).

3. References to the sexuality of children are scattered throughout the first volume of Foucault's *History of Sexuality*, but he discusses "incest," in particular, on pp. 108-110. What is peculiar about his discussion is his focus on its prohibition:

> ...in a society such as ours, where the family is the most active site of sexuality, and where it is doubtless the exigencies of the latter which maintain and prolong its existence, incest...occupies a central place; it is constantly being solicited and refused; it is an object of obsession and attraction, a dreadful secret and an indispensable pivot. It is manifested as a thing that is strictly forbidden in the family insofar as the latter functions as a deployment of alliance; but it is also a thing that is continuously demanded in order for the family to be a hotbed of sexual excitement. (109)

Again, Foucault's language in this passage is deceptive. Like the passage quoted in my text, the verbs in this example are also in the passive voice with the agency suppressed. *Who* is he talking about? *Who* "solicits" incest? *Who* "refuses" it? *Who* "demands" it? *Who* is "obsessed" and "attracted" by it?

4. Charlotte Cushman (1816-1876) was a highly acclaimed actress and a notorious "Lesbian" of her day. One of her closest friends (a crony, not a lover) was Harriet Hosmer (1830-1908), a highly regarded sculptor who lived in Rome, Italy.

5. Sarah Ponsonby and Eleanor Butler were widely known as the Ladies of Llangollen. In 1778, after a couple of failed attempts, Sarah and Eleanor finally escaped their respective families in Ireland, and made their way to Wales, where they established a home together. Several books have been written about them, including *The Ladies* by Doris Grumbach (New York: Ballantine Books, 1984), and *A Year with the Ladies of Llangollen* by Elizabeth Mavor (New York: Penguin, 1984).

6. Natalie Barney and her Paris salon must surely deserve to rank among the most notorious. Virtually every Lesbian in Europe who was "anyone" visited Barney's salon at least once. Her lover, Elizabeth de Gramont, the artist Romaine Brooks, the writer Renée Vivien, Mimi Franchetti, Renata Bogatti, Radclyffe Hall and Una Troubridge were among the nucleus of Lesbians who socialized there. Colette visited there, with "Missy," the Marquise de Belboeuf. Even Gertrude Stein and Alice B. Toklas are said to have visited once. Readers interested in knowing more about Natalie Barney and her circle can consult a number of books: Tee Corinne's *Women Who Loved Women* (Pearlchild, 1984); Sheri Benstock's *Women of the Left Bank, Paris 1900-1940* (Austin: University of Texas Press, 1986); Karla Jay's *The Amazon and the Page: Natalie Clifford Barney and Renee Vivien*

(Bloomington: Indiana University Press, 1988).

7. The Daughters of Bilitis (DOB) was founded in 1955 by Del Martin and Phyllis Lyon in San Francisco. They tell the history of the organization in *Lesbian/Woman* (New York: Bantam Books, 1972).

8. The differences in experience between lifelong Lesbians and ex-het Lesbians are discussed most fully in *Dykes-Loving-Dykes* by Bev Jo, Linda Strega, and Ruston (Oakland, 1990), but readers will also want to read the article by Marilyn Murphy, who describes herself as a "Lesbian-Come-Lately" in "Color Me Lavender" in *Are You Girls Traveling Alone?* (Los Angeles: Clothespin Fever Press, 1991), 17-20.

The Lesbian Perspective

I call this essay "The Lesbian Perspective," not because I imagine there is *one* Lesbian perspective, but to suggest the possibility of a Lesbian consensus reality—a Lesbian-centered view of the world—and to indicate that there are aspects of Lesbian experience on which we can ground a self-defined consensus reality. When Lesbians work and create together, we live a vision of Lesbian community. "That is the whole meaning of Lesbian works, magazines, videos, movies, research, all of which shape our collectivity into reality. A collectivity becomes flesh and bone each time one of us thinks of herself as partaking in an actual Lesbian community" (Grimard-Leduc, 494). Given the depth of the differences in the ways we understand ourselves, can there be such a being as "The Lesbian"? I think yes. Our perspective inheres in all our works. If we are not trying to articulate a Lesbian view of the world, why do we create the artifacts of a self-realizing culture? Although I am unable to flesh out the anatomy of the Lesbian Body, I want to emphasize the unique potential inherent in the Lesbian experience, a potential so dangerous to the heterosexual body politic that it's exhilarating.

Easy generalizations about *all* Lesbians are impossible; each of us participates in heteropatriarchal culture to varying degrees. We make different social, economic, and political choices in the context of our backgrounds and experiences and our interpretations of them. But I cannot use that fact to avoid generalizing. If we think that any generalizing about Lesbians is wrong, then we should also stop identifying ourselves as *Lesbian* and *Dyke*, and adopt the point of view that there is nothing significant about being Lesbians. By placing the Lesbian experience clearly in relation to male culture, however, I will show how our political differences arise from specific contexts and our responses to those contexts. I want to outline the common ground on which I think we can create a Lesbian community that will support even those who may not want it or know that it exists.

What I call the "Lesbian Perspective" is a "turn of mind," a stance in the world, that asks unpopular questions, that can be comfortable only when it confronts the sources of its discomfort, a frame of mind that refuses to accept what most people believe to be "true." This turn of mind I identify as "Lesbian." It is what enabled us to reject heterosexual bribery. It is a mind that must have its own integrity on its own terms. Just as being a living, breathing Lesbian exposes the lie of heterosexuality as "normal" and "natural," the Lesbian Perspective challenges *every* lie on which male society is founded. And there are lots of those. We don't submit willingly to the dogmas of authority. Even when we try to hide our "bad attitude" from those who have power over us by retreating into silence, we stand out like dandelions in neatly manicured lawns. Lesbians are the weeds that blossom proudly, stubbornly, in heterosexual families; no matter what lethal methods they use to eradicate us, we keep springing back. We are resilient, and our roots go deep.

What's Wrong with this Picture?

Where do we begin to define our Selves? How are Lesbians unique? In spite of an occasional craving to be "like everybody else," we know that we *aren't*. If we were, we wouldn't be Lesbians. Some deep-seated consciousness knows that the world presented to us as "real" is false. There's something wrong with the picture. The Lesbian Perspective originates in our sense of "difference"—however vague the feeling may be, however much we resist that knowledge—and in our certainty that what others seem happy to accept as "real" is seriously flawed. In order to conceive and define ourselves as Lesbians, we have to defy the "wisdom of the ages." Nobody held up a picture of a wonderful Dyke for us and said, "*You* could grow up to be strong and defiant like her." From the day a girl child is born, everyone who exercises control and authority in her life assumes that she will grow up to "fall in love" with a male (the verb *fall* suggests that it is an "accidental" misstep), and that she will inevitably marry one. All the messages she hears about *who* she is and *who* she's expected to become assume that there's only one kind of love and one kind of sexuality, and that's *heterosexual*. One of those messages informs us that we possess a biologically determined "maternal instinct"; another croons at us, "Every woman needs a man." Imagine how many Lesbians there would be in the world if we got the kind of airtime and publicity that heterosexuality gets. In spite of liberal feminist proclamations to the contrary, we're a long, long way from Marlo Thomas's world of "Free to Be You and Me." What we're "free to be" is heterosexual. That, and that only.

If we must speak of choice, it is the Lesbian who *chooses* to accept the terms of the heterosexual imperative, not the heterosexual. Heterosexuals don't choose their sexuality; they believe it's "natural"—the only way there is to be. Only Lesbians can choose how to define ourselves. Being a Lesbian or a heterosexual isn't a matter of "choosing" a lifestyle or a "sexual preference" from the table spread before us by parents, teachers, and other authority figures. There's only one dish on the social menu—heterosexuality—and we're given to understand that we swallow it or go without. The only options we have are those we create for ourselves because we must do so. Who we decide we are isn't a matter of "taste," although some Lesbians do try to acquire a "taste" for heterosexuality.

There's a large difference between "being heterosexual" and "being a Lesbian." "Being" heterosexual means conforming, living safely, if uncomfortably, within the limits established by men. "Being" a Lesbian means living marginally, often in secrecy, often shamefully, but always as different, as "deviant." Some Lesbians have sex with men, may marry one, two, three, or four men, have numerous children, and live as heterosexuals for some portion of their lives. Lesbians are coming out at every age, and, regardless of how old we are when we decide to act on our self-knowledge, we say: "I've always been a Lesbian." Some Lesbians die without once acting on their deep feelings for other wimmin. Some Lesbians live someone else's life. Deciding to act on our emotional and sexual attractions to other wimmin is usually a long-drawn-out process of introspection and self-examination that can take years, because the social and emotional pressure surrounding us is powerful and inescapable. There's no visible, easily accessible support in our society for being Lesbians, which explains why we have so much trouble imagining what "being Lesbian" means. In many ways, we remain opaque even to our Selves because we haven't yet developed a language that describes our experiences.

Some of our political differences (I'm not referring here to differences arising from ethnic, racial, or class backgrounds, although they influence those I'm talking about) have to do with our level of tolerance for discomfort, how thoroughly we've learned to mistrust and deny our Lesbian selves. Lesbians can deny ourselves endlessly because we're told that we "should." Being heterosexual is the only identity offered, coerced, supported and validated by male society. Male society makes it easy to deny our inner selves, to disbelieve the integrity of our feelings, to discount the necessity of our love for each other, at the same time making it difficult for us to act on our own behalf. Ask a Lesbian who has lived as a heterosexual if she knew she was a Lesbian early in her life, and most will say "yes." Maybe some didn't know the word *Lesbian*, but they'll talk about their childhood love for teachers and girlfriends. Most will say, after they've named themselves Lesbians, "I've always been a Lesbian." Most will say, "I didn't believe there were others like me. I thought I was the only one." This is reinterpretation of experience from a new perspective, *not* revision.

Once a Lesbian identifies herself as *Lesbian*, she brings all of her earlier experiences with and feelings for other women into focus; she crosses the conceptual line that separates the known (the "safe") of the social validation awarded to heterosexuals and the tabooed unknown of deviance. Crossing into this territory, she begins to remember experiences she had "forgotten," recalling women and her feelings for them that she had analyzed or named differently; she examines memories of her past from a new perspective. Events and experiences that once "made no sense" to her are now full of meanings she had ignored, denied, or discarded.

Reconceiving herself as Lesbian, she doesn't change or revise women, events, and experiences in her past; she reinterprets them, understanding them anew from her Lesbian Perspective in the present.

When we fail to be visible to each other, we invalidate the Lesbian Perspective and the meanings it attaches to our experiences. Each of us pays a price for Lesbian invisibility in our self-esteem, in years of our lives, in energy spent trying to deny our Selves. But it is a fact that millions of us name ourselves "Lesbian" even when we have no sense of a community, when we know no one else who is like us, when we believe we will live as outcasts and alone for the remainder of our lives. How do we become that which is nameless, or, once named, shameful, sinful, despised? The Lesbian stands against the world created by the male imagination. What *willfulness* we possess when we claim our lives!

The Lesbian Perspective develops directly out of our experiences in the world: how other people treat us as Lesbians, the negative and positive reactions we get in specific situations, what we're told (and believe) we "ought" to feel about ourselves as Lesbians, and the degree of honesty we come to feel we can exercise in our various relationships. What appear to be important differences among Lesbians are survival skills that enable us to survive in hostile territory. Some of us, for example, have had mostly positive, or at least less damaging, reactions to our Lesbianism from others who "count" in our estimation. Some Lesbians have experienced varying degrees of acceptance, tolerance, and open-heartedness from their heterosexual families and friends. Some Lesbians say they've had "no problems" in their lives connected with their Lesbianism. Not every Lesbian has had portions of her mind destroyed by drugs and repeated shock treatments, or been disowned by her genetic family, or had to survive on her own in the streets, but lots of Lesbians have suffered greatly, have been abused, rejected, ridiculed, committed to psychiatric hospitals, jailed, and tortured. For some, the pain of living as a Lesbian made death a reasonable choice, and many Lesbians have killed themselves rather than endure an existence that seemed to have no hope. Suicide is a valid choice. Whatever our personal experience is, we are always at risk in this society.

Choosing Our Selves

Being a Lesbian isn't a "choice." We *choose* whether or not we'll live as *who we are*. Naming ourselves *Lesbian* is a decision to *act* on our truest feelings. The Lesbian who decides to live as a heterosexual does so at great cost to her self-esteem. Heterosexuals don't have to question the assumptions on which they construct their lives and then defend them to a hostile society. I can't estimate the damage done to our emotional lives by the dishonesty forced on us by male dogma, but I know how much of my own life has been lies, lies, and more lies.

We live in a society where dishonesty is prized above honesty, and Lesbians learn the necessity of lying early on. Parents may tell us to "be ourselves," but we find out quickly, after only one or two "experiments," that honesty is punished, that "being ourselves" really means "Be who we want you to be." I know how much of myself I've tried to cover up, deny, and lie about in order to escape the most violent, lethal methods of suppression. The people who represent "society" for us when we're growing up teach us all we need to know about what being an "adult" means. "Growing up" for females in male societies means *choosing men*, and then lying about how "happy" they are. Naming ourselves Lesbian is one of the most significant steps we take to affirm our integrity, to choose honesty over deception, and to become real to ourselves. This is why the consensus reality of heteropatriarchy describes Lesbianism as "a phase," as something we're supposed to "grow out of." Adopting the protective coloration of heterosexuality is thus equated with "maturity." "Growing up" is a code phrase signaling one's willingness to perform in specific ways: compromise principles, deny feelings, provide *and* accept descriptions one knows to be false, and read along from the heteropatriarchal script. Some people are more adept and credible at acting "mature," but adults lie, and they lie all the time—to their children, loved ones, friends, bosses—but mostly to themselves.

Even after we've begun to explore and expand the meanings of our Lesbian Perspective, we bring our painful experiences about the cost of being honest and the resulting dishonesty we've learned into our communities. Unlearning years of heterosexual training isn't something we can expect to accomplish quickly or easily. Staying honest about ourselves takes lots of practice. We bring our lessons about the necessity of disguising ourselves, of lying about our innermost feelings, and a sincere reluctance to self-disclose with us when we become members of Lesbian society. The results can be far more damaging to our attempts to communicate and create a community than they are in male society.

On the one hand, lying, not being honest about who we are or how we feel, is a *survival skill* we have developed. We have to lie to get by in most heterosexual contexts. I realize there are exceptions to this. But a majority of Lesbians—today—are still *afraid* to be honest about their Lesbian identity, and with good reason. As an out-front Lesbian, I want to validate their fear. It's real, it's based on actual or likely experiences, and no Lesbian should feel she's expected to apologize for protecting herself in the only way she knows.

On the other hand, we've learned the ethic of fear and secrecy so thoroughly that we discover we can't simply shed it when we're in Lesbian contexts. Again, though, previous experiences suggest that self-disclosure and honesty aren't entirely wise even among Lesbians. Too many Lesbians simply don't feel "safe" among other Lesbians on an emotional level, and so we're constantly on guard, prepared to protect ourselves. If we're committed to creating Lesbian communities in which we can work together, we have to deal up front with the fact that Lesbians hurt other Lesbians, not just sometimes, but frequently. We can only stop it when we recognize it, name it for what it is, resolve not to do it, and eliminate it as a behavior.

Choosing Each Other

Those of us who call ourselves *Dyke* or *Lesbian* talk often about a Lesbian community, whether we're "in" or "out" of it, whether or not a community can be said to exist, whether we approve or disapprove of some events or behaviors. Some of our talk may be negative, bitter, wishful, even fanciful, but it is based in our experiences as well as our desire. However we feel about Lesbian community—negative, positive, or indifferent—we call it into existence because we *do* talk about it.

One Lesbian or another can be heard denying that there's any such thing as a Lesbian "community" because she hasn't gotten support for one thing or another. Denying the existence of something acknowledges its potential existence. It's easy to deny ourselves, to remove ourselves from a Lesbian context, to refuse to argue with each other. Those who say the Lesbian community doesn't exist are simultaneously asserting that it *should* exist, thereby calling it into being. I think we deny the existence of Lesbian community when someone or some group fails to meet our expectations of what we believe a Lesbian community *should* be. Rather than risk exposing our expectations of ourselves and other Lesbians, we elide the community we're working hard to create. Something that doesn't exist cannot be blamed for betraying or failing us.

However we conceive our Selves, when each of us decided to name ourselves Lesbians, we were simultaneously estranged from our first "community," the male society into which we were born and in which we were raised. Our decision to be Lesbians cut us off from the forms of validation available to non-Lesbians. Even if a Lesbian gladly embraces male values in every other aspect of her life, if her only act of rebellion is her decision to relate sexually and emotionally with other Lesbians, she will never be rewarded as heterosexuals are. Our Lesbianism isn't valued by male society; it's systematically devalued—discouraged, derided, punished—no matter how we choose, individually, to accommodate estrangement in our lives. We may find occasional support and validation here and there among heterosexuals, but it's not something we can rely on or count as permanent. Our greatest hope for steady, reliable support lies with each other, within the Lesbian community.

Community and Communication

I'm going to suggest that a lot, not all, but a lot of our internal dis-eases, are essentially language problems. They originate in how we talk or don't talk to each other and how we listen or don't listen to each other. Talking, which implies the desire to share ideas, opinions, and feelings, is the essential feature of two pairs of

44

words: *communicate* and *community*, and *relate* and *relationship*. The word *community*, after all, has the same Latin root as the verb to *communicate*, *communicare*, 'to share', and its adjective, *communis*, meaning 'common'. In addition to their more specialized meanings in English, these words also mean 'to share with' and 'to be connected'. If we break the words *community* and *communicate* down further, the prefix *com-*, as in *complete* and *commute*, means 'with', and *-mun-* is the root of the Latin verb *munire*, meaning 'to fortify'. If we think about all these meanings—being connected, sharing, having something in common, and being fortified—we can better understand why a word like *community* resonates in us. We communicate most comfortably with those with whom we have something in common, and we're most likely to find them within a community. By sharing with other Lesbians, we fortify ourselves and grow stronger.

Relationship, that tired, overused word, sounds empty these days, having been heterosexually reified as though it were an autonomous entity, or therapized into a banal abstraction. Whether we can save it or not, we need to remember what it once meant: the willing telling of our Selves to those we connect with. Our relationships aren't limited to those that're sexual; sexual intimacy isn't the defining characteristic of a "relationship." Our friendships are "relationships," and our disagreements are relationships, too. Both our individual relationships as Lesbians and our community are premised on the same sharing: our willingness to *tell* our Selves, our stories, our fears, and our imaginings. The more we talk and listen to each other, the stronger each of us becomes. The stronger we are, the stronger our community. Too often, though, we talk *around* or *at* each other rather than *to* or *with*. Arguing is one kind of communication, but it's something we seem reluctant to do publicly, as if by suppressing our disagreements we can coerce unity from silence.

When we disagree, when we criticize other Lesbians, we're sharing ourselves and our own ideas and opinions. Disagreement isn't only a way of affirming ourselves; we also affirm the significance of the individuals we criticize. Arguing and disagreeing are ways of paying attention to the ideas and beliefs of others. When we argue, we're implying that the ideas we disagree with are important and merit attention. Silence often signals indifference. What we don't find worth responding to, we ignore. When we argue with other Lesbians, we also grow. Total agreement is total stagnation and boredom.

Consider this: In this society, we learn to think of argument as war (Lakoff and Johnson, 4-6). ARGUMENT IS WAR is a cultural metaphor that turns up in the ways we describe the process of arguing. We talk about feeling "defensive," "defending our position," "shooting holes in someone else's argument," "holding opposing views," "demolishing an argument," "winning" and "losing arguments," having "weak points" in an argument, making claims that're "indefensible," "going on the offensive," and "being right on target." If we argue with each other as though ARGUMENT IS WAR, it's no wonder that criticisms are felt as "attacks" and disagreements are felt as "hostility." But arguing doesn't have to be experienced as a war. It's only the male description that makes the equation seem to be "inevitable" and "accurate."

If we believe that criticism is an "attack," and arguing is inherently "hostile," we're also likely to confuse unquestioning support with nurturance. If someone questions our opinions, behaviors, or attitudes, we may dismiss them as "unsupportive." Much is possible once we stop expecting to agree with each other on every single aspect of our lives. Like the members of any other society, we're not going to agree completely, ever. Yet, as a community, we don't handle our disagreements as well as we could.

I believe that inside each Lesbian is the headstrong, willful core of Self that enabled her to choose to act on her Lesbianism, and we need to reclaim that initial certainty, to fulfill the promises we made to our Selves. A first step toward a real Lesbian community must be relearning honesty, a difficult project when all we know is lies. If we are to talk to each other, we must be able to believe that what we're hearing is honesty, even if we don't like it. Let's drop the fine rhetoric and the pretense to perfect understanding. If we're going to make a commitment to a viable, strong, Lesbian community, we have to begin by talking honestly to each other and listening carefully, too. We must take responsibility for articulating and acting on Lesbian values, values that empower our Lesbian Selves.

The BIG Picture

The 1980s were a scary decade for Lesbians, and many of us slipped into an uneasy silence or slammed shut the doors of the closets behind us for a second or third time. We need to keep reminding each other that, as far as we know, *nothing like us has ever happened before. As far as we know*, there has never been a Lesbian Move-ment, and we are *global* in our connectedness. Too many Lesbians have learned, again, to think of ourselves as insignificant. We've heard so much about "broader issues" and "the big picture" that some may think that the Lesbian Perspective is a "narrow" one, restricted to an "insignificant" minority.

Narrow, when applied to concrete, physical dimensions, is used positively, because it refers to slenderness in width, and being 'slender' in heteropatriarchal society is a virtue for those born female. But *narrow*, used abstractly to describe ideas, implies a primarily negative evaluation of whatever concepts it's attached to. We speak, for example, of "narrow opinions," "narrow perspectives," "narrow concerns," and we're much taken by points of view that advertise themselves as part of "the broader picture," as affording us "a broader perspective," a "wider scope," or an opportunity to join the "larger revolution." The word *narrow* is used to trivialize, diminish, and discredit a point of view that some people, usually those with socially-validated power, find threatening, repugnant, and downright outrageous. It is my intention to be outrageous. The Lesbian Perspective is certainly no less "real" or compelling than the dominant perspective of the white, heterosexual majority, and it's by no means as "narrow" in the negative sense of that word. We rightly avoid the "straight and narrow path."

Our unacknowledged allegiance to male thought patterns can hypnotize us into passivity, and men frequently succeed in freezing us with the word *narrow* (and others). There is nothing "narrow" about being and thinking *Lesbian*. What I'm warming up to here is a discussion of "category width" in English and where we think we might "fit" into the categories of man-made frameworks. The language most Lesbians in the U. S. speak, by choice or coercion, is English (native American, black, Latina, Chicana, and Asian-American Lesbians know first-hand about the cultural imperialism of imposed language), and it's the semantic structure of English that binds our minds, squishing our ideas into tidy, binary codes: not-this/this, female/male, small/big, black/white, poor/rich, fat/thin, unseeing/seeing, insane/sane, powerless/powerful, narrow/broad, guilty/innocent. These are narrow concepts in the most negative sense of the word, but they are the semantic basis of the pale male perspective, and we need to understand the conceptual territory those semantic categories map before we can set about the task of creating a new map that charts the territory of the Lesbian Perspective.

Learning a first language socializes us, and we're dependent creatures when our minds are guided into the conceptual grooves created by the map of the territory men want us to follow. The language forces us to perceive the world as men present it to us. If we describe some behaviors as "feminine" and others as "masculine," we're perceiving ourselves in male terms. Or, we fail to perceive what is not described for us and fall back on male constructs, such as "butch" and "femme," as inherently explanatory labels for our self-conceptions.

Those of us raised speaking English weren't offered any choice in the matter. However, while we were passive in the indoctrination process for the first few years, there comes a time when we have to put aside the fact that we began as innocent victims, and undertake the active process of self-reclamation that starts with understanding what happened to us and questioning the conceptual premises on which male societies are based. Learning to think around categorial givens is hard, but it's something we have to do in order to think well of ourselves. If we refuse to do this, we abandon ourSelves.

What is called "consensus reality" is the male-defined, male-described version of "what is," and we are obliged to live around, under, and sometimes within what men say is "reality," even as we strive to conceive and define a Lesbian "consensus reality." The duality of our position as Lesbians—simultaneously being oppressed by a society in which we are unwanted and marginal, and envisioning for ourselves a culture defined by our values, with Lesbian identity at its core— is, I maintain, a position of strength if we claim it.

First, we must undertake the tedious process of examining and re-examining *every* aspect of how we've been taught to "think," including the process of thinking itself. Every one of us raised in an English-speaking household learned to perceive the world, and ourselves in the world, according to the selective map of the pale male perspective. Any map is always, and only, a *partial* description of the territory it claims to chart. Each map draws attention only to those topographical features that the map creator thinks are "relevant" or "significant"; each map creator perceives only some of the aspects of the territory while other, perhaps equally important, features remain invisible, unperceived. Some things are left out on purpose, others are distorted. Black and dark, for example, are given negative values in the pale male conceptual structure, while white and light are assigned positive values; being able to see is a "good thing"; not being able to see is a "bad thing"; accepting male versions of what is "real" is "rational"; rejecting them is "irrational." These descriptions and the values attached to them are not "the nature of the world," and it's not coincidence. Whatever conceptual changes are eventually condoned by male culture can occur only by enlarging existing category widths, in particular the referential scope of words like *people* and *gay*. The semantic categories themselves don't change; they aren't allowed to change. They expand and contract, but the essential thought structures remain the same.

One of our difficulties with describing a Lesbian consensus reality is a language problem: we use contradictory labels to name ourselves, terminology that's sometimes useful but often divisive. The way we name ourselves reflects how we understand what we mean in the world. We call ourselves, for example, "people," "human beings," "women," "gays," "Lesbians," "Dykes." Because we're biologically categorized as female, it seems meaningful to say that, by inclusion with heterosexual women, we're oppressed as "women," and our experience of socialization confirms this category overlap. Likewise, because we aren't hetero, we're also oppressed as "homosexuals," so some Lesbians identify with gaymen, in which case they call themselves "gay women," as I did for many years. Our invisibility, even to ourselves, is at least partially due to the fact that our identity is subsumed by two groups: women and gaymen. As a result, Lesbian issues seem to find their way, by neglect or elimination, to the bottom of both liberation agendas. The liberation of Lesbians is supposed to wait for the liberation of all women, or be absorbed and evaporate into the agenda compiled by gaymen. Instead of creating free space for ourselves, we allow men to oppress us invisibly in both categories, as "women" or as "gays," without even the token dignity of being named "Lesbians." How we name ourselves determines how visible we are, even to each other.

If we allow ourselves to imagine ourselves as something other than "woman" or "gay," if we try to conceive of our Selves beyond those labels, what comes into our minds? Is it no-thing, or is it some-thing? Even if it is hazy, vague, without clear definition, isn't it some-thing we know but haven't yet been able to articulate? The issue here is making explicit the basis of our prioritizing, which has been the idea that we are "sub-" somebody else. I think we are much, much more if we choose our Selves. The problem, as I identify it, is calling ourselves *women*. Monique Wittig (1988) and others have argued that the category 'woman' is a man-made category that serves men's purposes. In this case, the label *woman* diffuses Lesbian movement toward ourSelves, diverting our attention from Lesbian issues and Lesbian needs. The label shifts our focus, directing our attention away from Lesbian community. As soon as we name ourselves Lesbians, we step outside of the category 'woman'. What we experience as Lesbians and identify as "women's oppression" is the socialization process that tried to coerce us into 'womanhood'. As a result of this tailoring of our identities, when we change categories from 'woman' to 'Lesbian', we're still oppressed as 'female' and oppressed for daring to be 'not-woman'. While both Lesbians and hetero women experience misogyny as biological females, Lesbians' experience of that oppression is very different.

The L-word continually disappears into the labels *gay* and *woman*, along with our energy, our money, and our hope. So much Lesbian creativity and activity is called "women's this" or "gay that," making Lesbians invisible and giving hetero-sexual women or gaymen credit for what they can't imagine and haven't accomplished. We need to think *Lesbian*. We need to think *Dyke*. We need to stop being complacent about our erasure.

The male map cannot be trusted because the territory it describes isn't a healthy place for us to live in. Accepting male descriptions of the world endangers Lesbians. We can fight for inclusion within already sanctioned categories, such as 'people', 'human being', or 'woman', thereby forcing other speakers to enlarge them, or we can remain outside of patriarchally given categories and endeavor to construct a different, more accurate map of the Lesbian conceptual territory. We have internalized a description of the world that erodes our self-esteem, damages our self-image, and poisons our capacity for self-love. If the children we were lacked options for the process of self-creation, the Lesbians we've become have the potential, as well as the responsibility, for redefining ourselves, learning to perceive the world in new and different ways from what we were taught, and setting about making maps that accurately describe the territory of our envisioning.

We can choose whether or not we will conform to heterosexual values, and even the degree to which we'll conform to the map men have imposed on reality. How we choose to deal with the defining categories of male culture places us within its boundaries or at its periphery. (See my essay, "Heteropatriarchal Semantics and Lesbian Identity: The Ways a Lesbian Can Be," this volume, for an analysis of these defining categories.) We are never "outside" the reach of society, because even the negative evaluation of who we are can limit and control our lives. How we describe for ourselves that first wary step into an uncharted world determines how we think of ourselves as Lesbians. The Lesbian situation is essentially *ambiguous*, and that ambiguity provides the foundation of the Lesbian Perspective. We must start from where we are.

Terra Incognita

Deciding to act on our Lesbian perceptions requires each of us to conceive of ourselves as someone other than who male society has said we are. The Lesbian process of self-definition, however long it takes, begins with the recognition and certainty that our perceptions are fundamentally accurate, regardless of what male societies say. This is a *strong* place in us. In order to trust ourselves, we have to be able to push through the lies and contradictions presented to us as "truths," cast them aside, and stand, for that moment, in our own clarity. Every Lesbian takes that step into *terra incognita*: the undescribed or falsely described, the "unknown," beyond the limits posted by the pale male map of reality. Picture for yourself the map of the "known" world presented to us every moment, every day of our lives. Label that map HETEROPATRIARCHY out to the very neatly trimmed edges. Now read the warning signs along the edge: "Dangerous," "monstrous," "sick," "sinful," "illegal," "unsafe," "Keep Out! Trespassers will be violated!" Remember how long you deliberated with yourself before stepping across that boundary, before you decided you had to ignore the warning signs and take your chances in an ill-defined geography.

It's the clarity of that moment, the confidence of self-creation, that creates the "euphoria" so many Lesbians experience when we first come out. We do not forget that moment of clarity, ever. Lesbians think and behave differently because we've had to fight constantly to establish and maintain our identity in spite of covert and overt attempts, some of them violent, all of them degrading, to coerce us into heterosexuality. The Lesbian Self must stand alone, sometimes for years, against the force of the heterosexual imperative, until she can find other Lesbians who will support and affirm her. The out Lesbian has denied the validity of what men call "reality" in order to be Her Self. We do think differently. We perceive the world as aliens, as outcasts. No matter how hard some Lesbians try to "fit in," pale male societies define us as outside the boundary of the categories that maintain its coherence. We are made outcasts, but we can empower our Selves on that ground.

Although we may look back at times with yearning toward the heterosexual land of make-believe, we know that delusion for what it is: a man-made smog that pollutes and poisons all life. We must choose our own clarity, our willfulness, and reject the orthodoxy, "right-thinking," of men. Being Lesbian *is* nonconforming. The Lesbian Perspective demands heterodoxy, deviant and unpopular thinking, requires us to love ourselves for being outcasts, to create for ourselves the grounds of our being. The Lesbian Perspective isn't something we acquire as soon as we step out of our closets. It's as much a process of unlearning as it is learning. It's something we have to work at, nurture, encourage, and develop. The Lesbian Perspective is furious self-creation.

If we can imagine ourselves into being, if we can refuse to accept the labels and descriptions of men, the "possibilities *are* endless." We *are* outcasts from male society. We have no choice in that. What we can choose is how we define ourselves with respect to our outcast status. The Lesbian Perspective always asks "unpopular" questions. They're not popular because they threaten the interior structure of societies erected by men. What, exactly, does the Lesbian Perspective look like? Because we're already living in a way that men say is impossible, we gradually shed the dichotomies and distinctions we learned as children. The labels, names, and compartmentalizations that accompany them come to have less and less relevance in our thought processes, and we find new ways of interpreting our experience in the world because we perceive it differently. What we once memorized and accepted as "facts" no longer accurately describe our perceptions of reality. We realize that what we were taught to think was "real" or "natural" are only man-made constructs imposed on acts and events, ready-made representations of thoughts and feelings that we can, and must, reject. This is a difficult, gradual, uncertain process only because male societies don't want us to enjoy being outcasts. It's definitely *not* in the interests of men for us to like ourselves. Although it's men who established the boundaries that made us outcasts, what counts is how we organize that information in our minds and act on it in our lives.

The Lesbian Perspective challenges what heterosexuals choose to believe is "fact." As our joy in being outcasts expands, so does our ability to ask dangerous questions and dis-cover magical answers. We have no "givens" beyond that which is "other than": "deviant," "abnormal," "unnatural," "queer," false descriptions we begin with and cannot afford to forget. Indeed, we should wear them proudly. But our major endeavor must be self-definition. We have much to learn yet about ourselves, *our* culture, and we have new maps to draw that show the significant features of our worlds. The Lesbian Perspective makes it possible to challenge the accuracy of male consensus reality, and to create a reality that is Lesbian-defined and Lesbian-sustaining. Once we learn to perceive the world from our own perspective, outside the edges of the pale male map, we'll find it not only recognizable, but familiar.

Wimmin- and Lesbian-Only Spaces: Thought into Action

T here are women and Lesbians who take wimmin- and Lesbian-only spaces[1] for granted, perceiving them as efforts that aren't difficult or dangerous to maintain, on a par with sneaking beer into a movie theater. But such spaces are always endangered and vulnerable to trespass and infiltration. Attempts to discredit, disrupt, and destroy Lesbian- and wimmin-only spaces have persisted since Lesbians began establishing spaces and insisting upon our right to them. This isn't new information. We have learned that those who take the risks to create wimmin- and Lesbian-only spaces cannot assume that other Lesbians and wimmin will respect them. Unless we find a way to maintain male-free spaces, the intrusions typical of the 1970s and 1980s will persist through yet another decade.

- In June, 1987, Sisterfire[2] coordinators ignored male assaults on two Separatists and told them they didn't belong at the festival and "had no right" to deny men access to their booth.

- In 1989, Lesbian mothers brought at least four male children to the first East Coast Lesbian Festival even though the festival brochure said specifically: "Lesbians and Girl Children Welcome."

- A gayman, Bob Kavin, threatened to file a complaint against Crones' Harvest, then a new wimmin's bookstore in Jamaica Plain, Massachusetts, for advertising "wimmin-only" events in *Gay Community News*. He characterized such male-free events as "divisive" and said the ad "pissed him off."

- Also in 1990, Rex Wockner, a syndicated gay columnist, made Mountain Moving Coffeehouse, a wimmin-only space in Chicago, the center of a controversy in its fifteenth year of existence.

- A woman describing herself as "strayt" occupied a full page in a

1990 issue of *Dykes, Disability & Stuff* and promised (!) to send more "stuff."

- Two men have crashed into an issue of the Women's Braille Press newsletter.

In spite of their apparent dissimilarity, these events have several common features. Each violation is an attempt to force *normalization*[3] on Lesbians and wimmin who are consciously encouraging and cherishing attitudes, values, and behaviors devalued by the majority culture—what heteropatriarchal society labels "abnormal" and "unnatural": wimmin loving and attending to one another. These people insist that Lesbians and wimmin respect and condone the heteropatriarchal values they bring with them. In the heteropatriarchy, it is *normal* and *natural*, not deviant, for men to have unchallenged access to women. The gaymen trying to destroy Crones' Harvest and Mountain Moving Coffeehouse and the Sisterfire coordinators insist that men retain their privilege to invade and occupy wimmin's spaces. Men justify their intrusions by asserting that the privileges they have in the heteropatriarchy are their "natural right."

The claim of "natural right" is also used by a few mothers of male children who insist on bringing their sons with them into wimmin- and Lesbian-only spaces. Most mothers of sons support and respect our spaces, either by arranging to leave their male children at home or, for financial reasons, stay at home themselves. Why, then, do a few mothers *insist* that we tolerate their sons? For one thing, they have millenia of heteropatriarchal dogma behind their demands: Because breeding is considered "normal" and "natural," those mothers *expect* to take their offspring wherever they wish. When denied access for their male children, they protest as though their privilege were an "inalienable right." Some Lesbian mothers persist in demanding that we allow them to bring male children to wimmin- and Lesbian-only events. Their insistence on giving males access to wimmin- and Lesbian-only spaces reaffirms the breeders' privilege they enjoy in the heteropatriarchy.[4]

There is no space on this planet that men do not claim as theirs "by right." However much space they dominate, it never seems to be "enough" for them. Wimmin- and Lesbian-only spaces challenge the male "right" to occupy and control territory. In this culture, "it's a man's world." Whatever is "public" space is theirs. Men assume they have the right to occupy any "public" space because it's *their* world. Women's lives have been confined to the "private" sphere. But men control the private as well as the public sphere. As Catherine MacKinnon has pointed out,[5] men's laws operate only in the public sphere; they cease to operate in the private sphere, because that is where men "exercise" their freedom and do whatever they want to women and children. If Lesbians want to raise males, they should be teaching them that wimmin have the right to establish our own spaces; that no man has any right to be where we don't want him; that "No" doesn't mean

"Yes."

When we create a space we label Lesbian- or wimmin-only, we mean what we say. This isn't something that's open to interpretation! Yet, a few women and Lesbians feel compelled, year after year, to defend and insist upon men's "right" to unlimited access to other wimmin and Lesbians. By demanding that we admit them with their male children, these individuals make it clear that they value men more than they value wimmin and/or Lesbians *and* the desire we make explicit by creating these spaces. Each intrusion devalues wimmin-only space, negating it by introducing male presence, male values and male behaviors, sometimes all three. In every case, the Lesbians trying to establish and maintain wimmin-only space are trivialized and attacked, and the mothers of sons and their supporters justify their attacks by the tactic of reversal: they cast themselves as the "victims" of Lesbians who reject the claims of men and Lesbian mothers of male children. The violators attempt to coerce and intimidate other Lesbians and wimmin into supporting men and condoning their values and behaviors by describing themselves as an "oppressed minority."

In each case I've cited, some type of "discrimination" is alleged in order to deny our right to control the spaces we create: at Sisterfire, the two Lesbians were accused of racism and "provoking" a man's physical assault by telling him they didn't want him to enter their booth; Lesbian mothers of males portray themselves as taking "risks" to raise male children, as "pioneering" radical ways of parenting. They describe Lesbians who won't support them as their "oppressors." Men who resort to their legal system to redress the "wrong" done to them when wimmin or Lesbians create wimmin-only events claim that they are the "victims" of "sexist" oppression.

For some reason I don't understand, some Lesbians, women, and men either don't grasp the principles involved in wimmin- and Lesbian-only space, or they pretend not to understand. I don't understand why they don't understand. I've thought the ideas were easily grasped and the labels we use to describe them were literally interpreted: "wimmin-only" space means *wimmin only*; "Lesbian-only" space means *Lesbians only*. There is no ambiguity in either phrase. Sons are, by definition, inherently *male*; otherwise, they would be daughters. Where, then, is the problem? Why is the concept of "female-only" space so difficult to entertain and so frequently challenged?

I've been thinking about how we think about Lesbian-/wimmin-only space and trying to understand why there are conflicts when we stake out some area as our "own." What do we *imagine* we're doing when we say we're "creating" Lesbian-/wimmin-only space? Our thinking is based on the CONTAINER metaphor[6]: we imagine that we create a container (or draw a circle) that has an inside and an outside. *Inside*, within our circle, we say we want only wimmin or only Lesbians; individuals who aren't wimmin or Lesbians we expect to remain *outside* our circle. We *include* all other wimmin or Lesbians and we *exclude*, by default, anyone who doesn't identify as woman or Lesbian, and those women and Lesbians who prefer male company. There is, or should be, a process of self-selection: anyone who doesn't like Lesbian- or wimmin-only spaces needn't come.

Where do we imagine we "draw" our imaginary circles? Where do we think we've created our wimmin- or Lesbian-only space *in relation to* patriarchal space? Do we imagine our "space" to be "inside" or "outside" of male-dominated space? I, for one, have imagined Lesbian-/wimmin-only space as being "outside" or "beyond" patriarchal social space in a metaphorical sense. I know that I've thought of it that way in the past: Standing naked "downtown" at the Michigan Womyn's Music Festival, I have thought of myself as "inside" and of the patriarchal world as "out there" somewhere beyond the borders of the womyn-owned land. While I'm at the Festival, I rarely remind myself that the two worlds are connected by the public road that lies just outside the gates of the Festival. The spaces we create for ourselves may have physical boundaries, but, more importantly, they're an idea we nourish in our minds.

Whatever spaces we temporarily carve out for ourselves from the world of men and label wimmin- or Lesbian-only space are just that: temporary. Using the CONTAINER metaphor to think about wimmin- and Lesbian-only spaces tricks us into thinking of them as "insides" that have "outsides," but this isn't true. We are always *in* heteropatriarchy, never *outside* of it. For this reason, our spaces cannot be defended against intrusion. In spite of their vulnerability, we have been able so far to at least curtail men's access to wimmin- and Lesbian-only spaces. What we seem unable to discourage or halt are the persistent attempts of a few women and Lesbians to breach the spaces we claim as Lesbian- or wimmin-only. Such encroachments are more insidious than male intrusion. I don't *expect* men to respect wimmin-only spaces; nonetheless, some do. I *expect* other wimmin and Lesbians to respect such spaces; some don't.

For example, when Lisa Vogel and Barbara Price discovered that some workers had brought men's music to listen to at the Michigan Womyn's Music Festival, they were shocked that those workers failed to perceive their actions as contradictory or invasive, and were dismayed that the propriety of listening to male voices in that context could be an "issue." Why isn't it clear that the sound of male voices at a *womyn's* music festival introduces men's ideas, values, and behaviors? What some or many of us assume are self-evident labels—*wimmin's* music, *wimmin-only* dance, *Lesbian-only* workshop—are apparently labels that others feel compelled to violate.

More dangerously, such violations are often gradual or clandestine. For example, it was not "enough" when the Michigan coordinators responded to the protests of the mothers of boys by establishing the Brother Sun Camp for boys up to the age of ten. For the past two years, a special area has been set aside *at the center of the Festival* for mothers with children under three.[7] It is common knowledge among festie-goers that mothers of sons, apparently not satisfied by their successful encroachment into the "wimmin-only" space of the Michigan Festival, have deliberately proceeded to violate the essential idea of wimmin-/Lesbian-only space by disguising their male children as girls and sneaking them onto the land! Such purposeful disregard for the implied rights of other wimmin and Lesbians to define and control our spaces violates our trust as well as our declared boundaries.

Why are a few mothers of sons so determined to violate the spaces some of us cherish and work so hard to create? I don't think they even understand what all the fuss is about; I don't think they perceive their actions as betrayals or violations because they don't think of wimmin- or Lesbian-only spaces as *containers*. In their minds, they haven't yet distinguished between "the male world *out there*" and the world we create and think of as *in here*. To them, our spaces are the same as the rest of the world: males have and, thanks to the intervention of a few mothers of sons, *do* have access to both. We will continue to repeat this conflict until, or unless, these few perceive wimmin- and Lesbian-only spaces as we do, and come to think of them in terms of the CONTAINER metaphor.

How are we to deal with such women and Lesbians? Can we deal honorably and honestly with those who refuse to be honorable or honest with us? Since *some* mothers of male children seem utterly uninterested in or incapable of respecting the boundaries and definitions other wimmin and Lesbians have said we want them to honor, our options are limited. Some Lesbians think it is a contradiction to "exclude" wimmin and Lesbians from wimmin- and Lesbian-only spaces even though they have violated the boundaries we have said we wish to maintain when they sneak in their male children. For example, when I was explaining what I thought "Lesbian-only" space meant from the stage at the East Coast Lesbian Festival in 1989, someone in the audience screamed out, "The mothers are Lesbians, too!" But this is a diversionary tactic. The issue isn't whether the mothers of male children are or are not Lesbians. The issue is their demand that we accept their male children *as a corollary* to accepting them. An 18-month-old male child is *not* a Lesbian. About that there is no question. Yet, their reasoning seems to go something like this:

> I am a Lesbian. Therefore I have a right to be in Lesbian-only space. (So far, so good.) I have a son. Because I am a Lesbian, I have the right to bring my son (or exceptional man) with me.

Having identified themselves as Lesbian, they proceed to use that identity as an umbrella of immunity for any male *they* feel safe with. (But many of us have been raped and/or assaulted by boys and men that other females felt "safe" with.)

All of the examples I've mentioned represent *violations* of the boundaries of other Lesbians and wimmin and betrayals of our trust in their integrity and values. Those who insist upon their "right" to bring men into wimmin- or Lesbian-only space cannot seem to distinguish between the heteropatriarchal culture in which we all live and the small, temporary spaces we attempt to claim as our own for hours, days or weeks. Their demands force us to compromise and ignore our own values and priorities. Lesbian- and wimmin-only spaces give us many joys and opportunities we can't get anywhere else in this world:

- they provide us with some respite from the dangers and anxieties of our lives in heteropatriarchy;

- the atmosphere and joy we experience reenergizes us and enables us to go on surviving and working for change;

- in them, we can creatively explore and develop Lesbian values and ways of relating to each other;

- we can talk, roam, play, and sleep undisturbed by male intrusiveness and interruptions;

- we don't have to listen to men or the sound of their voices;

- such spaces are the *only* ones in which girl children can run free without fearing male predation and violence.

For all these reasons (and more), these spaces are important to many of us. They are one of the greatest and most lasting gifts we can give to girl children. *We have a right to them* and, as well, *the right to expect that others will respect them.*

If we are to maintain these spaces, what are we to do with women and Lesbians who demand access for their men and male children to them and *believe* that their demands and surreptitious violations have the weight of moral righteousness behind them? We have been explaining to them *for years* why we want them to respect our spaces, and they seem unwilling to understand their own hypocrisy in the situation. They fail to perceive how bringing their sons into Lesbian- and wimmin-only events violates the very spirit and intent of such spaces, when their ostensible reason for coming is to enjoy their unique qualities with the rest of us. They cannot have things both ways.

What is involved here is a choice that they must make, one they have, so far, refused to consider: Either they figure out how to leave their sons at home or they voluntarily exclude themselves. And, in so doing, they have to take responsibility for their choice. Their claim—that we "exclude" them when we exclude their sons—is false (unless we agree with the heteropatriarchal notion that mothers become indissolubly *merged* with their children), and most mothers of sons reject this claim by their ability to choose.

It's long past time to stop trying to reason with them and to acknowledge that our explanations are just not sufficient for them. One would think that the simple statement about what we want for ourselves would be enough to dissuade these few from continuing to violate our spaces. Judging from their behavior and what they say, this doesn't seem to be the case. Their persistent encroachments require an unsavory vigilance and a constant drain on our energies to defend the spaces we claim. If we continue to give in to these demands and ignore the tremendous toll these violations exact, we will no longer be able to enjoy even those few, isolated and extremely vulnerable wimmin- or Lesbian-only spaces we establish.

Again and again, a few women violate our spaces without any apparent regard for us. What are our options for dealing with Lesbians and women who prioritize men and male values over the expressed desires of other wimmin and Lesbians? Obviously, naming our events "Lesbian-" or "wimmin-only" has failed; they refuse to honor them. Explanations of the political and personal reasons for having wimmin- and Lesbian-only spaces have consistently failed us, but the alternatives to explanation are unappealing. We could think of these spaces as "wimmin-only-sort of" or "Lesbian-only-sort of," which seems to be the approach already in use. A space is wimmin- or Lesbian-only except for when it's not. Or, we could establish "strip searches" at festival registrations and have every mother with a child open its diapers or pants to prove that it's a girl child. Such a solution is repugnant. Yet, we cannot, it seems, trust each other, or, at least, not *all* of us. If we can't trust each other to respect our expressed wishes, whom can we trust? If some women and Lesbians who value men over the rest of us persist in their refusal to respect us, I don't know how we can continue to honor an illusory respect or trust that isn't mutual.

I do know that some of us will continue to create, participate in, and enjoy Lesbian- and wimmin-only spaces, and we will continue to repulse the intrusions of gaymen and sons of mothers: We will refuse to admit gaymen to such events and ask mothers to leave their male children at home or accept responsibility for their decision to exclude themselves.

Endnotes

1. I realize that my repetition of *wimmin-* and *Lesbian-only* will seem cumbersome to readers; for this, I apologize. I want to acknowledge that heterosexual wimmin as well as Lesbians support and enjoy male-free spaces. But I also want to represent a distinction that's important to me. In my own experience, both kinds of space are different in a number of ways: they establish very different frameworks, contexts, and expectations. What is talked about in an all-women context differs from the subjects Lesbians choose to talk about; the life-experiences discussed and validated are dissimilar; the perspectives with which participants approach each context reflect different values and assumptions. These differences became clear to me one night when I watched a tape of a female comedian who has taken women-only space mainstream and is performing to sell-out, *women-only* crowds! While I laughed out loud at some of her jokes, I found most of them either distasteful or boring because she focused almost entirely on men and women's feelings about and relationships with them. I have no quarrel with what she's doing; the women who attended her show seemed to be enjoying themselves and that's

enough reason to support what the comedian is doing. But Lesbian-only space is something altogether different and more pleasing to me: It is the only space in this world where Lesbians focus exclusively on each other, on our ideas, on our desires, on our relations with each other. And, for most of us, it provides us with a much-needed respite from having to deal with men and women who focus their entire beings on men.

2. Sisterfire was an annual music festival organized and produced by Roadworks, a Washington, D. C. collective; it was the only wimmin's music festival that attempted an explicitly multiracial, multi-ethnic focus that reflected the cultural diversity of our communities. Two years after the fiasco I discuss here, the Sisterfire festival ceased to exist.

3. For a thorough discussion of the many ways Lesbian motherhood co-opts Lesbian values and spaces, see *Dykes-Loving-Dykes* by Bev Jo, Linda Strega, and Ruston (Oakland: Battleaxe, 1990), esp. pp. 212-234. Kate Moran, in a conversation, described the process discussed here as "normalization," and I'm indebted to her for our many talks about this issue and how it affects Lesbians.

4. Many mothers expect privileges and certain behaviors from others. I meet them everywhere I go. They *expect* strangers to smile approvingly at them; they expect others to allow them to cut into long lines; they expect others to put up with their childrens' screeches and squalls in restaurants, theaters, and other public places. I don't know why. There're already too many people in the world. Once, I boarded a plane, expecting my reserved seat to be available. Instead, there sat a breeder with her baby spread out in what was supposed to have been my seat! As I approached and began checking the numbers of the seats to be sure I hadn't made a mistake, she smiled at me confidently. I asked, "Who do you think you are? Do you think that, because you're a breeder, you have the right to take over my seat?" The stewardess came rushing down the aisle, saying "Oh, I'm so sorry. I thought it would be all right." Why would someone assume that I wouldn't mind having my seat taken away from me?

5. In *Feminism Unmodified: Discourses on Life and Law* (1987) MacKinnon elaborates how the liberal concept of the "private sphere" is "an ideological division that lies about women's shared experience and that mystifies the unity among the spheres of women's violation" (102), with respect to abortion (100-102) and pornography (155 and 211).

6. Michael Reddy first identified the "Container Metaphor" in "The Conduit Metaphor— A Case of Frame Conflict," *Metaphor and Thought*, ed. Andrew Ortony (Cambridge: Cambridge University Press, 1979), 284-324. Readers interested in other ways the Container Metaphor structures how we think about other aspects of our daily lives will find a more detailed explanation in *Speaking Freely: Unlearning the Lies of the Fathers' Tongues* (Pergamon, 1990), in which I discuss the function of that metaphor in heteropatriarchal thinking, and illustrate how it shapes our understanding of language, writing, and ourselves as females as well.

7. When a Michigan festie-goer complained about the creation of the toddler camping area, where mothers can have male sons up to the age of three, Lisa Vogel explained that she and Barbara Price established the new area because too many mothers dropped off their infants and small children, and then apparently "forgot" the children and failed to return for them. Announcements, asking mothers to return to the daycare area for their abandoned children, have been a too common feature of the nightstage at Michigan. Understandably, Michigan workers are reluctant to accept responsibility for very young children and to bear the brunt of their mothers' neglect.

Do We Mean What We Say?: Horizontal Hostility and the World We Would Create

"Horizontal hostility"—the anger, frustration, and mistrust directed by members of an oppressed group, often inappropriately, toward other members of the same group—is nothing new. Florynce Kennedy coined the phrase very soon after the second wave of the Women's Liberation Movement (WLM) got underway. Horizontal hostility has been going on, pretty much without let-up, from then until now. Most of us have been the targets of another Lesbian's anger; we know how it hurts. Most of us have also taken out our anger and frustration on other Lesbians; we know how effective it is in silencing us. The more visible and vocal we are, the more likely we are to be on the receiving end of horizontal hostility.

Lesbians know a lot about horizontal hostility: we know when we're engaging in it and we know its origins in our experiences. We know that horizontal hostility allows us to direct our anger, which arises from our marginal, subordinate status in a heteropatriarchy and should be directed toward our oppressors, toward other Lesbians and wimmin, because we know it is safer. Other wimmin and Lesbians cannot (or do not) respond to our anger with physical threats and violence, as men do, nor do we have the power and authority to define and control the lives of others as men and their institutions do. Horizontal hostility functions to insure our on-going victimization within our own groups, and it keeps us silent when we most want to speak out; it keeps us passive when we most want to challenge, because we don't want to be the target of another Lesbian's anger. Our fear of being hurt by each other is a terrible barrier to being honest among ourselves. Yet, honesty is something we must have if we are to work successfully for our liberation. Horizontal hostility is the heteropatriarchy's best method of keeping us "in our places"; we do the work of men and their institutions for them.

Clearly, naming the phenomenon *horizontal hostility* hasn't stopped it or even curbed it. Just as clearly, horizontal hostility remains, along with the patriarchy itself, one of the major obstacles to the success of the Women's Liberation Movement. Horizontal hostility is one of patriarchy's most successful weapons in its self-perpetuation because it maintains our internalized oppression. Horizontal hostility has the *power to divide* because every single one of us has internalized divisive patriarchal descriptions of who and what we are. When we lash out at each other, we expose how much we hate ourselves. We expect verbal and physical violence from men. We don't expect it from one another. And so we are continually being caught "off guard," betrayed.

It's not that we've ignored horizontal hostility among ourselves; from time to time, those of us who've felt the brunt of horizontal hostility have spoken up. Most recently, Sarah Hoagland's *Lesbian Ethics* (1988) has presented an analysis and suggested ways we can work together in the creation of a Lesbian-identified community in which each of us is valued for what we do well and supported in spite of our shortcomings. I speak of "what we do well" and "our shortcomings" advisedly. One of the nasty things about horizontal hostility is that we can be made outcasts for competence as well as betrayal. Joanna Russ has addressed the tendency to attack those perceived and described as "stars" in her essay, "Power and Helplessness in the Women's Movement" (1981; 1985). Horizontal hostility doesn't distinguish between honest mistakes and outright betrayals, between the failures of "magic mommas" or the low self-esteem of "trembling sisters." Horizontal hostility is our own self-loathing turned outward against those who mean us well. It attacks us where we are least guarded, and denies our sincerest intentions. Think what we might accomplish if we stopped hurting each other!

Although others have discussed horizontal hostility, I'm going to approach the subject from a different angle. I have identified three layers in the construction of horizontal hostility. The first layer I call the perceptual-descriptive: one individual perceives another Lesbian acting or behaving a certain way in a situation. She then attaches a label to that Lesbian's behavior that she feels accurately describes her perceptions.

The second layer is interactional. The perceiver, she who chooses specific words to describe her perception, rarely does so in isolation or utter privacy. She shares her observations with friends, choosing her words and their ordering when she reports her perceptions. Even if she bothers to describe her perceptions to the offending individual, her reporting may not stop there. In addition to telling her friends, who will tell their friends who will tell their friends, she may write a letter to a newspaper or journal. The publication of her perception-description then extends the range of her reported perceptions infinitely.

The act of reporting one's perceptions and the descriptive language in which those perceptions are reported create the third layer of horizontal hostility: the layer of information use, or *acceptance-repetition*. What we think becomes what we "know." Whoever hears or reads her reported perceptions has at least three choices, maybe more:

1) They can choose to accept the first Lesbian's description as an accurate report of her perceptions of the other Lesbian;

2) They can choose to accept the first Lesbian's description as an accurate report of her perceptions of the second Lesbian but not, necessarily, as an accurate report of that Lesbian's behavior and beliefs, and/or

3) They can assume that her perceptions are inherently accurate and accept her description as an absolutely true report of the second Lesbian.

This third level is the most complicated. Its many strands form our community's "grapevine," binding us together in a cycle of action and reaction, accusation and rebuttal. The kind and extent of damage done to the Lesbian being talked about depends upon every single member of the community—in particular how much credibility both of the Lesbians involved have in the community, and how readily other community members accept negative reports. Within the warp and woof of these layers, in the descriptive language of the report, lie the origins of horizontal hostility. Everyone who participates in these interchanges and relays is personally responsible.

These three layers, the perceptual-descriptive, the interactional, and acceptance-repetition, are connected and mutually re-enforced by a naive belief in a close correspondence between experiences and the language we use to describe them. Language figures prominently in our worst conflicts. I say that believing in an inherently accurate, one-to-one correspondence between our language descriptions and reality is naive because language cannot ever be an absolutely accurate description or report. There is no simple, one-to-one correspondence between what we say and what we mean, or between what we say and the world beyond our skins.

Unfortunately, we tend to forget along the way that our perceptions, and our descriptions of them, are choices we make among a multitude of options; our listeners can be equally forgetful, and what we say is then quickly mistaken for *what is*. The relationship between what happens in the world and what we say about it is tenuous, yet we persist in believing that language works like the pneumatic tubes at drive-in banks. We imagine that we place our ideas into small containers, words, phrases, sentences, and toss them into the air, which magically transmits our ideas, intact and utterly accurately, into the minds of our listeners. But language—specifically when we use it to communicate—doesn't work that way.

Heteropatriarchal culture encourages us to believe two impossible things at once about language in the world: on the one hand, that language, and, by implication, words, are trivial, irrelevant, empty. A quick way to shut down disagreement is to tell someone that her argument is "just a question of semantics," or to dismiss her point of view by saying, "Let's not quibble over words." On the other hand, we have been taught, "educated," to use words loosely, to confuse labels with reality as though they can mediate and legitimate our experiences and actions in the world. We believe, without critical awareness, that the words we choose are insignificant and, simultaneously, that the words we use are absolutely *true*.

We also know that our perceptions, and our descriptions of them, can be distorted or downright false. There are contexts, however, in which the accuracy of our descriptions is irrelevant, and I'll mention a couple of familiar examples before turning to contexts in which the accuracy of our descriptions is profoundly important. We talk about tables and chairs as though our perception of them as "solid" were true, and no harm is done. Unless we claim that such descriptions are scientifically valid, perpetuating such false descriptions doesn't betray us. Books and plates stay on tables, and chairs (usually) hold us. We say that "the sun rises" and "the sun sets," knowing that those descriptions are based on inaccurate perceptions. We talk about the "morning star" and the "evening star" as different objects, when, in fact, both labels refer to the planet Venus. The language we use in these descriptions has nothing whatever to do with "reality," even if they reflect the way we perceive the sun's motion or the times Venus is visible to us. We know that our perceptions in these cases don't record reality. We know that what we say isn't accurate.

Now, consider another situation: You and a friend are walking through an apple orchard one afternoon and you both observe apples attached to a tree limb one moment, then lying on the ground in the next. Even though you've both perceived exactly the *same event* at the *same time*, your descriptions may still differ. You might say to your friend, "Look, the apples have fallen *from the tree*." Your friend might say, "Wow! The apples have fallen *to the ground*." These are *different* descriptions of the same event; both are *equally* accurate. One is focused on the earlier state of the apples (*from the tree*), the other focuses on their final state (*to the ground*).

But these examples don't reflect differing values or threats to our self-esteem. It doesn't matter whether they're accurate or true. However, our *values* determine how we perceive people and events; our language choices reflect the belief system that structures our perceptions. When values and value judgments are involved, as they often are, what we say to each other is *crucial*. The *words* we choose are crucial.

Consider the following description of an event in the Montana legislature: "Today, *the battle against marijuana was won* in the legislature." The reporter (a man) had several alternative descriptions to choose from: he could have said, "The battle to legalize marijuana was lost," "Montana legislators decided not to legalize marijuana," "Efforts to legalize marijuana suffered a setback in the Montana legislature today," and so on. Each choice reflects a different opinion about the event, different ways of perceiving it. Some possibilities are more neutral than others. Some are more biased. The reporter chose a biased description, and his belief system determined how he described the event. The language of his description, "The battle against marijuana was won," didn't inhere in the event itself. His linguistic choices tell us something about his attitude toward the legalization of marijuana.

What we say reflects our values—positive, negative, or indifferent. Because there is no inherent relationship between our language and what is happening in the world, the way we use language originates in the values underlying our choices. Our values mediate between our language use and the world we are attempting to describe. Do we mean what we say? Are we willing to be held responsible for the harm we cause with our words?

Many of us are sensitive to the arbitrariness of words when we hear or read misogynistic descriptions. "Woman is intended for reproduction; she has been appointed to take an active part in the reproduction of the race by pregnancy and childbirth." "The true heroes of the feminist movement can be found more easily in a kitchen in Dorchester than on a platform in the person of a weeper like Pat Schroeder." Likewise, we are, or should be, attuned to how language serves white male supremacy. "Integration is big business. Invest your daughter." And we are unlikely to be able to ignore the callousness of Himmler's description of the Nazis' genocidal plans. "The Eastern territories must become free of Jews."

The language of hatemongers may frighten us, chill us. And, although all of us may not be able to explain exactly why their descriptions scare us, we recognize the assumption of the authority to define women's "place" and "feminist" heroes, and the assumption of the power to dispose of. All four examples illustrate how white men's assumption of their superiority to women, Jews, and people of color determines their choices of vocabulary and syntax.

Perhaps some of us were able to ignore our disquiet when Reagan, describing his "innocence" with respect to the Iran-Contra scandal, said: "Mistakes were made." Few of us are surprised that Himmler, Reagan, Bush, and the Ku Klux Klan are our enemies. We expect them to hate us. But we have other enemies who endanger us even as they claim that they're our "allies." In the mid-1980s, gaymen and bisexuals in Massachusetts launched their attacks on Lesbians, and their hatred of us exploded into the local media in 1990, when they initiated a vicious letter-writing campaign because Lesbians protested the inclusion of bisexuals in the name of the 1989 Northampton Pride March and Rally.

But there was much more going on that most of the anti-Lesbians chose to ignore or trivialize. In 1989, there was no Lesbian speaker at the Rally. When Lesbians confronted Jeff Jerome (then a rally coordinator) about the erasure of Lesbians this represented, in print he said, "It was no one's intent not to have lesbian speakers,. . . Things fell through." (As reported in *Gay Community News,* March 25, 1990)

"Things fell through." Well, yes. Shit happens, but not without an asshole (*gracias*, Susan Wolfe). In private, Jerome had said that bisexuals could speak for Lesbians because he didn't know any Lesbians who didn't fuck men. Jerome is one of a growing number of bisexuals and gaymen promoting Lesbian-hating in a big way.

Since then, those "allies," their ranks increased by members of Queer Nation, continue to escalate the hostilities. Speakers from the gay, Lesbian, and bisexual group at the University of Massachusetts-Amherst tell classes that "All Lesbians are bisexuals," and a newsletter, *Outline*, publishes an article in which Lesbians are called "fascists from hell." In 1991, anti-Lesbian graffiti appears daily in public bathrooms around the Northampton-Amherst area.[1] In Bart's, for example, an ice-cream shop where Lesbians are regular customers, the language on the bathroom walls and doors is increasingly hateful. "Lesbians are sexual Nazis, and Bisexuals are their Jews." "Men are not your enemies; they are your superiors."

Bisexuals and gaymen are actively waging the smear campaign these graffiti represent. As quickly as Lesbians complain and Bart's paints over the graffiti, more appear, always variations in which Lesbians are called "Nazis," as though we had the power to eradicate entire segments of the population. The slogans are Lesbian-hating; they signal immediate danger to us: We have enemies in Northampton and Amherst, and they intend to do us, or someone we care about, harm. They intend to erase us.

But we don't expect Lesbians, of any color, of any race, of any nationality, to use the vicious and inflammatory tactic of name-calling against other Lesbians. Yet, we frequently hear and read similar uses of language uttered by Lesbians and women—much too frequently. Inexplicably, many Lesbians don't perceive name-calling as dangerous, or threatening, or false when other Lesbians do it; not only do they fail to perceive the danger, but they apparently believe that the names, like "Nazi," are accurately applied. Do the Lesbians engaging in name-calling mean what they say? If they intend us to take their hostile words literally, they should also be willing for us to hold them accountable for the damage done to the reputations and credibility of the Lesbians they attack. Similarly, those Lesbians who seem all too willing to believe the name-calling must accept responsibility for their own gullibility.

Names Can Hurt Us

Name-calling is one of the most dangerous uses of language. Used in the context of an on-going debate or argument over theory, analysis, or principle, it attempts to hide the name-caller's lack of an adequate response or rebuttal; name-calling is a feeble substitute for thoughtful analysis. It represents a refusal to take other Lesbians seriously, while it trivializes the horrors of racism and the Holocaust. Lesbians who use this tactic do so in order to divert other Lesbians from the inadequacies of their analyses, by attacking the integrity of those who disagree with them. At the same time, if name-calling *didn't work* so well, if Lesbians didn't *want* to believe it, it *wouldn't* work. Name-calling, whatever its motivations, is never justified, and it is time for us to stop listening to Lesbians who resort to name-calling and to hold them accountable for their horizontal hostility.

Among the labels most often used to discredit what other Lesbians have to say are *Nazi*, *racist*, *ageist*, and *classist*. However unjustified its use may be, once someone has called us one of these names, the label, and the evil it attributes to us, sticks. More importantly, name-calling often initiates a frenzy of scape-goating, during which the Lesbian so singled out is left isolated, and the original analysis and its context are altogether forgotten in the ensuing furor.

A familiar example of name-calling and scape-goating occurred in *Sinister Wisdom* (SW) in 1980, after the journal published Elly Bulkin's article, "Racism and Writing," in its thirteenth issue (19806). Bulkin had quoted passages from Mary Daly's *Gyn/Ecology* as *one* example, among others, of how racism appears in white wimmin's writing. In succeeding issues of *SW* (numbers fourteen through sixteen), there was a furious scurrying and covering of tracks as the letters condemning Mary Daly, and pointedly exculpating the letter-writers, were published. Now ex-friends of Daly's, some of whom had read and commented on earlier drafts of *Gyn/Ecology*—who apparently had not noticed racism on earlier readings—hastened to assure *SW*'s readers and the Lesbian-Feminist community at large that they were "innocent." Adrienne Rich condemned Daly for her "racism," and admitted—a little—that she was, in fact, one of the Lesbian-Feminist reviewers condemned by Bulkin for praising the Feminist daring of *Gyn/Ecology* "without questioning its racist blunders" (*SW* 14: 104). Worse, in a thinly disguised attempt to dissociate herself from Daly, Rich proceeded to circulate a petition among Lesbians condemning Mary Daly for her "racism" and urging us to join in her condemnation.

To this day, the label *racist* continues to follow Mary Daly's name. What started as Bulkin's effort to promote better communication and to offer specific ways Lesbians could deal with racism among us became a torrent of character-assassination that continues to flow beneath the superficial niceness of political discussions. Every so often, though, it erupts. In 1985, when a group of us at the University of Nebraska-Lincoln suggested Daly as a keynote speaker for a meeting of the Midwest Women's Studies Association, one Lesbian objected to the suggestion because "Mary Daly is racist." (Please note: Elly Bulkin did *not* call Mary Daly a "racist.") We did, finally, succeed in inviting Daly to speak at the conference, but only after weeks of acrimonious and exhausting debate. Nor is this an isolated incident. Yet, Rich escaped unscathed from the name-calling without being taken to task for her own "lack of consciousness." Apparently, her *mea culpa* came quickly enough to keep the shit from hitting her. More likely, no one noticed. The damage had been done, and countless hundreds of "feminists," gathering like vultures to feed on roadkill, continue to repeat the discrediting accusation. Only the label, not the original analysis and context, are remembered, reducing Daly's name and her integrity to a political chip to be cashed at the whim of anyone who wants to play more conscious-than-thou.

In citing this example, I cannot address Bulkin's intentions other than as she stated them in her article and in her response to criticisms in *SW* 16 (Spring, 1981: 94). (Bulkin pointed out that, of the 20-plus pages of her article, her critique of *Gyn/Ecology* occupied only five.) What does concern me is how *other* Lesbian-*Feminists* interpreted and *used* what Bulkin had said. Bulkin claimed that she had used *Gyn/Ecology only* as an *example* of unintentional racism. As she observed, we don't need to look very far for such examples. But members of the "community," especially those with visibility and prestige, seized upon the label *racist* and used it to flog not only Mary Daly but her allies as well. The label, once applied, however out of context, however originally intended, became an indictment of Mary Daly herself, of her character, her intellect, her integrity, and her friends. Adrienne Rich, by denouncing Mary, succeeded in further enhancing her own marketability. Why hasn't anyone questioned Rich's action or her integrity?

Sex "Radicals" and Sado-masochists

Name-calling is a very old technique for discrediting someone else and, at the same time, taking on oneself the mantle of virtue. Among the most skillful practitioners of name-calling are sado-masochists and their allies, the "sex radicals." The so-called sex "wars" are more than arguments about "lifestyles," "sexuality," or "political correctness." The fundamental issue is the inherent validity of one's perceptions. As the hostilities have escalated, the sado-masochists and their allies have generously indulged in name-calling in order to assert the rightness of their perceptions and the wrongness of those of us who disagree with their claims. To describe one's own perceptions of issues like sado-masochism, sex-change operations, or sex with children is, in this arena, quickly dismissed as "trashing" or, worse, "fascism."

Forgotten in the accusations and rejoinders is this: The *fact* of sado-masochism, or Lesbian role-playing, or the sexual use of children doesn't obligate Lesbians to support *or* condone the practices, nor does it enjoin us to be silent about our opinions. Yet, the sex "radicals" want to have it "their way," and they will go to any rhetorical lengths to discredit anyone who challenges their pronouncements in order to make themselves seem to be the innocent victims of someone else's meanness. It is no longer a matter of simply parting ways, leaving the respective disputants to their own perceptions, for better or worse. The sado-masochists assume the inherent validity of their perceptions, as though their perceptions were immune to challenge. She who suggests that they might examine the sources of their perceptions/"gut feelings," however gently, will quickly be labeled "anti-sex" and dismissed as a "vanilla vigilante."

At the same time, the perceptions of Lesbians who don't share these "gut feelings," who refuse to accept the claim that sado-masochism is the "cutting edge" of radical Feminist political analysis, are verbally attacked and trivialized. *Our* perceptions, it seems, are open to question; theirs are not. Our perceptions are flawed, oppressive, and politically regressive; theirs are not. In the midst of the furor, other Lesbians observing the fray seem to accept the labels the sex "radicals" use as true. But my disapproval of sado-masochism and sex with children doesn't make me "anti-sex"; anti-sado-masochism, yes—"anti-sex," no. By berating us for daring to question their assertions they have established themselves and their pronouncements about sex and desire as being beyond challenge. (Consider, for example, JoAnn Loulan's several books on sexuality and Pat Califia's *Sapphistry* (1980), which present sado-masochism as noncontroversial.)

Who Says?

Something is terribly wrong in this situation and in the manner in which the "debate" is being carried on. The assumption that only *some* Lesbians' perceptions are inherently true and accurate reflections of the world, and that other Lesbians are *required* to condone their "choice," has served the sado-masochists and sex "radicals" well. They perceive dominance and submission as necessary to their sexual satisfaction; they perceive pain as pleasure; they perceive humiliation as a necessary ingredient of their sexual enjoyment. And, by deceptively constructed syllogisms, they generalize their perceptions to all of us. The following quotation from a sado-masochist illustrates how *belief* in the first sentence becomes *fact* in the last, a sleight of syntax that enables the writer to cast the net of sado-masochism over all of us.

> I believe that most, if not all, womyn have S/M fantasies and desires. All of us live in this miserable patriarchy, and I doubt that any of us have avoided internalizing and eroticizing the victim and victimizer. The question, then, and this needs to be openly discussed, is, how do we deal with the fact that dominance and submission are an important part of our erotic selves?[2]

At first, the author sounds carefully personal: "I believe" and "I doubt." But she then moves very quickly from "I doubt that any of us have avoided. . .eroticizing the victim and victimizer" to ". . .how do we deal with *the fact that dominance and submission are an important part of our erotic selves?*"

Those of us who don't perceive pain as pleasure, who haven't eroticized dominance and submission, are left no room here for our feelings and our perceptions. Furthermore, should any one of us dare to question their assertions or assert the validity of our perceptions, we are called *Nazis, fascists, sex-police.* We are called *anti-sex, puritans,* and, the vilest label they can think of, *moralists.* I (and Kathleen Barry) have been called the Jerry Falwell and J. Edgar Hoover of the women's movement[3] because we don't agree with them, are not going to agree with them, and will continue to question their assertions. Such descriptions of Lesbians would be ridiculous if other Lesbians didn't believe them. The disagreement, on the other hand, is not ridiculous. At stake are our perceptions and interpretations of the world. At stake is how we understand ourselves in the world. At stake is the possibility of creating a world in which pain cannot be eroticized, a world in which difference and dominance and submission cannot be eroticized. At stake is a vision of people as capable of living and loving differently from what we have learned in the sado-society.

Name-calling is *easy*. It requires absolutely no thought, no analysis, and no justification. Unlike a carefully thought-out analysis, it is also *memorable*. A one-word epithet, like *racist* or *classist*, can hide one's utter lack of a cogent analysis. Its use among Lesbian-Feminists is also a fine example of what Daly calls "patriarchal reversal," a technique used and perfected by the Nazis to teach German citizens to perceive Jews, Gypsies, Lesbians and gaymen, the disabled, anyone the Nazis planned to kill, as *insects*, as sub-human, and so deserving of what the Nazis planned for them. Now we are made the victims of hate campaigns and called "Nazis" by other Lesbians, bisexuals, and gaymen, who call their attacks "dialogue" and spread lies under the guise of political "alliance"—as though the attacks were not only *not* hostile, but constructive. The language we use or allow to go unchallenged teaches us how to *perceive* each other, as though absolute truth inheres in the vilest names. If this smear campaign were instigated by the likes of Anita Bryant, George Bush, or Jesse Helms, it would be called "lying" and "bigotry." *When we accept degrading insults as accurate descriptions of other Lesbians or Feminists and allow name-calling to be substituted for argument, we are no better than the citizens of Germany who did nothing to stop Hitler and the Nazis.*

Because it succeeds, name-calling accomplishes several important tasks for the heteropatriarchy:

- It trivializes the real physical and social dangers posed by white supremacist groups like the Ku Klux Klan, the skinheads, and the neo-Nazis;

- It obscures the difference in intent and power between white men—who can *and do* reap material benefits from the oppression of targeted groups, who advocate violence against all of us who are different from them—and white and Jewish Lesbians who retain racist attitudes in spite of our best intentions;

- It conflates unintentional racism (also classism, elitism, and other prejudiced attitudes) with intentional, malicious, and violent hatred of others;

- It serves as a "divide and conquer" strategy that focuses on our differences at the expense of our similarities, keeping us distant from one another and unable (even unwilling) to identify ways we can work together;

- It pretends to prioritize some oppressions, such as class and race, simultaneously trivializing (by silence) our oppression as wimmin and Lesbians, without moving us to act effectively to eradicate even one of the oppressions;

- Labels like *racist, classist, anti-Jewish, ageist*, and so on, substituted for respectful argument, are used to discredit the work of white and Jewish Lesbians and, thereby, dismiss us as "evil" and "bad" people, without giving us the benefit of the doubt so easily dispensed to white men or credit for the changes in ourselves we have accomplished.

Lesbians should know better.

Why do we continue to credit name-callers? Because the act of name-calling places the Lesbian so attacked in an impossible situation there is no way out of. Here is what the Nazis knew about name-calling: in order to deny the truth of a label, one has to repeat the lie even as one denies it; the act of denial actually reinforces the original lie by repetition. Name-calling implies a willful, conscious bigotry that is, therefore, unremediable. There is no way the accused can emerge from the verbal attack with her reputation undamaged; yet, name-calling implies that her consciousness is somehow defective in a way (or ways) that she must purge from herself. Whatever response she attempts serves only to condemn her more thoroughly. Thus, once one of us is labeled a racist or a Nazi, her only viable option is silence. Attempts to disprove the accusation, even outright denial, do nothing but reinforce it by repetition. We have already lost too many friends and companions to the useless, and often vicious, effects of horizontal hostility. Somehow, we must figure out ways to acknowledge our mistakes, our omissions, and our harmful attitudes that don't trivialize or degrade a single one of us, that accept and celebrate our differences without denying and ignoring our similarities. Calling each other names and using labels to discredit and trivialize each other doesn't seem a kind or caring way to proceed with any political agenda. It certainly doesn't result in personal growth or change. Its only effects are pain, alienation, withdrawal, and silence.

I'm talking about the psychic and emotional damage done among us by name-calling. Labels like *racist, Nazi, anti-Semitic, fascist* (or their male personifications) have been used for years to silence us. As a result, many Lesbians are afraid to dissent from the latest tyranny for fear that those labels will be used against us. Rather than be described as the "oppressors" of others, we quietly disappear, and are often never heard from again. We cannot have a movement, any movement, in which dissent and honest disagreement are perceived as character flaws or threats to someone else's integrity, and we deserve better treatment from those who say they're our "allies."

Yet, the sado-masochists' and sex "radicals'" attempts to validate their perceptions by discrediting those of us who disagree with them persist. What is going on? Behind the issue of *whose perceptions are accurate?* is another factor: thought. How do we think? How do we frame our understanding of ourselves and others? In the Patriarchal Universe of Discourse (PUD),[4] specific linguistic structures constrain, limit, and/or contradict our perceptions of the world, denying us agency *in* the world, and coercing us into accepting the world as PUD presents it to us. If we ignore how English serves the heteropatriarchal world view, we find ourselves victimized by our best intentions, tyrannized by a tactic we thought would empower us. This has already happened. It is long past time to demand that name-calling stop, to refuse to accept insults as a substitute for respect and honesty.

Name-calling is a *power play*. It is an attempt to control the behaviors, thoughts, and actions of those we target for what Claudia Card has called "hostile attending." Name-calling is nothing less than *verbal abuse*, because it strikes at our self-esteem and our confidence, influencing what others think of us and, often, what we think of ourselves. What are the origins of the impulse to call other Feminists and Lesbians "racists," "fascists," "Nazis," "sex-police"? I think Claudia Card was correct when she pointed to the desire to *control others* as its source. As she observed, in her discussion of Sarah Hoagland's notion of "attending,"[5] "Hostile attending is a form of control available even to those otherwise relatively impotent" (*Lesbian Ethics*, 3, 3:96). Why do we single out other Feminists and Lesbians for verbal abuse? Card suggests that we attack each other because ". . .we have more *access* to each other than to those with power over us and because the *price* of harming us is not high" (*LE* 3:97). Nor is it an accident that the most virulent verbal abuse occurs in "personal" letters, in "private" correspondence. Abuse is a "private" activity, something practiced in *intimate*, rather than "public" contexts. "...[S]omeone who would not dream of [verbal] violence in the presence of outsiders will do incredible things to intimates in private" (Card, *LE* 3:97).

Most of us know that isolation is dangerous. We know that most direct male violence occurs in the private sphere, in the "home," away from the eyes of outsiders, more than in the public sphere. Here, in our small and intimate communities, because they are "private" and isolated, horizontal hostility perpetuates the violence we seek to avoid. We bring it with us, in our perceptions, in our descriptions, in our guts. We may have begun in the 1970s by wanting, even needing, to validate every Lesbian's perceptions. But *all* perceptions cannot be simultaneously valid, a fact substantiated when we disagree. The severe hostilities generated by these disagreements have devolved into the "sex wars": Whose perceptions are to prevail? If some of us are committed to changing the world, if some of us believe that there are other ways to be and to live than the ones we've been taught, we must figure out how to validate dissension, how to recognize and support differences that others would subvert or ignore. Are *all* perceptions accurate? Are the perceptions of *all* Lesbians equally valid?

Among Lesbians, this impasse is covertly resolved by treating only *some* of their perceptions as valid, in particular those saying they are being "oppressed": in this case, the sex "radicals" and sado-masochists. When some of us maintain that sado-masochism is inconsistent with Feminist principles, when we describe our perceptions and our feelings, we are answered by a barrage of name-calling that denies our perceptions and ignores what we have said. We are called "Nazis" and "fascists," although we aren't the ones carrying whips or adorning ourselves with swastikas; we are said to be "anti-sex" as though pain and humiliation were all the "sex" one can conceive of; we are compared to J. Edgar Hoover and his ilk, as though we could wield, if we wished, the institutional and personal power that he possessed. Because language is believed to point to something in "reality," these labels tend to stick and are repeated through Lesbian communities as "true." Both the sado-masochists' descriptions of their perceptions and their discrediting of others' are accepted as valid, and those who disagree with them are ignored, insulted, and ridiculed. We have now more than ten years behind us of the "sex debates." But these exchanges have been less "debate" than attempts to bludgeon dissenters into agreement or, failing that, then silence. As Shane Phelan has pointed out:

> Too many advocates of or participants in sado-masochism seem to take the position that any disapproval or criticism is oppression. This not only trivializes race and class oppression as well as that of women by equating it with simple ostracism or even dislike, it also vitiates the concept itself by removing any substantial distinction between these.. . .And, too, it serves as a political move to silence any debate. (1989: 132-133)

Among us, the "squeaky wheel gets the grease." Whoever screams "oppression" first, whoever claims they hurt the most, is the one Lesbians attend to.

Saying What We Feel

In the early 1970s, we had good reasons for wanting to validate each other and desiring the same acceptance for ourselves, but none of us realized how patriarchal language could distort and undermine the integrity of the perceptions we sought to affirm. To illustrate how the structure of English limits our descriptions of what we feel, I want to discuss a class of verbs that promotes verbal abuse among us, the *psychological predicates*.[6] The psych-predicates are the language in which we describe our perceptions of situations and interactions; they are the verbs we use to describe our feelings and reactions to other people: *nauseate, disgust, repel, intimidate, frighten, amuse, annoy, surprise, astonish, fascinate, excite, gratify*, *horrify*, *irritate*, *mystify*, *bore*, *threaten*, *puzzle*, *rile*, and *worry* are all psych-predicates.

They may seem, at first, a harmless bunch of verbs. But the way they force us to structure our thinking about our feelings is anything *but* harmless. They *require* the experiencer of the specific feeling named by the verb to describe herself as an object acted upon by someone else's attitude or behavior, and they figure most prominently as descriptions of situations in which *class* differences are invoked. *Intimidate*, for example, is a verb Lesbians use often to describe how they feel about someone else's carriage, speech or "presence": "She intimidates me," "I'm intimidated by you," "You're intimidating." All three descriptions locate the source of the speaker's feelings in the behavior of another person and assume that the behavior itself is (a) intentional, (b) an expression of "power over," and (c) that the speaker's interpretation and response are the only possible reactions because any other response is *inconceivable* to her. She denies responsibility for her feelings and "explains" them by blaming someone else's size or their way of talking, standing, or walking, as though actions, weight, or height in and of themselves were "intimidating." If we actually believe that what we're saying is *true*, these verbs force us to place responsibility (and blame) outside ourselves, thereby maintaining the heteropatriarchal fiction that we are emotionally dependent.

With verbs that describe a negative emotional response, like *intimidate*, the structure encourages experiencers to perceive themselves as the *victims* of others' behaviors and to treat that description as though it were valid. "You're intimidating," for example, allows the speaker to remove herself entirely from the "action" and attribute the underlying motivation and behavior to the character of the individual she blames. What the speaker feels can no longer be interpreted as an individual response. It becomes an allegation of malevolent intent on the other person's part, an inherent attribute of her personality. The experiencer's response is generalized, as though anyone who interacts with the individual so accused will also "be intimidated."

When we use psych-predicate descriptions, we forget that any habitual gesture or movement has several possible interpretations; we forget that our internal responses to physical or verbal expressions are often located in our personal histories and experiences with parents and other adults who had power over us and probably *did* intimidate us, intentionally or not. Relative physical size, for example, can arouse feelings of intimidation remembered from our childhood, and we may feel "intimidated" around people who are taller or fatter than we are. But those feelings are *ours*. We cannot assume that our perceptions of mannerisms and behaviors are truths, and we certainly cannot assume that the malevolence of another Lesbian inheres in the situation. These verbs enable us to project our internal self-valuation onto our interactions with other Lesbians, and we see and experience what we expect to. Of course, there are people who do set out to intimidate Lesbians, who want to assert their power over us. A verb like *intimidate* may accurately describe what is happening, but we simply cannot take for granted that our descriptions and the assumptions such verbs express are accurate, and we have to be careful about our use of psych-predicates and related structures.

The psych-predicates trap us. In English, there is no way for us to use one of these predicates *actively*, to name ourselves as responsible for our feelings. In every instance, when we feel repulsion, fright, disgust, or irritation we use a psych-predicate to describe ourselves as *acted upon* by some person or event. More insidiously, the psych-predicates enable us to blame someone else for our psychological responses, as though they cause us to feel as we say we do and, therefore, *they* are *responsible* for our feelings. When we use psych-predicates, we locate the origin of and responsibility for our feelings and emotional responses *outside* of us. If only so-and-so hadn't done this or that, we think, then we wouldn't feel like we do. Likewise, if these verbs force us to blame what someone else does or says for our feelings, they simultaneously provide us with a handy way of erasing our own responsibility, whether or not we're aware of it. That is, although something external to us may trigger our psychological response, that response comes from *inside* us. It is based on our accumulated experiences. More unfortunately, our emotional response may be utterly unrelated to the individual or behavior that we blame for it; our feelings, as real as they are to us, may be *out of context*. Our feelings may originate with something done to us years before, and not in the immediate situation to which we're responding. I learned this when I first began to deal with how I perceived and interpreted the behaviors of other Lesbians as a result of my incest experience. As long as we rely on psych-predicate constructions, we remain unaware of how our personal history determines our responses to specific contexts, and we continue to perceive ourselves as the victims of others' actions. If we believe that psych-predicates describe our perceptions of situations and other people's behavior in them as external truths, we won't examine the internal sources of our feelings or take responsibility for them, and we'll continue to think and act as victims.

I'm not saying that our anger, fear, and pain aren't real. I'm saying that when we use psych-predicates, we *blame* someone else for our feelings, and that we may falsely accuse someone today of causing us anger or pain when the responsibility for what we feel belongs to someone in our past. To say to another Lesbian, "You intimidate me," *and believe* what that description implies about her intentions in a situation makes us the helpless victims of the malevolence we ascribe to her. We allow our past experiences to control us in the present and to limit our choices of possible futures. When we cast her in the role of our "oppressor" and make her the culpable agent of the way we feel in her presence, we simultaneously disguise our internalized feelings of weakness and our sense of powerlessness and insecurity. *Some* Lesbians do set out intentionally to intimidate other Lesbians, but the language we use *hides* the fact that we could react differently and that we fail to consider the behavioral options we have. We don't have to allow her to succeed in intimidating us, just as we can resist men's attempts to intimidate us. This is one area in which we can control situations by conceiving of ourselves and others differently.

Omitting the psych-predicates from our vocabularies would be a significant advance, but English is full of similar cognitive traps. We have to learn new ways of thinking by self-consciously attending to the words we choose. Before we speak, we need to examine the words we're about to utter and weigh the risks and implications of their use, to ask ourselves if we really mean what we're about to say. We need to question our reasons for using the words we choose, and we have to be responsible for the consequences if we deliberately say something mean or degrading. We have to know *why* we say what we say, or zip our lips. As speakers, we cannot continue to use the structures of English unthinkingly to describe what we feel and what we perceive. The English language contains many linguistic resources, and we can become resourceful and conscious language users.

As speakers, we make a start by steadfastly insisting upon our own agency in the world, and then acting on what we think and say. As hearers, we need not "buy" the deceptive packaging of heteropatriarchal descriptions. The next time someone tells us that so-and-so is a racist, a Nazi, or an anti-sex puritan, we have to challenge her description and ask her if she means what she says. The next time someone tells us that so-and-so intimidated her, we need to question why she chose that particular description. We have to demand linguistic responsibility from ourselves and each other. We cannot continue to let our language use go without comment.

If we want to think beyond the conceptual grooves of the Patriarchal Universe of Discourse—and some may not want to—we can learn to avoid using verbs like the psych-predicates altogether, choosing instead other ways to describe ourselves. We have to start rejecting the descriptions English provides, or we'll be forever trapped by them. We'll do far less damage to ourselves and others if we take the time to construct sentences that describe, as accurately as possible, what we perceive and feel. More importantly, as we engage in the mental processes necessary for creating alternative descriptions we'll begin to reconceptualize who we are in relation to others. Rewording our perceptions will lead us to rethinking, and rethinking will lead to a self-knowledge that's impossible within the boundaries of PUD.

We have to change the way we think and the way we perceive the world. As we undertake this project of conceptual exploration and restructuring, our contradictory position requires that we live by a linguistic double standard. Our minds will have to live simultaneously in two universes of discourse: the patriarchal world we want to change, and the Lesbian-centered world we seek to create. On the one hand, because we live in a male-dominated society, we will have to improve our ability to use deceptive linguistic structures in our dealings with men. That is, we must become better liars, better verbal acrobats, in order to sustain ourselves in the world as men have made it. On the other hand, we must create radically different ways of perceiving and describing events in the world. We will have to live in transition, between what is and what we want.

Yes—we'll make mistakes. But the difference in the way we feel and act when we say what we mean is, I think, worth the effort. Learning to describe ourselves as agents in the world is a first step toward empowering ourselves. Further, if we are serious about freeing ourselves from male oppression and the many forms it takes, including horizontal hostility, we must be willing to commit ourselves to unlearning the map of reality presented to us as children. If Lesbians want to work together for our mutual liberation, we cannot go on speaking to each other in destructive, self-eroding ways. By refusing the distortions introduced by patriarchal linguistic structures, we can learn to focus on the features of our experiential landscape we fail to recognize because we lack ways of describing them. More importantly, we must find new ways to perceive our world and new words and descriptions for articulating those perceptions. In order to change the way we describe the world and talk among ourselves, we will have to find words that fit our perceptions and structures that organize our experiences with as little distortion as possible. As we find ways to describe our own perspective, the acts of renaming events and understanding relationships in new ways will be the first steps toward making our realities visible and functional in the world. Lack of ways to talk about our perceptions keeps them in the realm of the invisible, the "unreal." If we do nothing to stop uses of language (like name-calling) that forever make us the victims of what someone else is or is not doing, imagining ourselves into an age where oppression is obsolete will remain an unaccomplished "perhaps" in the long sentence of patriarchy.

We must stop the verbal abuse among us by demanding linguistic responsibility in all our communities. Very few of us had happy childhoods; many Lesbians were the victims of adult violence and predation. We are survivors of the heteropatriarchy's "sex wars," and the lies that kept us victims. But in our arguments among ourselves, today, we need whatever honesty we can manage among us. Our experiences are disorderly and unpredictable, full of chance encounters and casual conversations, and our memories of them are partial, selective, and inaccurate. Only when we gather our experiences in memory within the limits of language do they appear meaningful, orderly. We use language to impose an order that is illusory, and it is the ordering we choose that reveals us. We utter the world we would create.

Endnotes

1. The entire sequence of events surrounding the Northampton Lesbian/Gay Pride Marches, 1989-1991, has recently been recounted by Sarah Dreher in the first issue of *The Lesbian Outlook,* published by Lesbians For Lesbians, pp. 1-4. The examples I use in this

portion of my essay are quoted from p. 3 of her article, unless otherwise noted.

2. Ironically, the essay I am quoting here, Jeanne F. Neath's "Let's Discuss Dyke S/M and Quit the Name Calling: A Response to Sheila Jeffreys" (*Lesbian Ethics* 2, 3:95-99), was itself a call for "dialogue" between sado-masochists and anti-sado-masochists (99).

3. In her paper delivered at the Barnard Conference on Sex and Sexuality, "The New Feminism of Yin and Yang," Alice Echols referred to Kathleen Barry and me as the "J. Edgar Hoovers of the women's movement" (447). That paper was published in *Powers of Desire: The Politics of Sexuality*, eds. Ann Snitow, Christine Stansell, and Sharon Thompson (Boston: Monthly Review Press, 1983).

4. I describe the Patriarchal Universe of Discourse and illustrate the sort of descriptions that "make sense" within it in Chapter Three of *Speaking Freely: Unlearning the Lies of the Fathers' Tongues* (Elmsford, NY: Pergamon Press, 1990).

5. Claudia Card's discussion of "hostile attending" uses Sarah Lucia Hoagland's discussion of attending in Chapter Three of *Lesbian Ethics* (Palo Alto: Institute of Lesbian Studies, 1988), esp. 129-133.

6. My discussion here of the psych-predicates extends my discussion of those verbs in Chapters Ten and Eleven of *Speaking Freely*, especially on 183-185; 230-234.

Heteropatriarchal Semantics and Lesbian Identity: The Ways a Lesbian Can Be

Introduction

Of the "issues" that have disturbed and disrupted Lesbian communities during the past two decades, one, in particular, has the potential to destroy our efforts to mobilize Lesbians, to create a Lesbian *movement* grounded in a Lesbian stance: femininity. The repeated rationales offered for embracing femininity have generated anger and hostilities because they strike at the heart of what it means *to be* a Lesbian in a heteropatriarchy: one who *resists efforts to make her into "a woman"*; one who *defies the male descriptions and prescriptions that would limit her possibilities*; one who *refuses the very foundations of heteropatriarchal reality*. Our identity as *Lesbians* is at stake.

Whatever one chooses to call them, "lipstick Lesbians," "dykes for spikes," or "femmes,"[1] they have appeared in our communities and our movement in a variety of guises, demanding our support and approval for their appearance and behavior, asserting their "right" to wear make-up, high heels, and garter belts, to allow men to fuck them, and to exploit, use, and abuse Lesbians at will. When Lesbians like me object to their assertions, they insult us, belittle our lives, and call us their "oppressors." In short, their agenda is to destroy the Lesbian political movement by alternately playing the "victim" and then bullying, by lying, by coquetry, by manipulation, and by just plain stupidity.

I don't understand why some Lesbians feel so righteous, so sure of themselves, when they extol the virtues of Lesbian "femininity" and attack Lesbian "masculinity." I have trouble listening to Lesbians who use either word as though it were *meaningful* in a Lesbian context, because both *femininity* and *masculinity* are heteropatriarchal (HP) terms that establish the boundaries of what is "acceptable," "permissible" appearance and behavior for females, Lesbians included. Heteropatriarchal semantics (HS) equates femininity with femaleness and masculinity with maleness, as though behaviors and personality traits were determined by biological sex. On the basis of that equation, HP values femininity in females and masculinity in males. Only feminine females are considered "good" in HP, yet what is described as "masculinity" is held up to us as the ideal of what it means to be "human." As a result of these descriptions, the female who embraces the femininity forced on her by HP is trapped in a semantic double-bind. The woman who learns the behaviors and modes of thought attributed to femininity and becomes feminine is, by definition, less than "human." "Masculinity," in contrast, not only establishes the cultural boundaries for men, it taboos those behaviors and aspirations for females. Thus, femininity is made to seem attractive because females who act "like a man" are deviant, and, therefore, "bad"; women willingly acquire the appurtenances of femininity even though it inherently relegates them to second-class status because it's the only "positive" option available in HP terms. Within this framework, it's apparently better to be rewarded for accepting one's devaluation than to be devalued for defying the limitations imposed by male hegemony.

Sadly, Lesbians who challenge those who embrace and extol femininity are attacked as "oppressors," ridiculed for "aping men," and labeled "fascists" and "neo-Nazis." Lesbians who accept the HP dichotomy as meaningful remain trapped within the either/or thinking some of us are trying to unlearn. Lesbians committed to personal and social change not only want to rid ourselves of the HS dichotomy and the HP misogyny that values femininity, we want to learn how to think beyond the limitations imposed by words like *feminine* and *masculine* and imagine what it would be like to be *neither*.

In order to start this process, we have to start by asking: What does it mean to be a Lesbian in a Lesbian context? Our discussion can begin, I think, by identifying how Lesbians *differ* from heterosexuals, bisexuals, and gaymen, and acknowledging that our oppression is based on those differences. Just as blacks begin to establish their identity as distinct from their white oppressors, as native Americans resist the identities imposed on them by the white men who've destroyed their cultures, so Lesbians must make our difference the focus of our identity and resist those who wish to validate an identity constructed for us by men. We need to identify the features that make us uniquely Lesbian; it is, after all, the reason we're outcasts. We cannot ignore the heteropatriarchy or its values anymore than we can pretend that we weren't born into, raised, and live in HP, and the fact that many of our ideas and assumptions are heteropatriarchal in origin. But we can certainly start unlearning those values and assumptions, and the first step is rejecting femininity and the idea that it's a "good thing" for us.

Today, Lesbians remain divided by HP dichotomies, bouncing back and forth between the "feminine" and "masculine" poles, because we still accept as valid men's descriptions of "what is." A majority of Lesbians haven't even begun to imagine who we might be or to look for options outside of HP boundaries; they are still preoccupied with devising ways of surviving more (and less) comfortably within the HP context, which requires accepting as real the world described by HP terms.

The argument isn't about whether to be "feminine" or "masculine." It's about what being a Lesbian *means*. What *is* Lesbian identity? What does it mean to be a

Lesbian, live as a Lesbian, *think* as a Lesbian, *in a Lesbian context*? So we have to begin by identifying how we differ from heterosexual women and bisexuals and make our deviance the core of our identity. *Lesbians don't fuck men.* We are the only group in the world that refuses to place men at the center of our lives. We are the only group whose lives are focused on women.

But we are also not a homogeneous group. In our efforts to establish the basis of Lesbian identity, we are constantly engaged in confronting how the life histories we bring with us into Lesbian communities complicate and confuse our interactions. Because we each have different experiences and backgrounds,[2] we have to be willing to name and acknowledge the HP assumptions and values we bring with us into a Lesbian context. We must do this before we can rid ourselves of the HP elements that divide us from one another. We have to acknowledge the HP attitudes we still possess before we can unlearn them. And we *can* accomplish both. White Lesbians unlearning racism is a good example of this process; unlearning ageist attitudes is another.

I, for one, don't believe that femininity can be positively valued in a Lesbian context, and I will explain why rejecting femininity is an essentially Lesbian act.

Identifying the Problem

Lesbians are divided from each other by the descriptions of "the world" we accept as valid and accurate; we do not begin our Lesbian lives or enter our Lesbian communities untainted by HP ways of thinking and acting. Many of our political differences can be traced to how thoroughly we believe the version of reality men have presented to us. Some Lesbians believe that the HP description of reality is essentially accurate, while others believe that it's utterly false. Some Lesbians accept portions of HP reality that other Lesbians have rejected. Our commitment to the assumptions of HP is reflected in the ways we use English.

Our experience with acquiring a first language deceives us into believing that there is a single reality, the one encoded and described to us by that language. Many U. S. Lesbians learned English as our first language and, with it, the U. S. version of reality. English, like any language, describes the version of reality preferred by the majority of speakers in a society, and forces us to accept the reality agreed upon by those speakers. The United States is a heteropatriarchal society, a culture that assumes that heterosexuality is "natural," that male dominance is "natural," and that female subordination is "natural"; English provides its speakers with ways of expressing these assumptions as though they were incontrovertible facts. The words *masculine* and *feminine* exist only because they express concepts essential to the maintenance of HP reality. But the existence and continual use of these words doesn't mean that they denote "real" or actual things.

The English language is a grid, a conceptual frame, that a society imposes on the experience and perceptions of its speakers. There are ways of getting around that grid, ways of expressing values and perceptions not validated by the culture, but that takes work and thought that most people are unwilling to invest in talking and writing. As long as a Lesbian uses words sanctioned, supported, and accepted by HP culture, she risks being understood and interpreted within the limits of the reality described by English. To imagine that we can use English and totally avoid its HP assumptions is a delusion that's especially dangerous for Lesbians.

Lesbian speakers have a "semantic problem," but it isn't one of our own creation. It was imposed on us when we learned to think and talk in English. (I don't think dialect makes a difference here.) Some Lesbians may resist my assertion that our problem is semantic, because dysfunctional communication in heteropatriarchy is swept under the rug with statements like "It's just a semantic problem," "It's only a question of semantics," or "Don't play semantic games with me," as though semantics were irrelevant, or an excuse to muddy the waters that someone else thinks are "clear." I want to say that semantics *is* important, and we need to pay much closer attention to semantics than we do. We cannot adopt as workable the HP assertion that semantics is trivial, and we cannot continue to ignore the ways that semantics causes miscommunication among us.

Our semantic problems often stem from the divergent versions of reality we accept, and we get into trouble when we assume that our use of the same words means we're talking about the same things. A good example of semantic confusion occurred in *Lesbian Ethics* during 1985-'86 (the Fall, 1985 issue, in which Linda Strega's "The Big Sell-Out: Lesbian Femininity" appeared, and the Spring, 1986 issue, in which Paula Mariedaughter and Mary Crane responded to Strega's analysis.[3] In her article, Strega used the terms *butch* and *femme* to refer to differences among Lesbians because the labels are part of Lesbian tradition and so already have meaning for her Lesbian audience. Strega used the word *butch* differently than it has been and continues to be used among some Lesbians, investing it with political substance and, in the process, appearing to conflate the reference of *butch* and *Lesbian*. But butch and femme carry with them a lot of semantic baggage from our Lesbian herstory. What the terms have meant in the past, and the way Lesbians like Mariedaughter and Crane use them, wasn't the way Strega wanted to use them. Their use of the same words made it seem as though they were talking about the same aspects of Lesbian living, but they weren't. One of Strega's most important points was her observation that Lesbians in general value feminine Lesbians much more than they value masculine Lesbians. The Lesbian community generally discredits, even shuns, (life-long) masculine Lesbians because we fit the twentieth-century stereotype (promulgated by the nineteenth-century sexologists) of "the real Lesbian," while, in contrast, it listens to, even lionizes, feminine Lesbians, because they fit the HP stereotype of "the womanly woman."[4]

That valuing femininity more than what is perceived as masculinity among us reflects an especially nasty form of Lesbian-hating is, I think, beyond question. Why conformity to a male ideal would give feminine Lesbians more credibility among us continues to puzzle me. In order to understand our confusion and move toward a resolution of it, I think we need to begin with its sources in the heteropatriarchal semantics (HS) of English.

Heteropatriarchal Semantics

Why do Lesbians follow heterosexuals in valuing feminine women and devaluing "mannish" women?   The answer lies in the semantics of English. Diagram 1 presents the basic semantic dichotomy of HP and its internal logic. It represents an important piece of the HP semantic system called "consensus reality." "Consensus reality" refers to that version of reality which most people accept as true and act upon as though it were true. The diagram is a way of visualizing how this portion of semantic "space" is stored in our long-term memory, a picture of the grid that heteropatriarchal teaching has imposed on our experiences. (I've substituted words at each level for semantic features.)

LEVEL	CATEGORY	FEATURE	
		+ MALE	- MALE
I	BIOLOGICAL	Male	Female
II	FUNCTIONAL (Breeders)	Man Father	Woman Mother
III	BEHAVIORAL	Real Man Masculine Manly	Real Woman Feminine Womanly
		Womanish	Mannish

Diagram 1. Heteropatriarchal Semantics

The semantic grid of Diagram 1 represents the HP version of what "being human" means. The essential dichotomy that gives this grid its meaning is based on the much-touted sexual dimorphism of "our" species. That is, *homo sapiens* (sic!) is described as having two sexes which differ from each other in primary and secondary sexual characteristics. But this is only a partial description of the world we comprehend through our senses. For example, the existence of hermaphrodites exposes the inadequacy of the grid as a description of the world, while the word *hermaphrodite*, a compound (*hermes* [+MALE] and *aphrodite* [-MALE]) based on the dichotomy, isn't much more than a clumsy attempt to preserve the HP semantic structure in spite of contradicting evidence. What we have here is a description of reality that isn't accurate, one that tries to account for aspects of reality not covered by its dichotomy by simply repeating the dichotomy itself.

Sexual dimorphism is the foundation of HP semantics, politics, and personality. Personality, according to HP, is based on biological sex. Biology determines behavior, mannerisms, appearance, emotional style, and how one thinks. This is a monocausal ideology. Sexual dimorphism is the reproductive strategy for numerous species, but it's neither necessary nor inevitable, nor is it biologically superior to other reproductive methods (as is commonly believed). Many species in addition to our own are now known to reproduce parthenogenetically (for example, lizards, fish, seagulls, and some plants). Only humans seem to be obsessed with their reproductive capacity, as though they'd invented and perfected it. Contrary to popular thinking, it's not at all obvious that biological sex or reproductive potential should be the basis of personality. One might just as well posit height, weight, or the position of constellations with respect to the earth at the time of one's birth, as astrology does, as the source of personality. (Conventional astrology incorporates sexual dimorphism in its descriptions of personality types.)

Heterosexuality doesn't appear overtly in Diagram 1 because it's integral to the HP description of the world. The logic of HP assumes that heterosexuality *necessarily* follows from sexual dimorphism, expressed as "The Stick-in-the-Hole Theory of Behavior" or, "Function Follows Form":

1) Men have pricks, women have vaginas;
2) Pricks can be stuck into vaginas;

ERGO: Vaginas exist *because* pricks exist.

The possession of genitalia of a specific kind is believed to necessitate its usage in a specific way. The assumption that function follows form and is, therefore, "natural," is deeply ingrained. It isn't surprising that Lesbians as well as heterosexuals believe this. That which is assumed, primary, and implicit is difficult to challenge. Heterosexuality is hard for Lesbians to question because our outcast status depends on it; in a binary view of the world, we are its antithesis.

The ideas of heterosexuality and its "naturalness" cannot be questioned in HP: they aren't "open to question," like yours or mine, and aren't supposed to be challenged. If you doubt this, put a bumpersticker on your car (or bike or skateboard) that says, "If Abortion is a Crime, Fucking Should be a Felony." A female's right to terminate a pregnancy is open to question; the "necessity" of heterosexual coitus (fucking) isn't. Other cultures deal with sexual dimorphism differently, and this is reflected in their languages. I am concerned here *only* with the culture imposed in the continental United States. Some Lesbians, in an effort to deny the privileges they get for being feminine, get into "cultural relativity," and how this or that behavior or mode of dress differs from one culture to another (as in

Lesbian Connection 9, 1 [July/August 1986], p. 17). I'm not talking about saris or mu-mus or the kilts worn by men of the Scottish clans, but about what skirts, dresses, high heels, and make-up mean in the U. S., in the twentieth century.

Sexual dimorphism underlies HP semantics, along with its corollary assumption, heterosexuality. Dividing a species into male and female is only the first step. If one accepts the idea that biological sex is a significant feature, one might suppose that that distinction would result in semantic features like +MALE and +FEMALE. But this isn't the case in English. Instead, sexual dimorphism is coded as +MALE and -MALE. That females are -MALE in the semantic structure of English might not be immediately apparent to my readers, so I'll explain.

In English, the male sex is posited as the norm, the standard; the female sex is that which is non-male ("other"). The set of terms for occupations is a familiar example of how maleness is assumed unless the label is explicitly modified by a female term. Persons addressed as *doctor, lawyer, artist, author, engineer, surgeon, sculptor, mayor, jockey,* and so on, are assumed to be male unless a special form of the label is used, e.g., *woman doctor, lady lawyer, authoress,* or *sculptress.* This is true of all prestige occupations. In contrast, the occupational labels assumed to be inherently female, which require overt modification if the person is male, refer to low prestige, low pay occupations: *secretary, prostitute, nurse.* When a male holds one of these occupations, he is called a *male secretary, male prostitute,* or *male nurse.* Assuming that the male sex is normal and the female sex deviant also underlies the use of pseudo-generic *man,* men being "the measure of all things," and the pronoun *he* as though it encompassed females in its reference. In English, all "persons" are assumed to be male unless otherwise specified. (Lesbians are erased when we allow ourselves to be subsumed under male terms, e.g., *homosexual* and *gay.*)

The leftmost, vertical portion of Diagram 1 divides HP semantic "space" into three discrete levels: BIOLOGICAL, FUNCTIONAL, and BEHAVIORAL. I chose this particular order because the internal logic of HS posits an entailment relation between each level: Given that one is (usually) born either MALE or FEMALE (*female,* from the French *femelle,* was re-etymologized in the fourteenth century to make it look as though it were derived from *male*), it follows from this biological trait that one is either MAN or WOMAN in FUNCTION (FATHER or MOTHER), and from this functional description, it follows that one's BEHAVIOR will necessarily be culturally appropriate to one's FUNCTION and BIOLOGY— *masculine* or *feminine*—in HP terms. If one is born female, then one is also necessarily a woman and, being a woman in this HP culture, one is also *necessarily* "feminine" and "womanly." This entailment relation makes the two words synonymous in English, as when "being feminine" is used as though it means 'being a woman'. The meaning of being born female in the U. S. *is* being *feminine.* A female who is nonfeminine is an unacceptable contradiction in HP terms.

Most heterosexuals, and Lesbians as well, accept as "fact" the description of reality presented by English semantics. They assume that the descriptive limits of English are, in fact, the limits of reality. One is or is not a man; men are the standard of comparison. This assumption was expressed in a television advertisement for a magazine aimed at a female audience, *Savvy*: "You don't have to be *like a man* to succeed in business. You can allow yourself *to be a woman*." It's also the reason some Lesbians are repeatedly addressed as "sir" by heterosexuals. When we present ourselves at restaurants, gas stations, post offices, and other public places, whoever is dealing with us scans us for what they consider "relevant features": size, weight, height, voice, body posture, clothing, and length of hair. This information gives them a composite sex analysis, and, since they have only two categories, +MALE and -MALE, Lesbians who fit the +MALE composite are going to be addressed as "sir." They don't perceive us *as Lesbian*. They're matching bodies against conceptual maps. A rock and roll song of the 1960s expressed this operating assumption: "Just two kinds of people in the world." Likewise, Lesbians who describe another Lesbian as "like a man," "masculine," or "mannish" validate HP reality, and prioritize HP values by negating other Lesbians.

At the BEHAVIORAL Level (III), I've placed the most commonly used adjectives that describe the behaviors attributed to each sex. The significance of the +MALE/-MALE dichotomy and the rigidity with which HP must maintain it is explicit in Diagram 1 in two ways. First, I've included both "real man" and "real woman," which presuppose "unreal" men and women, i.e., "queers," as possibilities. This is one of the ways we're semantically viable, as a presupposition that reinforces heterosexual superiority. In usage, both expressions assume the accuracy of the logical entailments among Levels I, II, and III. If one is female, then one must be a heterosexual and a breeder, and behave in appropriate, "feminine" ways. If she doesn't, if she fails to symbolically enact (and validate) the logical entailments of Level II or III in some way, she isn't a "real woman." She's "something else" because she contradicts the logic of the HP semantic system. What she is is a Lesbian who defied every effort to turn her into a fembot! Some would call this Lesbian a "butch," erroneously, I believe (although many Lesbians who did resist feminization have called ourselves "butches" in the past).

Second, the importance attached to these semantic features is exposed by the final pair of terms, *womanish/mannish*. The usage of both words signals a feature negation (or "violation") within the system. A man who is described as "womanish" is behaving in some way thought to be "like a woman." He may cry when he's angry, frustrated, confused, or grieving; he may cross his legs at the knee; he may bend from the waist to pick something up off the ground. Whatever it is, he is behaving "inappropriately" according to HS. Likewise, a woman described as "mannish" has negated the feature dichotomy by "crossing the line." She may be aggressive, stoic, or withdrawn; she may wear her hair "too" short; she may be "too" tall, or weigh "too much"; she may take large steps instead of small ones. Whatever the specific behavior interpreted as a negation of her category, the attribute of "mannish" is intended by the user to be both an insult and a warning: Don't go "too far" or you're "out." Semantic violation becomes semantic exclusion; semantic exclusion becomes social ostracism.

HP semantic space is so well maintained that the attempts of some Feminists in the past decade to introduce "androgyny" (or "gynandry") were bound to fail. First, both terms validate the psychological dichotomy MASCULINE/FEMININE they're intended to replace. If two distinct kinds of behavior didn't exist, one reserved for the male, the other for the female, then there would be nothing to combine. Without the pre-existing distinction, no fusion would be necessary or possible. Second, gynandry (or androgyny), as proposed by such Feminists, was operational only at Level III, the Behavioral. They were talking only about personality traits, habits of behavior, as described by HS. Their substitution did not disturb or challenge the entailment conditions between the levels, and it certainly left the foundation, sexual dimorphism, untouched. Finally, trying to promote change "within the system" would work only if they started at Level I, and infiltrated Level III by establishing entailment conditions between the levels. But this strategy, too, is blocked by the adjective pair, *womanish/mannish*. The derogation of those terms interrupts attempts to blur the distinction carried by *masculine/feminine*.

In "Lesbian Separatism: The Linguistic and Social Sources of Separatist Politics" (1978), I listed definitions from the first edition of the *Random House Dictionary* (1967)[5] of the words *womanly*, *mannish*, and *manly*, *feminine* and *masculine*, then described and analyzed how the very existence of such terms could only be explained by the cultural values they denote and perpetuate. (Words become obsolete only when the speakers of a language no longer want to talk about the ideas or objects the words describe.) I'll repeat myself here, ask you to read the following definitions, and then tell me femininity is something Lesbians should try to "reclaim." I hope that reading these dictionary definitions and my analysis of their cultural significance will prompt other Lesbians to realize that we cannot, like Humpty Dumpty, continue to believe that words mean what we want them to mean.[6] Words exist and are created because they reflect and inscribe the values and attitudes central to a culture. When they cease to be useful, they become obsolete. Every time a Lesbian uses a word that carries HP assumptions, she is prolonging its existence. As one could predict, the "real meaning" of each word is revealed in the definition of its opposite.

> **womanly** — like or befitting a woman; feminine; not masculine or girlish. *Womanly* implies resemblance in appropriate, fitting ways; *womanly decorum, modesty.*

> **manly** — having the qualities usually considered desirable in a man; strong, brave; honorable; resolute; virile. *Manly* implies possession of the most valuable or desirable qualities a man can have, as dignity, honesty, directness,

etc., in opposition to servility, insincerity, underhandedness, etc. It also connotes strength, courage, and fortitude;...

feminine — pertaining to a woman or girl: *feminine beauty, feminine dress.* Like a woman; weak; gentle.

masculine — having the qualities or characteristics of a man; manly; virile; strong; bold; a deep, *masculine voice.* Pertaining to or characteristic of a man or men: *masculine attire.*

mannish — applies to that which resembles man:...Applied to a woman, the term is derogatory, suggesting the **aberrant possession of masculine characteristics** . (My emphasis)

You'll notice that the qualities listed under *manly* and *masculine* are the "good" things an individual might wish to be: strong, brave, determined, honest, dignified, etc. Notice that not a single one of many negative qualities commonly attributed to maleness is listed here. What happened to qualities like aggressive, violent, narrow-minded, self-centered, defensive, easily threatened, domineering, penis-obsessed, intrusive, predatory, immature, dependent, energy-sucking, or territorial, egotistical, and war-mongering? In which dictionary, do you suppose, one might find *those* qualities of masculinity listed?

In contrast, the adjectives *womanly* and *feminine* are not really defined. Please read them. Don't assume that you know what you're going to find there. Look closely at the long list of characteristics in the definition for *manly* compared to the circularity of the pseudo-definition for *womanly*: "like or befitting a woman." That's *not* a definition. The real definition for *womanly* is implied as "oppositions" to "manly qualities": "servility, insincerity, underhandedness, etc." Under *feminine*, we pick up two more adjectives, *weak* and *gentle*, and that's it. Positive attributes commonly associated with females, such as nurturing, kind, and loving, have been omitted. Those adjectives didn't make it into the dictionary. It should go without saying that, as a theory of personality, sexual dimorphism and the adjectives that express its assumptions ignore the fact that anyone can be strong *and* gentle. These traits, and others, aren't "opposites" and, therefore, mutually exclusive; it's only our acceptance of the HP description of reality that makes them seem so.

Lesbians shouldn't need to defend "femininity" or feel as though being gentle, kind, tender, interested in fabric and texture, or a host of other personality traits has anything to do with being a female or a "femme." We can be any and all of these things without subscribing to the HS dichotomy. Similarly, Lesbians can enjoy bicycling, playing softball, repairing cars, riding motorcycles, working in construction, and being hostile to men without calling themselves "masculine" or "butch." Accepting those labels to describe our predilections is a trap, and it perpetuates HP ideology as though it belonged in a Lesbian context.

The clencher comes when we consider the definition for *mannish*, "the aberrant possession of masculine characteristics," as though a female who is honest, strong, dignified, forthright, and brave were a *freak*. Men have reserved the positive attributes for themselves; women are "appropriately" weak, gentle, insincere, servile, and underhanded. Any woman who is honest, forthright, dignified, brave, or resolute is "aberrant," i.e., *mannish*. HS logic dictates that those born female who reject the HS dichotomy, who refuse to behave in feminine, "appropriate" ways, are labeled "masculine" by semantic default. Those who aren't visibly -MALE must be +MALE. This semantic trick makes it seem as though HS has described behavior accurately, but all it does is maintain HP consensus reality at the cost of Lesbian integrity. It's way past time for Lesbians to stop using HP words as though they were meaningful. Any Lesbian who defends femininity and compares another Lesbian to a man by labeling her "masculine" subscribes to HP "consensus reality."

The Ways a Lesbian Can Be

The purpose of semantic structure is to *create meaning*. Without a semantic structure, meaning does not exist. Lesbians aren't "meaningful" in HS, so we have to construct a semantic system in which we become meaningful. In the U. S., we turned to the only semantic system we knew as a model, Heteropatriarchal Semantics. Even in the 1950s gay community that I came out into, there was a tacit recognition that Lesbians didn't divide up neatly into "butch" and "femme." We had to make it up as we went along, and, although the resulting continuum of terms used the HS dichotomy to define its extremes, still a range of behaviors was acknowledged and labeled. Diagram 2 represents this behavioral continuum.

MASCULINE   FEMININE
dieseldyke—bulldyke—dyke—butch—nellybutch—ki-ki—femme

Diagram 2. The Lesbian continuum of the 1950s and '60s.

Diagram 2 uses some of the behavioral labels used among Lesbians of my acquaintance during the 1950s and '60s to illustrate how we expressed our perceptions of the continuum, and many of these terms are still in use among Lesbians today. We constructed a semantics in order to "make sense" of ourselves in HS terms, which ignored our existence. Since it was our denial of the entailment relation between the BIOLOGICAL and FUNCTIONAL levels of HS that defined us as "Lesbians," we accepted as given the validity of sex-specific behaviors as defined by HS and tried to "fit" ourselves in somewhere. Diagram 2 represents one attempt to construct a coherent, intelligible semantic system for describing perceived differences among Lesbians. Although we recognized a range of behaviors and the purported distinctions were fuzzy (to say the least), we were still bound by the basic dichotomy of HS as an explanation of personality. We used the most general terms, *butch* and *femme*, as though they were meaningful to us. We used them to talk about ourselves, to convey information about ourselves that seemed significant in our social context.

Ignored, however, in previous and current discussions of roles among Lesbians is the "ki-ki." She, along with her label, has disappeared, because our most recent dialogues have focused on the extremes as though one were necessarily either/or. This isn't accurate historically, and it's unfair to ourselves in the present.[7] I point this out because the term is obsolete as nearly as I can tell. When the Feminist second wave hit the Lesbian shore, *ki-ki* disappeared because it ceased, temporarily, to be "meaningful" among those Lesbians who became Feminists. (Maybe it's still used among nonFeminist Lesbians.) The Feminist analysis of heterosexual roles, male oppression, and sexism were adopted by Lesbian-Feminists and applied to the roles of butch and femme, and "sex-roles" among Lesbians became "politically incorrect." As Joan Nestle pointed out,[8] we lost a large part of our past, identities, and our tradition, such as it was. Being proud and honest about our past, however, doesn't mean its assumptions are or should be viable in the present.

I include the term *ki-ki* here because it named Lesbians who considered themselves neither "butch" nor "femme." The "role" they adopted depended upon who they were being sexual with at the time. In so doing, they affirmed the validity of the roles for those who chose them, but refused to make such a choice themselves. They didn't want to be "limited," and some of them regarded those Lesbians who were "into roles" as having made a bad choice.

One could be "ki-ki" in the "old days" (scarcely twenty years ago), when *dyke* and *bulldyke* (*bulldagger* among blacks) were strictly derogatory in their usage, within and without the Lesbian sub-culture. The more blatantly "mannish" a Lesbian was in her looks, dress, and behavior, the more negatively charged the label applied to her, by heterosexuals *and* Lesbians. Calling oneself a "butch" *might* correlate with one's physical appearance, including dress, but not necessarily. I knew a lot of "butches" who looked and were very "feminine," and we called them "nelly butches." "Butch" labeled their sexual behavior, not their appearance. One self-labeled butch I knew was extremely feminine. Not only could she pass as het, she was, in fact, a call girl, and the mistress of a wealthy man.

Also significantly absent from current discussions is another kind of Lesbian I remember well from the 1950s and 1960s: the Lesbian who didn't label herself at all. There were Lesbians, even then, who did not call themselves *butch* or *femme* or *ki-ki*. They disapproved of the roles altogether. Furthermore, they looked down on those of us who did role-play, and they said so to our faces. They may have even been a majority of the Lesbian sub-culture back then, or maybe it was 50-50, or maybe role-playing Lesbians were a majority. I can't quantify that from my remembrances. (Maybe it depended on the bars where one hung out, or whether or not one went to bars. I did know a few Lesbians who frequented the bars I did who refused to conform to the role stereotypes.)

In the late '60s, along came a female-centered political analysis (at least it claimed to be female-centered): role-playing among Lesbians was "out," and abandoning role-identified behaviors was "in." But—I know, you know, we most of us know—there is still a large, very large, Lesbian population who rejected Feminism and its analysis from the beginning of its influence among other Lesbians. They said, essentially, "We're happy the way we are; we have no intention of changing; we don't want to change, and you (meaning Lesbian-Feminists) aren't going to make us. Period." This "dialogue" in the Lesbian "community" was and is still being carried on by only a handful of us. Vast numbers are silent either because they don't know it's happening or don't care.

With the development of Lesbian self-consciousness about the political meaning of our lives, the reclamation of previously derogatory words began, *Dyke* among them, because it was so negatively charged for us. That this process *seemed* to move toward the "masculine" end of the continuum is a result of the HP version of reality, not anything inherent in being a Dyke. Given the HS dichotomy, "reclaiming" femininity is irrelevant because it's essential to HP. If Lesbians want to deny the "naturalness" of HP categories, and assert the positive value of our deviance, adopting femininity doesn't make any sense. To date, our efforts to use the word *Dyke* in positive ways, often equating the word with "high political-consciousness," have yet to be taken up by a majority of Lesbians. Other Lesbians say they're "reclaiming" femme and butch roles for themselves; *ki-ki*, as I've said, became obsolete. We haven't yet tried to reclaim *bulldagger* and *bulldyke*. Maybe there're good reasons for this even though we haven't articulated them.

What is the Locus of Lesbian Identity?

How is it that Lesbians, in spite of good intentions, continue to write and read in utterly opposed contexts? Why, for example, was Jan Brown revealing the misogyny she felt when she was a butch (in *Out/Look* 7:30-34), while Sabrina Sojourner was "reclaiming" femininity (in *Sojourner*, Feb., 1991)? Up to this point, I've left unmentioned two important factors: Political Consciousness and the continuum, Overt. . .Covert. I think it's because Lesbians conceive of ourselves in relation to the heteropatriarchy in conflicting ways, depending on whether or not we're Feminists and, more specifically, the brand of Feminism we've incorporated into our value system. I will call this "political consciousness."

Some Lesbians (I would say most) live *within* the heteropatriarchy, and would not even name this society as such; they think of themselves as being not so very different from heterosexuals, and so have only rudimentary analysis to account for their discomforts. Others conceive of ourselves as being *outside* the boundaries of the heteropatriarchy, as being quite different from heterosexuals, and so mistrust any aspect of our thinking and behavior that apes or mirrors the heteropatriarchal world. Lesbians don't share a "consensus reality"; that is, we have, as yet, no agreed-upon framework within which we make our decisions and evaluate options. We have no self-created description of what it "means" to be a Lesbian in HP, with the result that our valuations of specific kinds of behavior are diverse. Our willingness to challenge HP descriptions varies in terms of where we conceive of ourselves, as Lesbians, with respect to HP society. No Lesbian can ignore HP or pretend that it isn't there, although many try; none of us can deny its influence in our lives or in the ways we think. To ignore HP or claim that somehow we've "gotten past" it in our thinking is to trivialize the damage HP has done to us *as Lesbians*. These self-conceptions are in conflict each with the other, and they cannot be reconciled. There's no "middle ground" in this disagreement on which we can compromise, even if we were willing.

For the sake of argument, think of HP society as a circle. At various stages in her development and awareness, a Lesbian positions herself with respect to HP on the basis of her understanding of the meaning of her Lesbian life. Diagram 3 represents six possible Lesbian stances in her acknowledgment of HP: Conservative, Conventional, Humanist, Feminist, Radical Feminist, and Separatist. Each point on this continuum represents an approximate, not an absolute, political position. (I've used this terminology because I think it'll be understood by my readers.)

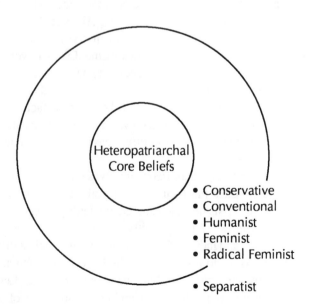

Diagram 3. Lesbian Self-consciousness as Political Identification

Conservative Lesbians accept HP descriptions of reality as accurate and all-encompassing, and they live as though the givens of HP were unalterable fact. Such Lesbians are usually white, financially comfortable, and living in the suburbs of large cities. In terms of the way they think, they are virtually indistinguishable from their heterosexual neighbors; they don't think of themselves as "Lesbian," and most of their friends may be heterosexuals. In spite of the fact that many Conservative Lesbians have never lived as heterosexuals, and must have, at some point in their lives, rejected the essential HP assumption, this fact has no political significance for them. They're "never-het," but covert. They believe that the "world" is fine just as it is. For them, no social or personal change is necessary or desirable.

Conventional Lesbians differ from the Conservatives only in that they may call themselves "gay" or "Lesbian," their circle of friends may consist of like-minded Lesbians and gaymen in addition to heterosexuals, and some—those who can afford it—may contribute money to "gay" causes as a substitute for active involvement. They may be never-het or ex-het, but their Lesbianism, or "gayness," is covert.

Humanist Lesbians believe that "we're all human beings," and that living as a Lesbian is no different from living as a heterosexual, even though they are aware that HP is oppressive in many ways. The oppressiveness of HP they interpret as some kind of misunderstanding, as though Lesbian oppression will end when heterosexuals understand that Lesbians are "just like" them. The political awareness of Humanist Lesbians may extend to pro-consumer, anti-war, anti-nuclear struggles; they are committed to saving the rainforest, the dolphins, pandas, and all living creatures; they may work as volunteers for AIDS crisis lines or on behalf of the United Way, because they conceive of themselves as having a stake in the outcome of political issues as HP identifies them. Like Conventional Lesbians, they may belong to any economic class. They may be ex-het or never-het, and they may be out as Lesbians or in the closet; neither aspect of their lives is politically significant to them. Their Lesbianism isn't the essential factor of their identity. Humanist Lesbians will agree that HP is flawed, but believe that all we need to do is make alterations in the social structure, leaving the primary assumptions unchallenged.

Feminist Lesbians have identified themselves with women's oppression, and they make women's issues the focus of their political activism. They may, for example, work on rape crisis lines, in battered women's shelters or abortion clinics, or teach women's studies. They correctly identify the fact that women are oppressed in this society, and they work actively to struggle against that oppression as they understand it. Most do not, for example, believe that men are the enemy—only some of them—and they attribute their oppression as Lesbians to their femaleness. They are committed to changing the structure of HP to varying degrees; they question some of the essential values and categories of HP; but heterosexuality remains, for them, an unchallenged given. Lesbian-Feminist consciousness is possible for the ex-het or never-het, closeted or out.

Lesbians who call themselves Radical Feminists position themselves some-where between Feminist and Separatist Lesbians, on the limits of reality as HP describes it. On the one hand, they identify their oppression as primarily women's oppression, not specifically Lesbian oppression; on the other they believe that men are the enemies of all women and have developed some of the best analyses of how HP society perpetuates itself and have proposed various methods of destroying "patriarchy." Although they don't identify as Lesbians first, they understand the threat that Lesbians pose to HP. They stop just short of identifying "patriarchy" as *heteropatriarchy*.

Separatist Lesbians think of ourselves as living *outside* HP society (although this is seldom true). Accepting the HP description of Lesbians as outcasts, we have chosen to stand in an antagonistic position to the HP, and it's Separatists who identify ourselves as Lesbians first and last. Whether never-het or ex-het, Separat-ists put our Lesbian selves first politically. The essential ingredient of Separatist politics is a rejection of everything vital to the structure of HP, which requires that all assumptions be challenged and examined. Whereas Humanist or Feminist Lesbians believe that behaviors and attitudes can be justified by appealing to the way they feel, Separatists (and Radical Feminists) want to know where these "feelings" originate. We're not interested in stopping our analysis with *how* we feel, because appealing to feelings is one way of resisting change. If we're going to change ourselves and unlearn HP's version of reality, then we're committed to examining our feelings and finding out *why* we have them and where they originate in our experience.

Toward a Lesbian-Centered Semantics

Because Lesbians have different backgrounds and experiences, communica-tion among us will be difficult as long as we use the same words with different meanings and values. But we should not stop arguing with each other. While our debates and discussions continue, though, we need other ways of talking to each other or, at least, explicit acknowledgments that our meanings may be vastly different. We haven't yet begun to work out our problems with the English language. As the debates about femininity and its effects among Lesbians illustrate, we don't have a "consensus reality," and any attempt to construct a Lesbian ethic are often met with arguments based on and fashioned out of HP descriptions of reality. Why are Lesbians so quick to resist Lesbian analysis and defend HP categories? Why do so many Lesbians resist what they derisively call "Lesbian conformity" yet defend their own conformity to HP categories? Where does this reversal originate and whom does it serve? Lesbians? I don't think so.

For Lesbians who are trying to live outside of or on the boundaries of HP, our attitudes toward and the values we attach to those behaviors have undergone important changes, but the diversity of behaviors observable among Lesbians hasn't. How are we to manage communication among us in spite of our disagreements? I've identified four options (there are probably others):

1) We can accept the valuation assigned to the MASCULINE/ FEMININE dichotomy by HP, as some Lesbians do, and continue to invest our lives with what those words mean;

2) We can reverse the valuation made by HP, as do those Lesbians who maintain they can "reclaim" femininity as "positive";

3) We can muddle along as we do now, sometimes assigning positive value to "masculine" behaviors, sometimes to feminine behaviors, and sometimes agreeing;

4) We can reject HP semantics altogether, move further outside the boundaries and terms of HS, and start anew to construct a semantic system of our own.

The first three options are already operational among Lesbians. Whether one values either masculine or feminine behaviors and looks, or neither, positively depends, I think, on where she places herself along the continuum of Diagram 3. This "makes sense," if one accepts the logic. Many Lesbians have constructed an identity dependent on the terms created and validated by HS; they have an investment in that identity, and any analysis which challenges that identity is suspect.

If my analysis of Heteropatriarchal Semantics is accurate, and if my analysis of how we have revised that framework in order to "make sense" of ourselves is accurate, then emotional health—thinking well of and feeling good about ourselves—requires us—those like me, who wish to change—to act on option 4: *creating a new semantic system for talking about who we are.* This is the hardest option of the four. It means we have to think differently about who we are as Lesbians in a world that hates us. (With good reason: a Lesbian who loves herself exposes the arbitrariness of HP consensus reality. If we're real, then their conceptual framework is flawed, partial at best.)

For starters, I'd suggest that we toss out HP semantics, including *masculine* and the labels derived from HS, *butch* and *femme*. Easy to say, hard to do. I don't believe we can ignore the label *feminine*, because so many Lesbians claim that "femininity" is an inherent trait of their "womanhood" and that femininity is a viable Lesbian mode. They still have an investment in HP descriptions of reality. Ideally, in some world that doesn't yet exist, it should be OK for a Lesbian to don a dress or blue jeans, high heels or boots, decorate herself or not, wear her hair long or short, cut her nails or grow them long; but it's not. Those aspects of behavior and appearance labeled "femininity" in HP are dangerous for us. We still live *in* a heteropatriarchy and Lesbians who incorporate male ideas of appropriate female behaviors into their lives signal their acceptance of the HP version of reality. What is more, they will continue to accept preferential treatment at the expense of Lesbians who defy HP authority in order to hold onto our identity.

Lesbians are a sub-culture trying to hold our own within the context of a large, hostile, HP society. Whatever we "choose" to wear, however we choose to look, those choices are likely to be interpreted within the HP semantic system by anyone who doesn't know us. Somehow, we have to acknowledge the existence of HP categories and their influence in order to unlearn them, without letting that acknowledgment become validation and acceptance of those categories as "true."

I believe that Lesbian femininity is politically corrupt and degrading, because Lesbians perceived as "mannish"—and described as "acting like men"—are shunted aside, marginalized, and trashed by Lesbians who value femininity.

How can we talk about the significant differences among us, the actual range of our observable behaviors, without accepting the assumptions of HP? In the past, the labels *butch, femme,* and *ki-ki* served Lesbians as a way of acknowledging and talking about behavioral differences among us, and they still serve that purpose in some segments of the Lesbian sub-culture. But those of us who want to reconceive ourselves in terms that don't carry with them the assumptions of HS will have to learn to describe ourselves in specific, sometimes lengthy ways that avoid both HS and its values.

In order to do this, we'll need to start with a radically different description of the "world," one based on Lesbian experiences and perceptions. Since Lesbians haven't yet worked out a "consensus reality," let's understand first of all that this dialogue is taking place only among Lesbians who are active politically. Let's find ways to talk to each other in a *Lesbian context.* (This will enable us to ignore, for example, those conservative, never-het Lesbians who are as Lesbian-hating and misogynist as the heterosexuals whose company they prefer to ours.)

We can make a significant start, as Linda Strega suggested, by valuing Lesbians who rejected and reject efforts to feminize them. We can value our deviance from HP reality, refuse to value Lesbian femininity positively—because it represents conformity to HP descriptions and values—and value nonfeminized Lesbians positively. Some of us resist HP training, to varying degrees; others do not, and to varying degrees. HP rewards those who conform to its version of reality; let's stop privileging HP conformity and, instead, reward Lesbian resisters. Strega posited that Lesbians must learn to value positively our resistance to HP programming and stop rewarding Lesbians who conform to it.

Most importantly, we must stand our ground outside of HP reality, occupy it with determination, and resist efforts to assimilate us and dilute the radical force of our perceptions. Lesbians who "pass" as heterosexuals do so because they don't want to live openly as Lesbians. Their choice clearly indicates that they value HP approval *more* than they value their Lesbian identity. A corollary of this is their avoidance and marginalization of Lesbians who cannot or will not pass. And I am weary of being exhorted in the Lesbian and Feminist media to value feminized Lesbians. While I recognize that many Lesbians try to pass in order to survive in HP, recognition of that fact doesn't mean any of us should value that deception positively or persist in according them preferential status in our communities. The fact of the matter is that Lesbians who pass do so in order to survive better, in economic terms, than those who don't.

Lesbians who can pass as heterosexuals must understand and admit that they acquire specific social privileges because they can hide their Lesbianism. The privileges and rewards of femininity, in addition to money and social approval, are a false sense of worth and self-esteem because they are grounded in hypocrisy and pretense. Furthermore, Lesbians who prize femininity either believe they are superior to "obvious" Lesbians or they sexualize the difference. In a Lesbian context, FEMININITY = HETEROSEXUALITY = CLOSETED = PRIVILEGE = LESBIAN-HATING. If Lesbians who pass as heterosexuals expect Dykes to condone their choices, as they seem to, they must also recognize that mutual respect is a two-way street. Describing nonfeminized Lesbians as "mannish" or accusing us of "acting like a man" is ignorant, degrading, and insulting. Dykes are accustomed to hearing such descriptions from heterosexuals; we don't expect or want to hear it from other Lesbians. It discounts our existence and disowns us. The fact of the matter is that *we* understand the fears and doubts of passing Lesbians, yet they've made little or no effort to understand us. Femininity in a Lesbian gives her access to heterosexual privileges, privileges that are tangible: they get better jobs that bring with them social prestige and money. Dykes know all about femininity, what it is, what it means, and the rewards it offers. Because femininity in women is so highly prized by men, femininity cannot be positively valued in a Lesbian context.

Endnotes

1. None of what I say here should be interpreted as referring retrospectively to the Lesbian femmes of the decades before the Women's Liberation Movement.

2. For example, one of the important differences among Lesbians, and one that most seem to want to ignore, is that between those of us who have always been Lesbians and those who lived and behaved as heterosexuals for long periods of their lives. That single difference—choosing to act on and live our desires, or choosing to live with/marry a man and bear children—has profound ramifications for how we behave and understand ourselves as Lesbians. For one thing, that choice frequently results in a class difference: lifelong Lesbians do not have the upward class mobility of passing, ex-het Lesbians, and remain poor and working-class because we can't get jobs that pay well.

3. I cannot do justice in this brief summary to Linda Strega's analysis in "The Big Sell-Out," nor to the responses to Strega from Paula Mariedaughter and Mary Crane, and I urge readers to seek out the issues of *Lesbian Ethics* in which the three pieces were published. Strega in particular provides specific examples of the HP attitudes she's in the process of unlearning with an analysis of why she wants to unlearn them.

4. Consider, for example, Maxine Feldman, who isn't feminine, who has never tried to pass as heterosexual, who isn't "pretty" in HP terms, in contrast to the recording "stars" of Olivia Records, who persist in trying to break into the "mainstream" of the music business. They purposely try to pass as heterosexuals, to look like heterosexuals. In fact, most of them refuse to use the L-word from the stage, even at events where they know that a majority of the audience is Lesbian. Such musicians not only betray those of us who are out-front as Lesbians, they exploit our desire for a music of our own in a cynical way, using our money and loyalty to them as a means to the financial gains they hope to acquire by appealing to a "broader" audience (i.e., heterosexuals). There is a cruel irony in this: with the exception of, perhaps, Holly Near (if one still thinks she deserves to call herself a "Lesbian"), none of them have succeeded in breaking into the mainstream.

5. A second edition of that dictionary appeared in 1987, but the definitions of these words remained virtually the same.

6. See, for example, the Sept./Oct., 1985, issue of *Lesbian Connection*, in which a couple of women maintain that they are "Lesbians" in spite of the fact that they fuck men! As one of them puts it: "I have broadened my definition of what a Lesbian is." Her use of the word *broadening* is, of course, intended to make readers interpret the statement as positive by opposing it to the word *narrow*, which has negative connotations in HS (unless it's used to characterize one's waistline or hips!). This kind of "broadening" is pernicious, hypocritical, and self-serving—and, besides, simply not possible. Like it or not, a Lesbian has sex with wimmin, not men; heterosexual and bisexual females have sex with men. That's what the words mean. I have no desire to "reclaim" heterosexuality as a lifestyle, and wimmin who do can't call themselves Lesbians. I have a personal investment in that word and I won't have it ripped off or diluted by those whose actions dilute its significance. Another word for *broadening* is *sell-out*.

7. With the notable exception of Merril Mushroom in *Common Lives/Lesbian Lives* 9 (Fall, 1983), 39-45.

8. In her article, "Butch-Fem Relationships: Sexual Courage in the 1950's," *Heresies: The Sex Issue* 12, 3: 21-24.

The Lesbian New-rotics:
Bogus or Breakthrough?

Introduction

These days, it seems that Lesbian political activism has been replaced by quick-fix Lesbian sex, at least in the popular Lesbian media. Lesbian "bed death" gets more attention than our survivors of psychiatric abuse. If my sexlife seems stale, I can "reclaim" the "erotic" in my life by reading one of JoAnn Loulan's books or "turn on" my VCR by popping in the latest, slickest Lesbian "erotica." The Spring, 1991, Naiad mailing brought with it an "invitation" to subscribe to *On Our Backs*, in which the *Bay Area Reporter* announced that that magazine "is the single most important event of the decade for lesbians." (If this is true, things are worse among us than I think.) The February, 1991 issue of *Sojourner*, a Boston Feminist newspaper, featured an essay by Sabrina Sojourner "reclaiming" not only "the erotic," but femininity, and words like *cunt, pussy, slit,* and *gash.* The Amazons and Edward the Dyke[1] have been succeeded by Pussy Galore.

It's not just the hard-sell, have-I-got-a-deal-for-you tone of the articles and advertisements that offends my sensibility, although the glitzy hype and the enthusiastic consumerism it encourages certainly are offensive. I am offended by the justifications for the "erotic" and "erotica" that want me to believe that these products are new and different because Lesbians are writing them, selling them, posing for them, and buying them. (Even Lesbians don't make things we can't sell.) I am offended that the dealers claim their products are politically "radical," and that I am an "anti-sex puritan," as though I couldn't possibly have legitimate reasons for not liking them. I am offended by the repeated assertions that my sexlife without such products must be lackluster and dull, and appalled when I contemplate the sums of money that some Lesbians are spending on "sex toys." But I am most offended by the words *erotic* and *erotica* themselves, borrowed uncritically from the male pornographic tradition as tony euphemisms for the sexual and the sexually explicit.

The production and consumption of sexually explicit material is a phenomenon of the 1980s that promises to stay with us through the '90s, but not a bit of the sex or the hype that sells it is new; Lesbians have read male pornography for years. What *is* new are the political claims used to rationalize its proliferation among us and the scorn heaped on those of us who don't buy the line.

My own opposition to the production of Lesbian pornography isn't new, either. In 1980a, I reviewed one of the first books to be advertised as "lesbian erotica"—Cedar and Nelly's *A Woman's Touch*—in *Sinister Wisdom* 15.[2] I return to the subject in 1991 not only because of the contemporary claims that fill the Lesbian media, but also because three contributors to a collection of Lesbian-Feminist literary criticism (co-edited by Susan Wolfe and me) objected to our suggestion that they change the word *erotic* to *sexual* in their manuscripts. They informed us that they objected to our editorial suggestion because Audre Lorde had "reclaimed" the word *erotic* in *Uses of the Erotic: The Erotic as Power* (1978). I don't think the ways Lesbians are using the words *erotic* and *erotica* have anything in common with the radical political agenda Lorde was talking about. Yet, I feel I must listen to their objections—all of these Lesbians are well-informed and committed to Lesbian-Feminist principles—and attempt a response to them.

On "The Erotic"

The appropriate place to begin is with Lorde's *Uses of the Erotic*, in which she set out her reasons why Lesbian-Feminists should "reclaim" the word *erotic*. In that work, Lorde explicitly associated both social and political change with "reclaiming" the word *erotic* and linked its reclamation to successful radical change of one's Self *and* the world.

> Recognizing the power of the erotic within our lives can give us the energy to pursue genuine change within our world, rather than merely settling for *a shift of characters in the same weary drama*. [My emphasis] For not only do we touch our most profoundly creative source, but we do that which is female and self-affirming in the face of a racist, patriarchal, and anti-erotic society. (p. 8)

This proposal urges Lesbians to undertake a radical political transformation. Lorde was clear: she wasn't interested in "settling for a shift of characters in the same weary drama." She disowned that easy solution. By "reclaiming" the word *erotic*, she intended to infuse it with more than a narrowly construed reference to sexual feelings and genital arousal. To "widen" our understanding and use of the word, she referred to its origin in the Greek word *eros*:

> The very word 'erotic' comes from the Greek word *eros*, the personification of love in all its aspects—born of Chaos, and personifying creative power and harmony. When I speak of the erotic, then, I speak of it as an assertion of the life-force of women, of that creative energy empowered, the knowledge and use of which we are now reclaiming in our language, our history, our dancing, our loving, our work, our lives. (pp. 3-4)

99

The scope which Lorde proposed for the "erotic" encompassed a variety of emotional reponses: satisfaction, joy, and a knowledge of one's capacities and capabilities as well. While I agree with Lorde's motivation and desire for a single, precise word to label what she calls "our deepest knowledge," I think she chose the wrong word.

Can the word *erotic* be "reclaimed," even though *Eros* was a male god in a major Western patriarchy?[3] What promise of radical change can that idea hold for us if we understand the process of reclamation to be founded on our will and desire to change *what we mean in the world*? As Lorde herself acknowledged,

> The erotic has often been misnamed by men and used against women. It has been made into the confused, the trivial, the psychotic, the plasticized sensation. For this reason, we have often turned away from the exploration and consideration of the erotic as a source of power and information, confusing it with its opposite, the pornographic....Pornography emphasizes sensation without feeling. (p. 2)

What Lorde warned against—confusing empowerment with the pornographic—is, I believe, exactly what has occurred. Some Lesbians have mistaken "plasticized sensation" for what Lorde envisioned, "the celebration. . .[within which] my work becomes a conscious decision—a longed-for bed which I enter gratefully and from which I rise up empowered" (3). Some Lesbians have chosen, I fear, beds to lie down on that delude them, and they rise up, not empowered, but oblivious to the work we must yet do. As Cherríe Moraga and Amber Hollibaugh (1983) put it, we need to examine what we are "rollin around in bed with." In order to examine the decisions we make, we need to consider the ramifications when we set out to "reclaim" a word from its heteropatriarchal context. We aren't only choosing words. We're choosing meanings and concepts inherent in the words we may not be able to transform.

As the Lesbian sexual materials being marketed indicate, *erotic* and *erotica* have their origins in a heteropatriarchal mode of thought that negates the empowerment Lorde sought to evoke, for they bring with them the assumptions, ideas, and values of the men who created them. Those words erode the political foundations of the Lesbian context some of us seek to create, because we cannot expunge the male sexuality inherent in their meaning.

In "Mystery and Monster: The Lesbian in Heterosexual Fantasies," also published in *Sinister Wisdom* 15 1980b, I analyzed how the idea of two wimmin making love was used in two kinds of heterosexual pornography: confession magazines, aimed at a female audience, and "adult" magazines, pornography served up to male prurience. One thing that had puzzled me from the beginning of my research was the contrast between the treatment of Lesbianism in the confession magazines and how it was presented in materials for a male audience.

The materials about Lesbians written and published for women were designed to scare them away from Lesbianism. By and large, Lesbians are presented in confession magazines as sick, degenerate predators intent on "seducing" innocent heterosexual women. In male "erotica" and pornography, in contrast, Lesbians are presented with great relish. The magazines marketed to a female audience used Lesbianism to scare their heterosexual readers; in the male magazines, the idea of two women having sex was clearly a turn-on. Men were not only *not* threatened by the idea, they jerked off to it!

While I pondered the implications of this, I noticed two distinct ways of representing Lesbians and Lesbian sexuality in men's magazines, each determined by the economic status of the audience to whom the material is marketed. The first type, the glossy, expensive male magazine, carries full-color photographs of supposed "Lesbians" that are hazy, indistinct, and romanticized. The women, posed as though they might touch each other, have what men consider "perfect" female bodies: without hair, without blemish. These images of models pretending to be Lesbians represent us to men's imaginations as mysterious but warm, provocative, and, through the lens of a camera, accessible. The accompanying descriptions of what the models have done or will do with each other elaborate these fantasies. These representations are called "erotica."

The second type of male magazine doesn't cost very much at all, as pornography goes. In them, the women posing as Lesbians are presented as coarse, vulgar, unattractive, and lewd (in male terms). These models have pimples and moles on their bodies, warts around their genitals, and hair all over their bodies (just like we do). The physical imperfections of the models haven't been airbrushed out of sight. Many of the black-and-white photographs in these cheaper magazines cater to male fetishism: the models wear garter belts and net stockings; some brandish whips.

I did that research between 1976 and 1980. The words and images I was looking at then are being marketed today as Lesbian "erotica" in magazines like *On Our Backs* and *Bad Attitude*. While I wasn't explicit then about the distinction I was trying to draw, I will be explicit now. Class is the significant feature that always distinguishes "erotica" from pornography. The glossy magazines and expensive, hardcover editions of treatises (like the *Kama Sutra* and *The Pillow Book*) · are published for rich men, the privileged, those who govern. The cheap ones—printed on newspaper, with gray, poorly-developed photos of crotch shots—are sold to working-class men. What rich men can afford to buy is called "erotica." What poor men buy is "pornography," "porno," or "porn."

The difference in cost—the class difference—dictates the different treatment given to "erotica" and "porn." Not surprisingly, this difference in cost (what a man can or will pay) also underlies the distinction between *mistress* and *wife*, *whore* and *call girl*. The indulgences and vices of wealthy white men are always valued as cultural treasures, and so are protected, preserved, institutionalized. The vices of poor and working-class men, whatever their race or ethnic background, cannot claim "socially redeeming value," cannot expect to be protected or preserved.

"Erotica" is marketed as "art," as "literature." "Pornography," in contrast, is easily and cheaply obtained; it is fragile, ephemeral, throwaway: trash. "Erotica" is preserved in the Special Sections (X) of libraries; porn ends up in garbage cans.

Now I must undertake what I did not do when Lorde first published *Uses of the Erotic* in 1978: complete my analysis of *erotic* (and *erotica* and *eroticism*) and explain why those words aren't appropriate to describe Lesbian sexuality *if* we intend to deconstruct our heteropatriarchal selves and construct new Selves that are radically *different*, thereby extricating our bodies from the male gaze. The following discussion, like Audre Lorde's, assumes an audience of Lesbians who intend to change what it means to be a Lesbian, who want to live differently from the ways we've lived in the past, and who look forward to a future much different from the familiar past and present. These Lesbians, like myself, are dissatisfied with the world as men have made it, and our goal is the destruction of the heteropatriarchal world order. Part of our project is challenging and discrediting male descriptions of *how the world is* and replacing them with our own, more accurate (we hope) descriptions. If thorough-going political change is not our goal, then how we think of ourselves, how we describe ourselves, and the words we do or do not choose, aren't relevant. Certainly, assimilation, integration, imitation, or acquisition will not require changing the way we talk and think.

Notice that folks like George Bush, John Doe, and Phyllis Schlaffly are not trying to "reclaim" words from patriarchal English. The desire to "reclaim" words is limited to deviants—those of us who don't fit the white, male hetero mold: blacks, Feminists, Lesbians. Those who enjoy and benefit from the *status quo* are satisfied with how men have named reality for them. The urge to "reclaim" is part of the desire to change the accepted shape of reality. It is an inherently deviant enterprise.

Reclamation Projects

What do we mean when we say we're going to "reclaim" a particular word? What is the impulse behind our desire to reclaim words from the patriarchal vocabulary? How do we decide which words *can* or *should* be reclaimed? The *impulse* that leads us to want a word is obvious and noncontroversial: We want labels for ideas, activities, events, and processes that are essential to our visions of who we can be and how we might live. Being able to name, for ourselves and other wimmin, our changes in consciousness, subtle shifts in perception, more sweeping transformations of how we conceive of ourselves in the world is, or should be, important to us. And we want to communicate all these events which we've experienced in our lives to other wimmin clearly and without ambiguity. Unfortunately, I think we choose the expedient, the ready-to-hand, without thinking through what that choice may entail.

There are three ways of achieving a new, transforming kind of naming that

Lesbians have tried: (1) making up new words and phrases; (2) resurrecting original and now archaic meanings of words, as Mary Daly has done; or (3) "reclaiming" patriarchal words and making them our own.

The first approach, making up new words, has failed, virtually without exception. In order for a new word to take hold in our minds, it has to be used many times by many Lesbians and wimmin. It has to become familiar. That happens only when a new word seems to fill some previously empty conceptual niche that we've ached to have a name for. Words like Kate Clinton's *fumorist* and *dedyking*, *na* (June Arnold's generic third person pronoun [1973]), *hasbean*, and *lovher* suggest themselves. Some we don't hear or use, such as *fumorist* (a blend) or *na*. Neither seems to have entered our daily vocabulary (at least not mine or my friends').

Dedyking, a noun turned into a verb, and *hasbean*, a blend based on *has been* and *lesbian*, are exceptions that do seem to have caught on. I've heard both *dedyking* and *hasbean* several times from festival stages and seen them in print. Their relative success may be attributed to the fact that both words refer to something familiar. *Dedyking* describes something many of us have done in our lives: removed every visible evidence of our Lesbianism—books, posters, records and tapes, paintings, T-shirts—and moved beds apart or even set up a fake "second" bedroom before the arrival of identified heterosexuals, usually parents, whom we aren't out to. Like *dedyke*, *hasbean* describes a situation Lesbians talk about: it labels a woman (ex-Lesbian) who decides to choose men rather than wimmin as her primary emotional and sexual focus. *Dedyking* isn't an activity and being a *hasbean* isn't a sort of woman that heteropatriarchal English has named for us. Both are alien concepts; they aren't just unnecessary, they are *unthinkable* in the Patriarchal Universe of Discourse (PUD). Lesbians wanted names for those concepts, and now we have them.

Notice, however, that both *dedyke* and *hasbean* aren't entirely unfamiliar, as was *na*. The verb *dedyke* is derived from an already widely known noun, *dyke*, with the prefix *de-*, also comfortably familiar in our daily use. However, the noun *dyke* is acceptable *only* if one regards it as *reclaimed*, an issue that isn't yet resolved. • Some of us like it, others don't. I still read comments in letters and short stories indicating that Lesbians in the U.S. continue to interpret *dyke* as it is commonly used in the heteropatriarchy: as an insult, a slur, a very negative label, especially on the lips of men, but also when it's used by some Lesbians, who equate "being a dyke" with "wanting to be a man." I would say though, that *dedyking* has had some success. *Hasbean*, a blend of two familiar words, has also been successful, maybe because Alix Dobkin has used it in her song, "Lesbian Code."

Lovher, like *fumorist*, is another blend (*love* + the pronoun *her*, which nicely substitutes for the *-er* suffix). It appeared in 1986 as the English title, *Lovhers*, of Nicole Brossard's *Amantes*, and has since turned up in a letter in *Lesbian Connection* and in the *Guide to Gracious Lesbian Living* (1989), but it's too soon to predict whether *lovher* will become more widely used. The fact that it, too, is a blend, rather than an entirely new combination of sounds, suggests that it has a chance. But *fumorist* hasn't caught on; at least, I've heard only Kate Clinton use it. Perhaps it's the way the word sounds to us, or maybe there's just not that much call for its use. (If we associate it with *fumarole*, a vent in the side of a volcano through which steam escapes, we might find uses for it.)

The second method, resurrecting the original meanings of words, has had more success: Mary Daly's revival of scores of words, including *crone, hag, witch, a-maze*, to name only a few, again indicates that we adopt into our usage coinages based on already-familiar words, or we can use familiar words with a renewed valuing more easily than we accept and use utterly new creations.

Familiarity seems to be a significant aspect of our linguistic process. For this reason, the third approach to language change—reclamation—has been the most popular and successful of the three approaches to providing ourselves with the names we need. As I suggested in *Speaking Freely: Unlearning the Lies of the Fathers' Tongues* (1990), and implied in my earlier discussion of *dedyking*, reclaiming heteropatriarchal words requires a "sifting" process in those Lesbian communities considering using the words. We weigh the pros and cons of accepting such words into our daily use; some make it, others don't. At least one aspect that some Lesbians consider is whether or not we *feel* that using a particular word will reinforce the heteropatriarchal programming we're trying to get out of our minds.

For example, many Lesbians have stopped referring to ourselves as the *victims* of incest and now say we're *survivors*. In *Wildfire* (1989), however, Sonia Johnson suggested that we stop calling ourselves "survivors" because it "perpetuates women's feelings of powerlessness and their perceptions of themselves as victims" (footnote, 130). I disagree. Her suggestion ignored how the words *survivor* and *victim* are used by Lesbians and wimmin who've been raped and/or battered. We choose our terms carefully. For some, it is the word *victim* that "perpetuate[s] feelings of powerlessness." Some of us interpret *victim* to refer to a woman who is still using the defenses she needed in earlier contexts to deal with events in the present. By *survivor*, in contrast, we refer to ourselves as having somehow interpreted past experiences from a newly gained perspective, a stance from which we acknowledge those events and the damage they caused, and as now having learned to distinguish between painful past experiences and their meanings and present words or acts that may *appear* to be the same but aren't. Other survivors of rape, battering, and psychiatric abuse call themselves survivors because they survived their experience. In our on-going dialogue about naming ourselves, Sonia Johnson has made a suggestion, I would say, without adequate information. Those of us who have gone through a transformative process want to distinguish between who we were and who we are becoming. *Victim* is, to us, a way we have conceived of ourselves; *survivor* names an important passage we have navigated or are navigating in our lives.

Our ability to determine the power of heteropatriarchal meanings isn't, so far, unambiguously evident, as the example of *victim* and *survivor* indicates. A significant factor in the reclamation process is *what the word means within the patriarchal universe of discourse.* To date, we have been most successful reclaiming words that men use negatively. But the negativity is in their (and our) *usage*, NOT in the word itself. What we've changed is how we *feel* about the word. We've changed the connotations of such words, but not their *denotation.* We haven't had to go through the process of creating entirely *new* meanings for the words. Mary Daly reinterpreted *crone, hag, witch,* revaluing them for us as positive labels, as names we could use among ourselves with glee.

Yet, even this method of reinterpretation isn't easy. You may recall Marilyn Frye's speech at the 1990 meeting of the National Women's Studies Association, published in *off our backs* (Aug./Sept. 1990), "Do You Have to be a Lesbian to be a Feminist?," in which she proposed using the word *virgin* in its early sense: "a female who is sexually and hence socially her own person." The outpouring of mostly hostile letters to *oob* about Frye's essay revealed that many readers hadn't understood what Frye was saying. They didn't get what Frye was trying to accomplish by using the word *virgin* as synonymous with *outlaw,* because *virgin* has only one meaning in PUD: For a woman to be a virgin, unfucked, is sort of a good thing. It means she isn't easy. For a man to fuck the unfucked is a good thing. It means he's "special," a man that the hold-outs give in to. As teenaged wimmin will tell you, being unfucked for too long isn't a good thing. It means there's something "wrong," and there's lots of pressure for young wimmin to get themselves fucked, at any cost, before they turn sixteen. *Being* a virgin is now an ambiguous situation, so some *oob* readers couldn't reinterpret the word *virgin* in the strong, positive way Frye was suggesting.

Like *crone* and *hag, dyke* is an extremely pejorative term when men yell it at us out of car windows, which accounts for our ambivalence about using it among ourselves. Nevertheless, I confess that the word *dyke,* because of what it meant to me in my past, now resonates with a deep and joyous pride. Lesbians who are still appalled at its usage don't feel proud about it. Hearing it *still* makes them cringe. *I* cringe when a Lesbian talks about enjoying "erotica."

What are We Reclaiming?

With some examples and discussion behind us, let's return to Audre Lorde's proposal that we "reclaim" the word *erotic.* Deciding to "reclaim" a word implies that we've rejected other solutions: coining a new word or reinstating obsolete, forgotten meanings for already existing words. As I suggested with respect to *survivor* and *dyke,* reclamation isn't a simple, unambiguous undertaking. Our reactions are predictably idiosyncratic, often boiling down to whether or not we like the way a word sounds.

What does Lorde's proposal have going for it? First, a lot of people *like* the way the word sounds. Lorde asserts that patriarchal society is "anti-erotic," but I think she's wrong. American society is notoriously loud in its lipservice to anti-sex morality, but talk is talk. In fact, this society is obsessed with hetsex. We *know* that even those most vehement in their opposition to anything explicit about sex, including sex education—especially the likes of the Moral Majority, the televangelists, and all their allies—are numbered among the consumers of the various sex industries. They're not "anti-erotic." They just don't want to talk about sex; they don't want anyone else to talk about sex. At least not in public. Keeping sex in the closet (and porn under the bed) makes it more—how shall I say?—titillating.

Contrary to Lorde's assertion, the word *erotic* (and its derivatives) is highly valued in patriarchal society, precisely because it dresses up sex, makes sex sound appealing, all silky smooth and luscious. Talking about our "erotic" feelings sounds so much better than saying, "I'm feeling *pornographic* tonight."[4] *Erotic* conjures for us exactly the images of Lesbianism found in male "erotica" (the expensive stuff, like David Hamilton's photographs): anatomical perfection (no unsightly warts, or hairs or scars); a misty, vague sensuality that goes beyond the nakedness of bodies to the atmosphere, the lighting, the air around us. *Erotic* suggests candles or other dim lighting, perhaps incense (for those not allergic to it), soft music, a warmth, coziness, and intimacy—in short, safety and security—that we cherish and enjoy. It's the underlying *class* meanings of *erotic* that seduce us. *Erotic* implies leisure, sophistication, the arts, and, most importantly, the MONEY that makes their consumption possible. "Porn," on the other hand, is "bad stuff." Its images are intentionally ugly, frank, unadorned, unimproved by the artist's airbrush. Pornography is unapologetically exploitive, specific, explicit, unashamedly there for men to jerk off to. Pornography emphasizes exactly what erotica tries to disguise and make palatable. The subjects, poses, and positions in "erotica" and porn are identical, but the packaging is very different.

The *erotic* carries the fragrance of wealth, luxury, time on one's hands, and, yes, the exotic. The exotic is that which is "not us." In PUD, *difference* is "sexy." Erotica *and* pornography make a lot of money because men sexualize differences. Whatever is not "of the man" is other, is prey, is "sexy." Difference, of whatever brand, introduces the alien, the unknown, to be conquered, beaten, degraded. Difference introduces tension, fear, dominance, submission, conquest, feelings of being powerful or powerless, feelings of being in control or out of control. In her discussion of Lesbian desire and its relation to our political perceptions in *Lesbian Ethics* (1988), Sarah Hoagland elaborated how perceiving difference as "exotic" works against our desire for each other:

> We. . .are attracted to difference as exotic, not as something to discover and learn from but rather as a mystery and hence something we objectify and keep

at a distance. As a result, we use vulnerability or alternatively a stoical approach with each other, rather than developing intimacy. (p. 168)

In PUD, there is no gray area to difference. It is all dichotomies, oppositions, polarities, like "masculine" and "feminine." It is the differences of us that underlie and justify the violence of the pornographic or erotic image. Both trade on misogyny, assume classism, require racism, and promote male rule.

Aside from its euphemizing and unreality, is the idea of "the erotic" hopelessly tainted? As we consider whether or not we want to reclaim the word *erotic* and apply its meanings to Lesbian sex and sexuality, we have to consider what it means in PUD, what it refers to when men use it.[5] We have to consider the context that makes it sound so good. Unlike *dyke* or *victim* or *bitch* or *cunt*, *erotic* is a sweet word, a deceptive word, a lying word. On the surface, it refers to sex and sensuality. Covertly, it drags with it misogyny, racism, classism, and more besides. *Erotic* is a positive word in PUD.

Most of the words we've tried to "reclaim" have extremely negative meanings; I can't think of a word we've reclaimed that is positively valued in PUD. Can we try to "reclaim" a word so laden with positive associations in male discourse? Is it possible to eradicate all of its meanings and replace them with our own? I don't think so.

In order to examine the possibility, we can look at some of the places the word *erotic* has taken those who, with Audre Lorde, claim to have "reclaimed" it. What they say reveals the path that their reclamation has taken them down. The first step on that path has turned out to be "reclaiming the feminine." Sabrina Sojourner (*Sojourner*, February, 1991: 9) described herself as "a lesbian feminist who writes erotica" and as a "femme." Addressing herself to the on-going debate about erotica and pornography, she said that "the argument seems to come down to 'What turns me on is erotica and what turns you on is pornography'." Having implicitly acknowledged the differential usage of those words, Sojourner refused to examine them more closely:

> Without falling into the trap of defining these terms, I would argue that this problematic stance requires a true dialogue—not a wrestling match of ideologies—among women with the idea of developing *new* paradigms for sexuality. [Her emphasis]

Why defining one's terms would be "a trap," I don't know, and Sojourner didn't explain. Without so much as an acknowledgment of the radical purpose that motivated Audre Lorde's proposal, Sojourner echoes Lorde's pamphlet in her next sentence:

> I enjoy writing erotica because I believe in celebrating the goodness and vitality of passion and Eros. Like power, passion and Eros are not evil. How

Eros, power, and passion are used determines the positive, negative, or neutral effect they have on our lives. [Her capitalization]

This is a familiar argument: nothing is inherently anything, it's what we make of it or what we do with it. By asserting that words, actions, and behaviors have no inherent meaning, Sojourner accomplishes two rhetorical aims simultaneously: she can imply that individuals have a lot more control over meanings than we actually do, and then omit to mention the already-entrenched, socially-approved meanings assumed by a majority of people, including some Lesbians and Feminists. No word or behavior or attitude comes to us without its PUD meanings, and to pretend otherwise is a delusion.

The result of Sojourner's rhetoric is predictable. She goes on to claim that "the outward appearance of being a femme is about celebrating the feminine. . . 'Femme' is a definition of femaleness which goes beyond heterosexist and white Western definitions about the feminine." *Femininity* attributes to wimmin certain specific behaviors. Yet, we know that not one of those behaviors is innate. Wimmin learn to be passive, docile, silent, silly, and weak. Wimmin know, from our own experience, that all those behaviors are faked. Beneath their feminine façades, wimmin are strong, determined, purposeful, resilient, courageous, risk-taking, and very, very smart. Unfortunately, the very concept of *femininity* is a lie that many wimmin eventually succumb to and try to live out, at the same time accomplishing the day-to-day struggle to survive, often in perilous circumstances.

Of course, Sabrina Sojourner isn't the only Feminist who wants to "reclaim 'the feminine'." Hetero women and Lesbians have often put forth the word *feminine* as a candidate for reclamation. Those who argue for "reclaiming" it point to the implicit associations of the word: nurturing, nonaggressiveness, tenderness, caring. But the explicit meanings of *feminine* and *femininity* in PUD cannot be ignored just because some women want to focus on the implicit meanings attached to them. Nor should we pretend not to notice the class parallelism between *femininity* and *erotica*. The cultural ideal of women that the word *femininity* refers to was created by white men, and the attitudes and behaviors of femininity were then used to judge both a woman's worth as a cohort to men and her status as a woman. Significantly, only women attached to males with the money to spend on the outer trappings of femininity had the leisure and wherewithal to indulge in the useless behaviors the ideal required. Women of color, poor women, rural woman, working-class women didn't have the time, money, or energy for femininity; that ideal was quite beyond their resources. Class privilege is inherent in *femininity*. Like "erotica," femininity requires both money and leisure, a "consumer mentality," and it serves rich men.

Because of the history and oppression of black people in the U. S., I can understand why Sojourner, a Lesbian of color, would want to "reclaim" a concept of "femininity," one, she says, "beyond heterosexist and white Western definitions." Neither, however, can we ignore the history of "the feminine" in white male cultures. One cannot claim to be "celebrating" a concept outside those definitions while using the English labels that name the concept. If Sojourner were talking about a radically different way of being, the word *feminine* would not suggest itself as an adequate name for her idea. (Perhaps we could borrow a word from another non-Indo-European language that means 'strong, caring woman'.) Like *erotic*, *feminine* is a seductive word that names only what men have intended it to name. Reactivating the words that name the limitations and restraints constructed for us does not, I think, create a wide road to freedom and independence.

I don't think I misjudge the consequences of Sojourner's proposal. She says she wants us to "begin a new sexual healing. Let us begin the creation of a female-centered and -defined sexuality which honors a woman's choices of sexual expression." I don't disagree with her goal, but I doubt that the words she has chosen to bring along will enable us to reach it:

> As I reclaimed *lesbian* in the '70s, I now reclaim the words that our heterosexist and sexist culture have tried to "pervert": *pussy* and *cunt* and *box* and *crack* and *joybox* and *lotus blossom* and *dripping gulch* and *hole* and *split tale* and *purse* and *pudenda*. I use these words in my writing because in the quiet of my bedroom with my sex partner, I do not say, "I want to lick your vagina;" I say, "I want to eat your pussy."

Sojourner's proposal is explicit about where using such words will take us. By "a female-centered and -defined sexuality," she means one "that recognizes the power of *surrender* and *capture*, that explores what *surrender* and *capture* and power and intensity mean to women. . .." The ideas of 'surrender' and 'capture', along with 'submit', 'yield', and their counterparts, 'conquer', 'overpower', and 'dominate', belong to the vocabulary of the LOVE IS WAR metaphor. The LOVE IS WAR metaphor originated with men, but Sojourner isn't the only Lesbian who likes the idea. Other writers advocating the appropriateness of roles in Lesbian relationships have also used the LOVE IS WAR metaphor.[6] To think of sexuality in those terms is to behave within the limits they name. Men capture prey and enemies; a defeated enemy submits to torture and surrenders. One who is preyed upon is a victim. Men's words mean what men intend them to mean, and we will not change those meanings in our minds by murmuring them to each other in the seclusion of our bedrooms.

We cannot really "reclaim" something that hasn't been ours. We might more accurately say we're going to *claim* a word from the the male vocabulary, with the intent to change its denotative and/or connotative value(s). Using such words will not help us to create "a female-centered and -defined sexuality," because we cannot "reclaim," and shouldn't claim, them. We should be very careful about which words we choose, and clear about why we want to include them in our program of change.

The words and phrases Sojourner wants to "reclaim," with, perhaps, the exception of *cunt,* belong to the vocabulary of male misogyny. Surrounding each of them are the scorn and disgust men feel toward us. (We still don't know the origin of the word *cunt,* which might be a possibility for a Lesbian-centered vocabulary of sexual experience, although many Lesbians and women say that they would never consider using the word *cunt* because their associations with it are so negative.) Such exceptions aside, those words were coined by teenage boys of successive generations and taken with them into adulthood. There are more than 300 such words accumulated to date and more are undoubtedly on their way. The negative and objectifying meanings of such terms would appear to make them likely candidates for claiming, but, unlike *Dyke,* they belong to male pornographic discourse where their use cannot be dissassociated from male sexual uses of women. We have to decide very carefully *which* words we can claim, and we can't do that by pretending they don't have PUD meanings or that we don't know or understand those meanings.

Examining the claims of those who, like Sabrina Sojourner, say they're writing "erotica" because they're seeking "new" paradigms or creating female-defined sexuality, I find that they're "reclaiming" exactly the same meanings and using the same words that I've expunged from my usage, if not entirely from my mind. If they mean to celebrate sexuality, they need look no further than the word *lesbian* itself (a word we have, I think, successfully claimed for ourselves). In the second edition of the *Random House Dictionary* (1980), the third definition of *Lesbian,* as an adjective, is 'erotic; sensual'. So much for our efforts to politicize meanings.

Sojourner and Lorde both argue that "reclaiming" "the erotic" (and *erotica*) will lead us to radical personal and social change, but the words they've chosen and the ideas those words denote lead us *not* to radical change but to what Lorde explicitly wanted to avoid: "settling for a shift of characters in the same weary drama." The endeavor brings us full circle: the LESBIAN IS THE EROTIC. *Erotic* leads to *feminine; feminine* leads to *femme; femme* leads to LOVE IS WAR and all the words associated with that metaphor: *submission, surrender, conquest, domination,* and *captivity.*

Time has demonstrated that Lorde's "reclamation" effort hasn't achieved the goal she hoped for, as evidenced by how Lesbians use the words *erotic* and *erotica.* Familiarity, feeling comfortable with a word may, in fact, be a danger signal we should attend to. "Reclaiming" can too easily become separated from its antecedent roots in the desire for political and personal change, and degenerate to a widespread, thoughtless activity of perpetuating the vilest, most derogatory terms in the PUD vocabulary. It's an easy game, because we already know the words. We've heard and, yes, used them all our lives. We don't have to learn anything; we don't have to risk anything; we don't even have to change. We don't have to live in the unknown, wondering how we're going to say to the woman next to us that we want to nibble and lick her clitoris. Most importantly, we don't have to think. Familiarity and its comforts seduce the word-weary and the unwary alike. Contrary to the empowering effects Lorde sought by trying to legitimize uses of *erotic* in Lesbian discourse, we're back in the 1950s, which some of us remember very well—still butch or femme, still slit, hole, or pussy, still thrashing about in the misogyny of PUD's vocabulary.

Trying to change how we talk, how we think, and who we are is a difficult and drawn-out process. No one of us goes to bed saying "Today I became a Feminist" and arises the next day with her mind wiped clean of heteropatriarchal cacagraphy (literally, 'shit-writing'). Sarah Hoagland, speaking of Lesbian desire, urged Lesbians to a careful, thoughtful exploration of our language.

> We need new language and new meaning to develop our lesbian desire, especially as we explore and develop what draws us, where our attraction comes from, what we want to keep, what we want to change and why, how our attractions vary, how our desires change over time, and so on. And this is an interactive, not an introspective matter. (1986: p. 168)

If writers like Audre Lorde and Sabrina Sojourner want to use words like *erotic* and phrases about "celebrating the feminine," so be it. But I think they delude themselves, and all the other Lesbians who follow them, into settling for a rehash of all the language of misogyny and the ideas it perpetuates. And that creates a linguistic barrier between us that will make communication difficult. They may insist on their "right" to use a certain vocabulary, while I insist on my "right" not to read their writing. The result is not a radical change in ourselves and the oppressive society we live in, but a stalemate and a terrible loss to all of us.

I would say that we must find ways to negotiate the words we choose, ways that acknowledge everything we know about English, its vocabulary, and what words mean—not just to each of us, but also to others who hear them from our lips. I don't read anyone who says she's writing "lesbian erotica" because I know, nine times out of ten, that I'm going to be sickened by what I read. I may miss the one that I'd really like, but, more importantly for me, I spare myself the exposure to recycled heteropatriarchal garbage in the other nine.

I have changed a lot since I first became a Feminist in 1972, and I value the changes I've made to the core of my being. I will not undo myself again in order to "fit in" with an agenda that contradicts my most deeply held principles. For me, that would be a going back to a Lesbian (actually, a "gay girl") I acknowledge as who I was in the past, and I no longer want to be her. I reject the alleged "reclamations" of the *new*-rotics because they don't take us forward into lives created and informed by a radical envisioning, but backward, toward an understanding of ourselves I've rejected and have no desire to resurrect. Like Marilyn Frye, I look forward to "a collective vocabulary crafted from our tenderness and our joy" (1988:54). Until then, I am content to do without.

Endnotes

1. Edward the Dyke is a character in Judy Grahn's "The Psychoanalysis of Edward the Dyke," in *Edward the Dyke and other poems* (1971).

2. One sentence of that review has been much-quoted by the self-styled "sex radicals," such as Alice Echols: ". . .the more we rely on internal fantasies during our interactions with other wimmin, the less we are relating to each other as wimmin." This single sentence is so well known by now that writers who've followed in Echols' tracks quote it without bothering to cite its source or list the review in their bibliographies. Yet, on the basis of that statement, I have been compared to J. Edgar Hoover and Jerry Falwell.

3. Sarah Hoagland (1988) has discussed the problems with the concept of 'eros' in detail.

> . . .'Eros', as developed in the homopatriarchal greco-christian tradition is quite the opposite of life-invoking; it is death or other-world oriented.. . .In religious terms, 'eros' represents an ecstatic loss of self, a love which is directed toward a god and whose climax, in christian mysticism, is self-annihilation (perfection). (Thus christian mysticism and sadomasochism embrace the same ideology, share the same erotic roots.) (p. 165)

4. For an excellent exploration of what the word *sex* might mean in a Lesbian context, see Marilyn Frye's "Lesbian 'Sex'," *Sinister Wisdom* #35, 46-54, in which she argues that the English vocabulary for "doing it" is devoid of wimmin's meanings with, at its semantic center, "male-dominant-female-subordinate-copulation-whose-completion-and-purpose-is-the-male's-ejaculation" (51-52).

5. Sarah Hoagland explicitly describes several elements of what sex and sexuality mean in PUD in *Lesbian Ethics*:
   (1) sex is necessary to a man's health,
   (2) sexual desire involves a death wish (eros),
   (3) male sexuality is a powerful and uncontrollable urge,
   (4) rape is natural behavior,
   (5) sex is an act of male conquest,
   (6) sexual freedom includes total male access to females,
   (7) sexual feeling is a matter of being out of control,
   (8) sex is a natural phenomenon such that women who resist male sexual advances are 'frigid.' (p. 164)

6. Lesbians who identify themselves as "butches" talk about how powerful they feel when another Lesbian "surrenders" to them (Rachel Brody, in *Common Lives/Lesbian Lives* #11, Spring, 1984).

Controlling Interests, Consuming Passions: Sexual Metaphors

Background

In spite of the politicization of sex among Lesbians in the past decade, a lot of the Lesbians I meet are insecure about their sexuality, and given to lengthy, often inarticulate, introspection. I think it's because we're still talking about our sexuality in the terms given to us by the heteropatriarchal (HP) society we live in, as though the vocabulary of heterosex had some inherent, universal validity. With a few notable exceptions (for example, Marilyn Frye's "Lesbian 'Sex'" [1988]), Lesbians don't question the terms and assumptions of the English vocabulary for sex and sexual activities, a vocabulary in which the concepts of sex and power are metaphorically linked. This cognitive/linguistic link has been treated in the Lesbian/Feminist Great Sex Debate as though it were accurate—indeed, as though it were inevitable rather than as the social construction that it is. It is no coincidence that Lesbians turned inward in the late 1970s to examine our sexual desires at just the time that we withdrew from active confrontation with the heteropatriarchy of the U. S., nor is it a coincidence that sado-masochists claimed authority about "Lesbian" sexuality as the right-wing acquired political credibility in 1979-80. At just the time that Lesbians felt alienated from the direction of political change in the U. S., the debate about "good" versus "bad" Lesbian sex became a frequent topic in the Lesbian-Feminist media. Most of the examples I'll use here to illustrate my discussion are quoted from Pat Califia's *Sapphistry: The Book of Lesbian Sexuality* (1980; hereafter *S*) and the Samois anthology, *Coming to Power* (1981; hereafter *CTP*).

I'm going to focus on what sado-masochists have had to say about their sexuality for two reasons. First, their claims initiated The Great Sex Debate and keep it going. Second, in arguing that Lesbian-Feminists should support sado-masochism as an oppressed sexuality, their language, and the stance presented by their language, demonstrate how our language choices follow from how we think of ourselves in the world.

The "debate" (now often referred to as the "sex wars") started when sado-masochists claimed that sado-masochism was the *avant-garde* of the "sexual revolution" and defined their ideology as "Feminist," thereby equating the politics of Feminism with the *Playboy/Penthouse/Hustler/Screw* "sexual revolution." Feminists, however, said that sado-masochism is a sexuality constructed by the heteropatriarchal (HP) values and assumptions that Feminism seeks to eradicate. Indeed, because the values and assumptions of those who've participated in this "debate" differ so greatly, the resulting debate hasn't been an altogether amiable, tender, or enlightening exchange of views.

Yet, some of the consequences of this debate have been, if not good, at least motivating. Radical Lesbians must now, I think, take some responsibility for having neglected Lesbian sexuality. Our failure to address Lesbian sexuality, especially its problems and ignorance about them, created a vacuum around sex and how to "do it"[1] that the sado-masochists gladly filled. Where there is ignorance, shame, inexperience, secrecy, and even puritanism, partial, even partisan, information is better than none. The Lesbian sado-masochists did what no one else seemed willing to do: to take Lesbian sex seriously and to attempt to educate Lesbians about our anatomies, sex techniques, and the importance of talking about what we like and don't like sexually. Because all of the information available on "what Lesbians do" for hundreds of years has been written by men (and *for* men), there are almost no reliable sources for Lesbians to consult on the subject of sexuality. Because most of us have to learn somehow "what to do," the sado-masochists have made the totality of Lesbian sexuality their "domain," virtually without challenge.

The Debate

Ideally, a forum permits the expression of diverse, even conflicting ideas. Early on, however, the discussion about sex ceased to be a "dialogue" and became, instead, a polarized opposition between the sado-masochists and those they described as having "vanilla" sex. The resulting animosity has made it seem as though there are only two possible sides in this argument: those who resist evaluation of sexuality and describe themselves as "pro-sex" (the sado-masochists and the "sex radicals," *their labels*), and those, like me, who believe that even our sexuality and sexual feelings cannot be placed beyond scrutiny and challenge (the "puritans," "fascists," and the "anti-sex;" again, *their* labels). In exactly the same way that the right-wing "pro-lifers" took a positive label, rather than call themselves "anti-abortionists," to imply that those who favor legal abortions are "anti-life," the "pro-sex" label has been used as a rhetorical ploy to discredit dissenters in advance, with about the same substance as the "pro-life" line. This facile word-trick attempts to stifle disagreement by forcing dissenters to start out in a negative and, therefore, hostile position, as though the sado-masochists' libertarian arguments were inherently positive. But there has to be a wider range of opinion than that allowed by the "pro"/"anti" polarity. The lines in this conflict have been so firmly drawn, however, that the two sides now can't speak to each other. Non-practitioner analysis of sado-masochism, however well-intentioned, has been perceived as inherently hostile, and our criticisms dismissed and trivialized as unspeakably ignorant.

Although Pat Califia, one of the most visible speakers for sado-masochism, has conceded that "the gross inequities in our society affect sexuality, and no lifestyle or activity ought to escape criticism and evaluation" (*S*, 107), criticism and evaluation of the assertions of sado-masochists have been received with outrage and indignation. The following description by Gayle Rubin, another vocal proponent of sado-masochism, typifies the way non-sado-masochistic analysis and criticism have been received by sado-masochists: "Current radical (mostly feminist) writing on S/M is a hopeless muddle of bad assumptions, inaccurate information, and a thick-headed refusal to accept evidence which contravenes preconceptions" (*CTP*, 223).

A corollary assumption of this kind of rhetoric is the notion that one must "have" an experience in order to "really" understand it. For a sexual proclivity that extols the powers of the imagination—the tension between the "real" and the "illusory"—this assumption devalues our ability to imagine ourselves into someone else's experience. An extreme expression of this idea is Juicy Lucy's statement to non-sado-masochistic Lesbians who object to the language of sado-masochism: ". . .if you haven't taken the risks you don't get to make the rules" (*CTP*, 31). Such assertions function both to stifle challenges to the claims of the sado-masochists and to discourage disagreement. If challenging assumptions and questioning the framework of an ideology isn't possible, and sado-masochism *is* an ideology, then talking about it is absurd. While sado-masochists have been most eloquent about their right to challenge and question the ideas of non-sado-masochists, they have been less than generous with their critics, substituting name-calling for argument.

I'm aware, therefore, that my analysis will be heard by the "sex radicals" and sado-masochists as "anti-sex," "anti-sexuality," and "inhibited," labels borrowed from the masculist cant of *Screw*, *Forum*, and *Hustler*. If only agreement can reflect thoughtful consideration, and some opinions are inherently "better" than others, then the sado-masochists and their allies should stop claiming they want "dialogue." If they insist on placing our "gut feelings," the heritage of our childhood experiences, beyond challenge or analysis, then there's no point in talking about sexuality at all. Why questioning how we *think* about sex and sexual acts should be interpreted and characterized as "anti-sex" can only be explained by supposing that the questions raised *threaten* the definitions of sexuality held by those doing the name-calling.

If it is true, as the "sex radicals" claim, that the heteropatriarchy is fundamentally "anti-sex," its population is also *obsessed* with the *idea* of sex; otherwise pornography wouldn't be a billion-dollar-a-year business. The tabooed and the unspeakable (like sex with children) become the conceptual focus of sexual excitement and titillation, and sado-masochistic practices find and exploit them. Because the "sex radicals" continue to "hold the floor" on the subject of Lesbian sex, the language they use is a significant reflection of their perspective, one Lesbians need to examine more closely. As Marilyn Murphy has pointed out in "The Power of Naming," there are no good reasons why Lesbians who aren't sado-masochists should contemplate accepting the sado-masochists' definition of what is or is not "healthy" Lesbian sexuality (1991: 168).

Not surprisingly, sexual language and communication have figured prominently in sado-masochistic writing. Pat Califia, for example, devoted a chapter to communication in *Sapphistry*. In a later chapter of that book, she says "S/M is a language of passion with its own conventions, signals and sexual techniques" (*S*, 120). That language, however, far from being the sado-masochists' "own," is a wholesale borrowing of the primary dichotomies of HP reality. The "conventions" of sado-masochism exaggerate and dramatize HP oppositions, and the "passion" frequently described in sado-masochistic literature reflects the sexualization of conceptual oppositions and hierarchies of domination such as racism, classism, anti-Semitism—in fact, every social construct in which an individual or a group wields power over another individual or group.

Califia, describing her own introduction to sado-masochism, spoke of learning ". . .the real (as opposed to mythological) content of S/M sex" (*CTP*, 246). What, then, is the "real" content of sado-masochism? The ideology of sado-masochism originates in the symbolic content of power-over relationships and enacts their metaphorical contrasts in sexual "dramas." Primary HP dichotomies—male/female, good/bad, powerful/powerless, give/take, and dominant/submissive—are labeled sadist/masochist, strong/weak, active/passive, butch/femme, and acted out in sado-masochistic "scenes" as master (mistress)/slave, top/bottom, superior/inferior, Nazi/Jew, boss/employee, teacher/student, parent/child, police officer/criminal, punisher/victim. (Sado-masochists are also "into" uniforms, but only some kinds of uniforms. Band uniforms and baseball uniforms, for example, seem to lack an essential titillation factor and so haven't caught on as sado-masochistic paraphernalia.)

Through the pain/pleasure polarization sado-masochism assumes and enacts more abstract dichotomies: freedom/bondage, safety/danger, being in control/being out of control, authority/lack of authority, and open/closed. These abstractions are made tactile in descriptions of sado-masochism in which the approach to orgasm is described either as "going through a wall" or "beyond the edge" of some imagined boundary or limit. The sadist forces the masochist through her "wall," the symbol of her resistance to losing control, by purposely pushing the masochist "beyond the limits (or boundaries)" of her tolerance for pain. The sadist must always be "in control" in order for the masochist to "let go" of her control, her self, her will, her boundaries. The masochist is forced "out of control."

In the literature of sado-masochism, the focus of the sado-masochistic scene is said to be an "eroticized, consensual exchange of power" (*S*, 118), an exchange best described, I think, by Susan Farr in *Coming to Power*:

The victim, by accepting her submissive role, is allowed to play out the illusion of complete powerlessness. She can no longer do as she wishes, and is thus completely free. The punisher, in accepting responsibility for the direction of the scene, is allowed the illusion of complete powerfulness. She can do as she wishes, and is thus completely free. Through different paths both parties have arrived at a feeling of complete freedom. It is only temporary, and it is an illusion, *but it is very compelling.* [My emphasis.] (p. 188)

What makes these shared illusions so "compelling"? I think it's the conceptual tension we acquire from heteropatriarchal (HP) dichotomies, the either/or descriptions of reality we learned as children in this society, and the idea that an abstraction can be experienced as "complete." The much-vaunted sexual "charge" of sado-masochism (and butch/femme sex, as well) depends upon accepting the opposed abstractions, for example, parent/child, teacher/student, and acting out the "power over" associated with the privileged member of the opposites—the same opposites that define social relationships in heteropatriarchies. What is "compelling" is the discovery that one can choose to humiliate or be humiliated. Equality removes both the oppositional structures of relationships and the associations of inherent privilege and authority. Without the idea of "power over" another person assumed to be one's inferior, taken unapologetically from heteropatriarchal structures, sado-masochism would not exist. The dichotomies defined by oppositional structures establish and maintain the tension translated into "sexual" behaviors.

Sado-masochism must have dichotomies; they are essential to the sexual tensions that motivate its behaviors and thinking. The process of dichotomizing figures significantly in, for example, the rhetoric that sado-masochists use to present themselves as an "oppressed" sexual minority. By casting those of us who don't condone their behavior as "fascists" and "Nazis" and themselves as our "victims," they attempt to coerce us into their framework, imposing, by their description, their way of perceiving events in the world. The dichotomies of good/bad and right/wrong also figure prominently in sado-masochists' descriptions. Those who engage in sado-masochism defend their behavior as "right" because "it feels good," and describe non-sado-masochists as "puritans" who believe that an experience is "bad" if "it feels good." This description is *theirs.* I enjoy activities that feel good; I disagree with the sado-masochists about *what* "feels good." Another dichotomy is implicit in the phrase "safe sex." The necessity of talking about "safe sex" among sado-masochists presupposes that dangerous or "unsafe" sex exists, and is a possible outcome of their activities. If this were false, no one would talk about "safe sex."

Difference, and the "power over" that heteropatriarchy attaches to it, is essential to successful sado-masochism, just as essential as it is in the language of the heteropatriarchy. Without polarized concepts, sado-masochism couldn't exist. Those who practice sado-masochism, however, don't agree among themselves on this subject. Juicy Lucy, for example, describes her understanding of semantic polarization and its function in sado-masochism as follows:

> Sadist & masochist are terms I have a schizophrenic reaction to.. . .In a sexual context sadist & masochist are roles that define erotic poles of power & have meanings of passion, trust & intensity that flow from a fully consensual situation. In a non-sexual context sadist & masochist are roles in power-over situations involving pain & cruelty where the consensual agreement to these roles is unacknowledged or absent.. . .These roles, of sadist & masochist, are the roles of heterosexuality & patriarchy. (*CTP*, pp. 30-2)

She distinguishes between heteropatriarchal roles and the sado-masochists' reliance on them by saying that "Heterosexuality & patriarchy attempt to freeze power, to make one side always dominant & one side always passive." In contrast, in sado-masochism, "Sometimes we give & sometimes receive but the energy, the power, always flows" (*CTP*, 32).

Acknowledging that the language and roles essential to sado-masochism "appear" to retain their HP meanings intact, yet attempting to discourage analysis and the possibility of criticism on that point, sado-masochist rhetoricians have resorted to a sexual relativism that assumes sex can occur in a cultural vacuum, cut off from its social meanings. In her chapter on "Variations," for example, Califia warns off skeptics with the following paragraph.

> We should be wary of making broad statements about the worth or value of another lesbian's sexual style, especially if it involves behavior we don't understand or have never participated in. No erotic act has an intrinsic meaning. A particular sexual activity may symbolize one thing in the major- ity culture, another thing to members of a sexual subculture or religious sect, and yet another thing to the individuals who engage in it. The context within which an erotic act occurs can also alter its meaning. (*S*, p. 107)

Fundamental to this line of argument is the claim that "No erotic act has an intrinsic meaning." Establishing the distinction between context-free and context-bound meaning is crucial to the rhetoric of sado-masochism, in which it is asserted that sex acts are meaningless in and of themselves, and acquire whatever meaning they have only in the contexts in which they are executed. By this device, any sex act is converted into an ambiguous, polysemous symbol whose meaning is totally context-determined. This is Humpty-Dumpty rhetoric: "Words mean what I want them to mean," and, by extension, sex means what I want it to mean. Severed from its associations and semantic identity with HP symbology, sado-masochism is meaningless. The emptiness of Califia's semantic relativism is clear in her asser- tion that the context of an act *can* "alter its meaning." For example, the testimonies of the victims of sadism in cults reveals that the "religious" context doesn't change the "meaning" of pain, torture, or murder. Furthermore, if specific contexts can "alter" the meaning of what are called "sexual" acts, like torture and humiliation, then those acts must have some already-established, understood meaning that they

118

bring to the context. That is, Califia's claim assumes the meaning of heteropatriarchal terms and actions; otherwise, there would be nothing to change.

Essential to the ideology of sado-masochism is the claim that meaning is context-bound. In *Sapphistry*, Califia carefully qualifies her assertions with phrases like, "In an S/M context" and "outside an S/M situation," and she makes much of distinguishing between the institutionalized violence against women sanctioned by heteropatriarchy and the "consensuality" of sado-masochistic "scenes." The writing of sado-masochists, however, depends upon descriptions of humiliation, degradation, force, and domination. The ideas of sado-masochism are identical to those expressed by raped and battered women when they describe their experiences of violence. Is Califia right? Do the ideas differ or change in different contexts? Compare, for example, how sex and violence are linked as though they were inseparable concepts and actions in the following quotations: *Now I see that love and struggle were fiercely joined.* (Kate Hurley, NTV, 60) *The desire to be sexual and the desire to be combative are complexly intertwined.* (Susan Farr, CTP, 183)

Hurley describes her battering experience as "love and struggle fiercely joined," a euphemistic variant parallel to Farr's "desire to be sexual and. . .combative." "The desire to be sexual" becomes "love," and "the desire to be combative" becomes "struggle. . .fiercely joined," but both describe the perception that sex and violence are inseparable. Such descriptions suggest that we risk, as Johanna Reimoldt says, "More blurring of the line between what is pleasurable to partners and what is violent assault" (*CTP*, 84).

Yet, Pat Califia claims that the fusion of violence with sexual activities inherent in the language of male descriptions of sexuality is altered or neutralized in sado-masochistic contexts (*S*, 27). Kitt, another sado-masochist, believes that "The strong, negative reaction to S/M is due in part to the fact that we have hand-me-down words, still clothed in many layers of patriarchal connotations" (*CTP*, 61). I don't think the division among Lesbians caused by sado-masochism is merely a result of the fact that words they use are the same as those that describe violence perpetrated on women against our will. Rather, I think that the sado-masochistic context enhances and normalizes, rather than alters or transforms, the meaning of the vocabulary of domination. If sado-masochism is distinct from HP violence, its writers and proponents should have sensed the danger for confusion and produced a new vocabulary for sado-masochistic sex that differs radically from the HP vocabulary. Instead, the sado-masochistic writing called "Lesbian erotica" reads exactly like male pornography, and the lack of difference in vocabulary, style, and tone cannot be attributed merely to "hand-me-down words. . .clothed in. . .layers of patriarchal connotation," nor to a failure of imagination. Lesbian and male pornography cannot be distinguished because they're identical.

Sado-masochists have frequently expressed outrage when non-sado-masochists equate the violence and humiliation of rape or battering to sado-masochistic sex, as I've just done, and they say that sado-masochistic "scenes" enable them to work through earlier experiences of rape and battering. Juicy Lucy, for example, says: "I am tired of being accused by hysterical dykes who beat up their lovers of being a rapist/brutalizer/male-identified oppressor of battered womyn. *I* was a battered womyn for years & claim the right to release and transform the pain & fear of those experiences any way I damn well please" (*CTP*, 30). Like other defenders of sado-masochism, she says that a lot of Lesbian relationships are sado-masochistic emotionally and physically. But the sado-masochistic context doesn't alter the meaning of words like *combat, pain, humiliation*, and *degradation*. If it did, then different words would better express the difference. Since sado-masochists don't change the language or symbols they use, and know this, Juicy Lucy shifts the ground of her argument. The difference, she says, is that the sado-masochistic content of such relationships goes unacknowledged, that there is no mutual consent to the violence, humiliation, and pain.

Neither the HP meaning nor symbolism of sado-masochistic acts *is* changed because two (or more) Lesbians participate in the actions. As a result, another argument often used by sado-masochists, like Juicy Lucy, above, claims that sado-masochism isn't a "power-over" situation, because the mutual consent of the participants produces a "flow" of power back and forth between the sadist and the masochist.

Defining Consent

Mutual consent, then, becomes the essential element that distinguishes the sado-masochistic context from the heteropatriarchal context that fuses sex and violence. If two adults agree to a sexual act, then no one should intervene. Right. (Agreement in principle with one's right to behave however she pleases does not imply support or agreement with the behaviors.) The "sex radicals" and sado-masochists don't stop with sex between consenting adults. The issue of "consent" figures most tellingly, I believe, in their arguments supporting adult/child sex. This is no surprise. The ideology of sado-masochism, and the polarities that make it "work" for some Lesbians, incorporate our experience of power and control as children. Sado-masochism depends upon our memories of the power differential that exists between those who have power, adults, and those who don't, children, and our experience of the violent acts adults committed against us because they could.

Gayle Rubin, also a vocal supporter of adult/child sex, has described the function of statutory rape laws as "not so much to protect young people from abuse, as to prevent them from acquiring sexual knowledge and experience," and goes on to say that "the vast majority of non-consensual incidents [of cross-generational sex] are heterosexual (older male, younger female)" (*CTP*, 196).

The first part of Rubin's assertion is simply false. Adults and their laws do not (and cannot) "prevent [children] from acquiring sexual knowledge and experience." Adults may *try* to keep children from acquiring sexual experience and information, but, having been children, they know that their efforts will fail. Adults may have power over children, but children find ways to subvert the efforts of adults to control them. (Children's skill at finding ways to subvert adult power reflects the reality of that power without successfully challenging it.) Sexual activity among children is frequent. It is also, I would argue, rarely consensual, because the activity is most often suggested by an older and bigger child, who uses the power of differences in age and size to coerce or intimidate a younger, smaller child to participate. The fact that older brothers, cousins, and their friends cajole, bribe, or force younger children into performing sexual acts with them has become commonplace even in the malestream media.

Under the guise of advocating the sexual rights of children, sado-masochists like Rubin promote a very different agenda: adult sexual exploitation of children. The "sex radicals" seek Lesbian support, not only for sado-masochism, which acts out the power differentials we learn from heteropatriarchy, but also for adult/child sex as well. We are asked to perceive sexual acts between adults and children as we do activities between adults, as though consent could mean the same thing in the two different contexts. I cannot, however, extend my own own understanding of "consent."

For one thing, adults have more power in the world, more control over their environment, and greater mobility, whereas children have no power in the world, almost no control over their environment, and no mobility. Children can't just decide they don't like a situation and move out of it. The younger a child is, the more dependent it is on the benevolence of adults. In most cases, children are stuck with whichever adults have accepted responsibility for them, at least until they reach adolescence and can seriously consider running away. Even then, they will find themselves at the mercy of other adults who will exploit their need for food and shelter and their inability to take care of themselves. Prostitution and hustling are virtually the only occupations open to young people on the streets.

The power of adults over children and the powerlessness of children in their relationships with adults are facts. That sado-masochists have sexualized the differences in power and authority, like the relationship of parents to child, con-structed by HP society, is a fact. If the difference in power between adults and children did not exist, the situation wouldn't be sexual for sado-masochists. They do not deny this. In contexts where one person has socially-condoned power over another, "consent" is a meaningless abstraction. Coerced "consent" is no consent at all. For a sado-masochist to suggest that "consensual sex" between adults and children is *possible* is double-talk. But arguing that other Lesbians ought to condone, support, and fight for the "rights" of adults to engage in sex with children asks us to ignore the difference in power between adults and children at the same time that we're being asked to support and condone a sexuality *dependent* on social power differentials. If we fail to endorse either part of the contradiction, we're "bad people."

If raping children (Rubin's "non-consensual incidents") is primarily a hetero-sexual activity, is "consent" a Lesbian issue? Yes—especially for those of us who were victimized as children by adults we trusted. We bring our memories of childhood rape into our sexual intimacy with other Lesbians. I speak now from my own experience as a survivor of incest. I was sexually molested by adults from the age of eight until I finally got away from my mother and stepfather. I was molested by my mother's boyfriends, a stepfather, and a man in a movie theater. Even though my mother had warned me about "strange men," she never thought to warn me about "familiar" men. In each situation, I didn't know what the man was doing or understand what he wanted. All I knew was that I didn't feel good about it. I had no idea, at first, what my stepfather was talking about when he kept asking me to "be nice" to him, and I was too willing to trust him to think of questioning him. I was eleven, old enough to know the mechanics of heterosex, but I thought he was talking about our being friends with each other! Moreover, when I did finally realize that he intended to fuck me, saying "no" didn't make any difference to him. It didn't stop him from trying to rape me. (A kick in the balls, however, did.)

Pat Califia has said that "Children need to know that they are entitled to say 'no' to anyone who wants to engage in sex with them" (*S*, 88). I agree. But Califia doesn't mention how hard, usually impossible, it is for a child to say "no" to an adult. When a child does muster the courage or desperation to say "no" to adults, she has almost no way to enforce the limits she sets. Adults, on the other hand, don't honor or heed the child's assertion of her boundaries because they don't have to. Does a child "really" mean "yes" when she says "no"? Califia assumes an equality of power and control in a situation where it cannot and does not exist.

Teaching children to say "no" to adults is a good idea, but it's not enough to protect them from adult predation. And the incidence of adult rape of children indicates that it isn't enough. Most children aren't old enough to know what their boundaries are, much less to defend them. While adults have to take responsibility for their actions, some of them seem unable to restrain themselves from taking advantage of the powerlessness of children. Nor do statutory rape laws "protect" children. Perpetrators are seldom stopped before they've already done serious damage to the emotional development of the children they rape. (And they often do considerable physical damage as well.) The power imbalance between adults and children is also easy to exploit because many children feel unloved and unlovable. Some children are so emotionally needy that they'll say "yes" to all kinds of propositions, including sex. But that's not all. Children are extremely curious, about their bodies, and adult bodies, and about their sexual feelings.[1]

Many incest survivors report having said "yes" to the adults who sexually molested and raped them, myself among them, and, thereby, having "consented" to what the adult wanted. That "yes," however, came out of an uncomfortable mixture of wanting to please, wanting to be loved, wanting to be touched and valued, and curiosity. As a result, incest survivors tend to carry around an unwelcome quantity of guilt, particularly if they feel they "agreed" to sex somehow, either tacitly or by saying "yes." Children aren't in a position where saying "no" to adult requests is easy for them, and the more tenderly those requests are made, the harder and less likely it is that the child will say "no." (Child molesters often say that *they* are the only ones who "really" love children.) What does it mean for a child to give "consent" when she has no way of knowing or evaluating the circumstances or consequences? I suspect that when we say "yes" in many HP contexts, we most often mean "no," and we are aware that our intention is meaningless and irrelevant.

Finally, I simply cannot believe what adults *say* children *want*, and I suspect them of imposing their own misinterpretations of children's behavior in order to rationalize their getting what they want. Even the curiosity of children can't be interpreted as necessarily sexual in intent, even though the adult perpetrator wants to interpret it that way. My capacity to trust was violated by adult perpetrators at an early age. I've worked hard regaining the ability to trust myself, and it's what I need most. It's taken me years to regain a still very shaky trust of myself and my perceptions. That's common among victims of adult rape and molestation; as a survivor, I can't predict that I'll ever be able to heal myself completely. I'll be dealing with my childhood experiences until I die, and I wouldn't wish that, ever, on another child. I know the barrier or wall so often described in the literature of sado-masochism, I know what it feels like, and I know how frustrating it is to try to breach that wall. And I also know the origins of my own wall—I built it as a last defense to protect my autonomy and sense of self against the perpetual assaults of adult predators. Many adults aren't trustworthy, and neither are some children.

The issue of "consent" is a false one, I think, in discussions of adult/child sex. What, then, of the adult female and her "consent" to sado-masochistic sex? Is it necessary to resort to what Reimoldt calls the Idiot-Woman argument? I don't think so. As Sheila Jeffreys pointed out in *Lesbian Ethics* (*LE,* 1986): "The triggers to a sexual response built around masochism are the symbols of power and authority. Particularly powerful symbols are those which represent abusive, cruel and arbitrary power and authority" (73). Sadomasochism is "built into our personalities from the. . .kinds of authority we are subjected to throughout childhood and growing up" (72). It's no coincidence that the symbolic content of sado-maso chists' scenarios sexualizes childhood pain: spanking, discipline, punishment, humiliation, and powerlessness.

Illusions and Reality

In the rhetoric of sado-masochism, what we were never asked to "consent" to as children, since consent is premised on the possession of power, the adult Lesbian can "consent" to. The pain and humiliation children learn becomes the sadist's power over and the masochist's pleasure. Administered as ritual or drama, pain is the catalyst for the masochist's ability to "lose control," to "go beyond her limits," or to "break through the wall." According to some writers on sado-masochism, its essence is theatre, the ability to create an illusion so powerful that the participants are transformed by their shared experience. The proponents of sado-masochism argue that the distinction between "reality" and "illusion" distinguishes the sado-masochistic context from the heteropatriarchal context.

Susan Farr, addressing the issue of reality versus illusion, says, "One clue to how much of drama and how little of reality is involved is that the roles change" (*CTP*, 185). She returns to this distinction at greater length:

> The apparent power relationship being enacted in a punishment ritual is that the dominant person is in control, the submissive person completely vulnerable. This is indeed the scenario being followed, but the reality behind the scene is more complex. The first rule of discipline games is that they are played by mutual consent and end immediately when either party wishes them to. It is the 'victim's' consent that is crucial because she must endure the pain. It is the victim's tolerance for pain that sets limits to the severity of the punishment.. . .Thus the behind-the-scenes senior author of the production that features an imposing punisher is the victim herself. The illusion, however, is the opposite. (*CTP*, pp. 187-8)

This sounds familiar, an echo of the masculist assertion that women *really* rule the world from their prone position. According to this description, the masochist, the "victim," is "responsible" for her punishment; the sadist, who appears to be "in control," does nothing more than give the masochist what she "asks for." How, then, is one to interpret the many instances in sado-masochistic literature that describe a masochist saying "no more," or "stop," or otherwise protesting, and sadists saying, "I'll stop when it's time. I know what you can take. And I know you need it, too" (*CTP*, 49)? It cannot be true that what are described as "discipline games. . .end immediately when *either* party wishes them to" [my emphasis], because *either* means that one may want to end the "games" *before* the other(s) do. Furthermore, the role of the sadist is to force the masochist past her own self-defined limits, which means that the sadist, in order to fulfill her role, ignores the masochist when she says she wants to stop. Someone is lying, either the masochist or the sadist, because the "games" often continue far past the "victim's" use of the agreed-upon "safe word."

"No" and "stop" are meaningless in a sado-masochistic context. Neither can be used in a sado-masochistic context as "safe" words precisely because they're meaningless in HP contexts of violence and abuse. If they have any meaning in a sado-masochistic context, it's the opposite of what they should mean: "no" means "yes" and "stop" means "continue." The drama of sado-masochism strips the vocabulary of intentionality, and takes us back to the masculist cliché, "When a woman says 'no' she means 'yes'," because she doesn't know what she wants (or means). Where is the line between consent and coercion to be drawn, and by whom? The sadist, as superior, is the only hearer and interpreter.

Sado-masochistic "theater" get its scripts from our childhood. The voices we hear are those of our childhood—the voices of ourselves, the powerless, dependent child who had no control, and of the powerful parent who ignored our cries and told us what we "needed."

Sado-masochists, however, say that what we hear is the *illusion*, the drama of childhood, being re-enacted in "highly controlled situations" (*CTP*, 181). Sado-masochistic sex, according to its practitioners, "involves playing with the issues of power and control" (*CTP*, 62). Who is "really" in control? According to Kitt, in *Coming to Power*, "Everyone who is playing" (62). But Califia, in her chapter on the "Erotic Imagination," contrasts fantasy and reality: ". . .the essential difference between an arousing daydream and a real sexual encounter [is] in the fantasy, you are in *complete control*" [my emphasis] (*S*, 9). In the real, illusory sado-masochistic scene, the participants aren't in "complete control." You might recall my earlier quotation of Susan Farr's description, "The dominant person is in control, the submissive person completely vulnerable" (*CTP*, 187). The "control" of the masochist, according to Farr, lies in her "consent" to the game.

But the crucial idea of "consent" isn't really viable in a sado-masochistic context because sado-masochism is "a real sexual encounter," *not* a fantasy.

Sex and War

Metaphors give meaning to form. The most fundamental values in a culture are encoded in its central metaphors. The sado-masochistic context is framed by the metaphors created by HP culture and its values. These metaphors form a coherent system that structures the way we perceive and interpret our experience. Calling sexual violence "combat" or "struggle" fails to disguise the essential metaphorical equation with fighting and war. War and its associated activities are often the comparative term in heteropatriarchal metaphors: ARGUMENT IS WAR, ATHLETIC CONTESTS ARE WAR, LOSING WEIGHT IS A WAR.

Here I'll illustrate how the metaphor SEX IS WAR, found in commercial pornography, permeates the "theater" of sado-masochism. In male pornography, females exist to be subdued and conquered; women's resistance must be overcome, and a successful fuck is a "sexual conquest." In sado-masochistic writing, there is a lot of talk about "fucking" another female and her desire to "be fucked." It's no accident that the English word *fuck* is cognate with the Latin verb *pugnare*, 'to fight'. The emotional "charge" of the word *fuck* in sado-masochism derives from its association with fighting, struggling, resistance, conquest, and violence.

In the world of men, wars are fought because someone wants to have control of a territory and power over its inhabitants. In war, there are boundaries to be attacked and defended, held and challenged, established and overrun. If we accept the metaphor SEX = WAR as true and accurate, then incest and rape are "good, clean sex," just as men claim. Those aspects of rape that continue to terrorize women long after the physical act of violence—the loss of control, the powerlessness, the coerced consent, and the on-going, pervasive fear that rape will be repeated—are irrelevant, or merely a nuisance, because they're business-as-usual, "normal" sex.

In sex, the boundaries to be controlled are nothing less than the self, or identity, of the female. The struggle focuses on *who* will control her boundaries, and orgasm, the "little death" of men's poetry, is the locus of that "battle" for "control." If we take the SEX = WAR metaphor to its "logical" conclusion, we end up with something that the metaphor hides: The final act of war is death. Those who don't die incur permanent physical and emotional wounds they will take with them to their graves. Can we enjoy our sexuality if we persist in using a metaphor that equates an act of living with dying? Perhaps death, the final edge, is the only way men can understand what it means to "have control" or "lose control."

Control is a central issue of HP society, and so it becomes crucial to the child's developing personality. As a metaphor it's the underlying concept that holds the SEX = LOVE = POWER = VIOLENCE equation together. CONTROL/ LACK OF CONTROL is the conceptual axis of that equation. Early in our childhood we are taught, forced, to control our bodily functions. We learn that "controlling ourselves" is a good thing and "losing control of ourselves" is a bad thing. These lessons establish for us the dual orientational metaphors CONTROL IS UP/LACK OF CONTROL IS DOWN. In HP English, we speak of "losing control" of our emotions, tempers, anger, bodies, and weight. Ads for diets routinely talk about "the battle of the bulge," "losing the battle against fat," and "controlling weight." Fat people are described by the medical folks as having no "willpower" and being unable to "control ourselves." Being "fat" is understood as a "control" problem. Since being "out of control" is bad, fat people are bad. Those who are "out of control" are the powerless. Since we cannot "control ourselves," someone else will step in to do it for us.

Our childhood powerlessness and the ways adults manipulated and controlled our lives underlie the equation of control with power. Lesbians talk about power and control as though they were identical. We approvingly talk about friends who "have control of their lives" and disapprove of those who don't. Lesbian rap groups often have as a stated goal "getting control," and, therefore, "power over" our lives. In incest groups, this takes the form of talking about one's boundaries and limits, setting boundaries and not allowing them to be crossed or violated. We have accepted the twin ideas that "having control" is the same as "being powerful," and that "being out of control" is identical to "being powerless."

The issue of control is central for incest and rape survivors because our inability to be powerful in a dangerous context resulted in numbing our minds and bodies to external stimuli. Because feeling anything was so threatening and painful for us, because our need to repress painful experiences was so strong, many of us have spent years of our lives in a numbing fog.

This self-numbing, which I used to think was "self-control," was really lack of control. My past controlled me. Defenses that had served me well as a child had become obstacles to the adult. My mind and body were disconnected from each other, especially with respect to pain. A body that's out of control doesn't feel pain. The pains that signal the onset of serious illness or disease aren't felt or recognized as the danger signals they are. The body's messages are so "damped down" that illness isn't identified until the pain is so excruciating that it has to be named. By then, some illnesses are serious, even fatal. Only extreme pain can get through that numbing, and the more numb we become, the more pain it takes to get through to the mind's pleasure/pain center.

In the language of sado-masochism, "being in control," "letting go of control," and "taking control" are frequently used to describe the feelings of the participants, and are associated with "loss of the self" during sex. The metaphors CONTROL IS UP/LACK OF CONTROL IS DOWN are acted out by the "top," who takes control, and the "bottom," who must be forced to abandon her control. In this "exchange of power," having control is "good" for the sadist, being "out of control" is "good" for the masochist. These conceptual metaphors function as a pivot for sado-masochistic behavior, and are used often in descriptions of "scenes" (quotations from *CTP*):

". . .she knows I can control her physically. . ." (21)

". . .I had let go, leaving her to end it. I had, after all, given myself to her. I was hers,. . ." (49)

"I lie there, spreadeagle, arms out of my control, as her breasts, covered in the cool, self-contained silk, rub over my body." (64)

"Clearly it is time to control this youthful exuberance." (68)

"It was exciting to be tied down and to give up the power to Jan." (88)

". . .it [bondage] gives you a chance to be sexual without any responsibility for your sexy feelings, without any control over what happened. You were being 'forced' to submit." (88-9)

"It feels good (at times) to let go of the struggle to be powerful and just relax and give up all claim to that power." (90)

"She's got this wall around her that I don't know how to break through. It feels a lot like Jan, in control, controlling." (91)

"Sex puts me in someone else's power.. . .I'm scared to death,. . .of. . .losing myself, liking it too much, not liking it at all." (93)

"I like the feeling of giving up control, and I like the feeling of taking her to that edge—. . .Being given such power and responsibility is as erotic to me as giving it up." (103)

"i begin to lose myself (you have me).. . .you push me over the edge. . ." (138)

"When I'm to deliver a spanking,. . .I feel powerful, responsible, and in control, both of myself and of the situation." (183)

Summary

Sado-masochism is a *constructed* desire based on a circular equation familiar to all of us:

SEX = LOVE

LOVE = POWER

POWER = VIOLENCE

VIOLENCE = SEX

SEX = LOVE, ad infinitum.

Those who have power and authority control the child. Power and authority, especially the violent abuses of power and the arbitrariness of control, are sexualized by the powerless child. Parents tell children, "I'm doing this because I love you," "This hurts me more than it hurts you," "If you love me, you will behave, be good, do what I tell you to do, jerk me off, suck my cock, please me." The authority figures who make demands of us, who force us to perform for them, who control our bodies and our environment, are perceived as wielding absolute, complete power over our lives. Because we have no control and no power as children, we internalize the message that being powerful is the same as being "in control." In the mind of the beaten child, violence as an exercise of control equals love. In the mind of the raped daughter, sex as an exercise of power equals love. Love, sex, and violence are intertwined in our minds, and that conceptual network is created by the HP metaphors that lie at the "joints" of the network. We take that construction with us into our adult lives to enact and re-enact in intimate contexts.

I think it's unfortunate that the control issue for Lesbians has been raised in a sexual context, because it makes it seem as though control is an issue important or resolvable only in a sexual context. The equation of sexual energy with power among Lesbians goes back at least to Audre Lorde's pamphlet, *Uses of the Erotic: The Erotic as Power* (1978), in which Lorde says, "When I speak of the erotic, then, I speak of it as an assertion of the life-force of women; of that creative energy empowered. . ." (3-4). I Think Lorde intended her equation to be affirming and expansive. Instead, it has been used in a reductive way that limits both our understanding of and feeling about energy in general, and sexuality in particular. Identifying sex with energy reappears in the literature of sado-masochism as part of the rhetoric of justification. Juicy Lucy says, for example:

> Our sexual energy is literally our life force at its rawest—. . .This is especially true with S/M. Sexuality is energy as tangible as that which turns the earth. It is both power and a pathway to power. I see most lesbians being terrified of their power. . . (*CTP*, p. 38)

Susan Farr makes the equation more absolutely: "Power is the capacity to make things happen—power is energy—and we would do well to know as much as we can about it" (*CTP*, 182). Problems rooted in control and power issues permeate the lives of Lesbians. To imagine that they can only be dealt with successfully in a sexual context seems, to me, an over-idealization of our sexuality, however we think of it.

Making sexuality, sex, desire, the *locus* of our power and the grasp of our energies is, I think, a mistake. First, it is reductive, because it again makes sex the focus of Lesbian identity. Second, it denies our strength and power in other ways we can act in the world. Third, it repeats the masculist, HP fallacy of equating sexuality with identity, will and action. Finally, it reinforces the connections between power and control, manipulation and guilt, strength and coercion, joy and pain, pleasure and evil. These are links I think we must at least question; at best, dissolve.

The childhood linkages among the concepts power, control, violence, and sex are explicitly sexualized in sado-masochism. The sadist forces the masochist over the "edge," and destroys her "barrier" or "wall." The context of sado-masochism is the sexualization of control as the focus of sexual energy. It gives the masochist permission to be "out of control" and the sadist permission to be "in control," as though control were identical with power. But the HP description of control and lack of control isn't changed or transformed by the sado-masochist context; it's essential to the existence of sado-masochism. Perhaps a more accurate description would be to say that the sado-masochist context provides one way of understanding that many of the sexual frustrations Lesbians experience as "blocks" occur because our bodies still respond to the signals of the heterosexual code we learned as children. As long as we're controlled by our past, we cannot be the agents of our present lives and actions.

Practitioners of sado-masochism claim that they're learning control of their bodies, getting in touch with their own feelings. But masochists describe their experiences as a process of leaving their bodies. Sometimes this is described as a "turning inward," but it's still a dissociative process by which one loses touch with her body, becoming numb. Putting ourselves "in our heads" distances us from our bodies and what we're feeling physically. A body at the mercy of the mind isn't a body "in control"; it's a body denied and abandoned. We cannot learn how to be centered in our lives, how to identify what we do or do not want, by denying our bodies, by continuing to ignore what we're feeling. Sado-masochists say that intense pain focuses all awareness in one's body, but they learn to transmute that pain, to "transcend" it. If we translate this sexuality into life, however, it no longer matters whether or not I'm oppressed because I'm so numbed I don't recognize it. What I don't or can't feel doesn't exist to my mind.

As Jeffreys has said, "It is very hard to fight what turns you on" (*LE*, 73). But we must. If, as she suggests, sado-masochist sexuality is constructed, we can deconstruct it. "We are not to blame for the way our sexuality is constructed, though we have total responsibility for how we choose to act on it" (*LE*, 73). We can begin the reconstruction of our sexuality by untangling the unlovely intertwining of sex = love = power = violence = sex. The "turn on" of sado-masochism is grounded in the powerlessness we experienced as children.

In spite of its dependence on the way HP conceptually organizes experience, sado-masochists seem determined to present sado-masochism as something "new" and "heretical." Gayle Rubin, describing Feminist treatments of sado-masochism, says: "I think feminism has always dealt bad[l]y with dissent and *new ideas* [my emphasis], and it's important for feminists to do better with these issues if they want the women's movement to stay current, flexible, and democratic" (*CTP*, 253). Well, sado-masochism isn't a "new idea," even among Lesbians. Sado-masochists have been among us ever since I can remember, and Califia is quite honest when she observes that "The most accessible images of sado-masochism are found in commercial pornography" (*S*, 120). Far from being "new," sado-masochism has its own long tradition and a literature that promotes its ideology. Nor are Feminists, to the best of my knowledge, going to go somewhere and vote our consciences on the subject of sado-masochism. Rubin sounds like she's making a salespitch worthy of an MBA when she warns that Feminists should "stay current [and] flexible." Comparing a liberation movement and its members to institutional democracy is blatant rhetoric.

Given the deep-rootedness of the SEX = VIOLENCE cycle in the way we think and talk about sexuality, I don't think we can afford to have "complete trust" in our "gut feelings." I know this will anger many Feminists, but I believe that not questioning our feelings will lead us to continue to act on our feelings without understanding why we have them, where we got them, and what they mean in our lives. The idea of "complete trust" itself is suspect to me. Like any absolute, it is meaningful only in an either/or context. I don't think there's any abstract idea that can be said to be "complete," whether it's trust, control, or freedom.

We carry the idea that abstractions can be complete and absolute into our adult lives from our remembered dependence as children, when we believed that adults were all-powerful, all-controlling, and all-knowing because that's how they presented themselves. But we know now, or should know, that in areas of their lives where they didn't have power over another individual, their control was considerably less than "complete," as ours is. What we learn is that power and control are relative, not absolute or fixed, concepts.

Lesbian sex should be fun. I say "should be." Is it possible for sex to be a joyous, exciting, celebratory rollick when we are surrounded by our oppressors and constant reminders of our oppression? Can Lesbians create sexual contexts that are original, that don't borrow from HP sexual frameworks? Maybe. But first we have to stop relying on the HP patterns of sexuality reflected in the ways we think and talk about Lesbian sex and sexuality. We comprehend our lives through metaphorical concepts. The metaphor SEX = WAR isn't a harmless "figure of speech." The only way to change our situation is to come up with our own constructs and metaphors for interpreting and enjoying sexual desire.

Endnote

1. My description of a "vacuum" concerning Lesbian sexual practices follows the common perception among Lesbians, one that isn't, strictly speaking, accurate. There were, in fact, at least two books about Lesbian sex and sexuality published in 1975: *Loving Women* by the Nomadic Sisters (illustrated by Victoria Hammond) and *what lesbians do* by Godiva. (Neither book has any publication information beyond the copyright; both appear to have been self-published, but I can't be sure.) In any case, these books probably disappeared from the shelves of bookstores that carried them and are difficult to find now, more than fifteen years later, accounting for the perception of Lesbians who never saw them that Lesbian-Feminists ignored our sex and sexuality.

2. Both their need to be loved and their curiosity make children easy victims of adults who want to take advantage of them.

"Killing Us Softly": A Murder Mystery

Prologue

On Saturday, March 28, 1987, after working for two weeks on the original version of this essay, I had a dream. I dreamed of nomadic groups of women, tribes of women, always moving through the cover of forests—women on the run, hiding, seeking a place where we could close our eyes and sleep soundly, space where we could sleep without fearing that we would be awakened from our sleep.

We were nomads because we were hunted. Sleeping soundly meant death for one of us. None of us could ever be sure that she'd wake up if she slept, and, if she did awaken, what she'd awaken to find. We struggled against the lure of sleep because sleep itself had become a trap, an enticement we could not afford. But there were those nights when we dared to sleep, slept because our bodies demanded it of us, and we knew those who awakened would find yet another companion dead. Her sleeping bag would be blood-soaked, and the bloody pieces of her body would be scattered around our campsite.

What was terrifying was the knowledge that we had slept through her murder and the slow process of dismemberment. We had slept on, hearing nothing. What was terrifying was our ignorance of her murder and the *silence* in which this act had been executed. She hadn't sounded an alarm. She hadn't cried out for help. Each night, a companion was silently murdered.

Each night, one, and only one of us would be murdered and mutilated. What was terrifying was the singleness of the murder, as though our hunters knew they didn't need to slaughter all of us at once—as though they could afford to wait, murdering us one by one. And those of us who awakened each day wondered why we were still alive, and when our time would come.

What was terrifying was our inability to stop the murderers, and their ability to find us. What was terrifying was not knowing who our murderers were, not being sure that they were actually outsiders. There was no place where we could safely lie down to sleep, because the murders would cease only when all of us were dead.

The Body of This Paper

It was a dark and stormy night. (Harlequin Romances, murder mysteries, and horror stories require such an opening.) A meeting was held. A vote was taken. Testimonies were given, evidence was heard. These artefacts ('made-up things') were interpreted to mean that Feminism was no longer alive, no longer necessary, no longer "viable." It was declared that, henceforth, the second (or third, or fourth or fifth [depending on what one counts]) wave of women's liberation was dead. It was announced that we had entered the "Post-Feminist Era."

You may be able to imagine some of the things that went through my mind when I read the Midwest Women's Studies Association's "Call for Papers." There, among the suggested paper topics was "surviving in a 'post-Feminist' era," protectively buffered by "lessons from Feminist history" and "Lesbianism and Feminism." What, I wondered, can the phrase "post-Feminist" mean? Who decided that women's liberation was over and done with, and whose interests would it serve to make such an assertion? What, I thought, does the label *Feminist* mean in "post-Feminist"? Well, it's always been difficult to come up with an adequate definition of *Feminist*, but there ought to be *some* limits to its possible meanings.

A few examples from 1987 television will illustrate how meaningless the word *Feminist* had become. The Joan Rivers Show provided several unpleasant surprises. Early in 1987, Gloria Steinem appeared on that talk show. In the course of that appearance, Joan Rivers twice used the word *feminine* instead of *Feminist* to describe women's political activism. Somehow, she had confused the labels *Feminist* and *feminine*. Wimmin's political activism synonymous with the adjective that means 'weak' and 'passive'? Gloria Steinem, however, didn't correct her. She allowed the error to pass without comment.

Later that year, Joan Rivers asked Estelle Getty (Sophia on "Golden Girls") if she considered herself a "Feminist," and Getty said, "Oh yes, I was a Feminist long before it was a fad to be one. I did it all—career, marriage, family." ("A fad"?) To which Rivers added, "Me, too." Joan Rivers a "Feminist"? Much of her "humor" is based on presenting herself as a stereotypical "dizzy" female; her career was made on "jokes" about how much she hates her body.

Then, on March 27, 1987, the actor who played both the "exceptional lizard" in the defunct television series, "V," and Freddie in *Nightmare on Elm Street* appeared on Joan Rivers' show, bringing with him his "hand," a glove on which each finger ends in a 5- or 6-inch talon. He waved that "hand" around as he bragged about how his female fans surround him at sci-fi conventions, wanting to touch, stroke, caress the "hand." *Who* are Freddie's female fans? *Who* are the women enthralled and captivated by an instrument of terror and violence? And, again there's Joan Rivers herself, a woman with exceptional media visibility, who claims she's a "Feminist," but thinks that *feminine* and *Feminist* mean the same thing!

If mainstream women like Joan Rivers and Estelle Getty believe that being a

Feminist means being "feminine," being SuperWoman, SuperMom, SuperWife, is it possible that Feminism has changed the way men think about women? How *did* men think about women in 1987? To judge from the media, women were still an inferior form of life. Consider how the murderer of John Lennon reduced women to conceptual *zeros* in his self-description:

> Maybe my problem was I kind of sounded feminine. . .One time about a year ago in a store I was just trying to make up my mind what to get, you know, and this salesgirl, she says, "You're just like a woman—can't make up your mind." You get somebody saying something like that and it just crushes me . . . I just felt like I wasn't worth anything. (James R. Gaines, "The Man Who Shot Lennon," *People*, p. 65)

Note how being compared to a female stereotype, how being thought of as feminine, made him feel "like he wasn't worth anything," and was used to explain his "pathology." But, this man isn't "sick"; he's described a "normal" male reaction. The Marines use the tactic of comparing recruits to women and girls to shame them into killing automatically and without feeling, and it works. Under patriarchy, being a woman is the *worst* thing men can imagine.

If women, generically, are zeros, where, on a scale of peoplehood, do Lesbians fall? Listen to the way Lesbians as a group are dismissed by May Sarton and Jill Johnston in the front page teasers they wrote for *Long Time Passing: Lives of Older Lesbians* (1986), published by Alyson Publications:

> . . .it is really about human relations and the universal quality rather than a book just about lesbians. I want people, all people, to read this book.
> (May Sarton)

> I enjoyed *Long Time Passing* a lot.. . .The spectrum of class and professional affiliations also affords a certain comprehensive view. This should be an enlightening book for everybody, not just lesbians. (Jill Johnston)
> (This description was also incorporated into the ad for the book in *Feminist Bookstore News* 9, 3 [January 1987], p. 6)

How quickly we—the principal audience for the book—are shunted aside! "*Just* lesbians" resonates with dismissal and scorn.

Should we celebrate Joan Rivers' "conversion" to Feminism? Have we "come a long way, baby" when the female stereotype is used derogatorily by a sales*woman*; when being compared to that idea of a woman justifies a man's violence; when female movie-goers flock to caress Freddie's taloned hand; when Lesbians are dismissed as an insignificant readership of a book about Lesbians (but are probably a majority of those who bought it); when an obnoxiously pregnant "business woman" is featured in an ad for Chevrolet vans; when Doritos is advertised as the "nacho with the real *macho* bite"; when Milk of Magnesia is peddled as M.O.M.?

Is Feminism alive and well in the United States? If it is, what are we to think about the "interview" with Andrea Dworkin published in the April, 1987 issue of *Penthouse* and the use to which it was put? When freelance writer Michele Mayron asked to interview Dworkin for the Israeli daily newspaper *Yedioth Ahronot*, Dworkin consented, taking Mayron at her word. Mayron then turned around and sold the interview to *Penthouse* for an undisclosed sum of money, and the magazine used the interview in an attempt to discredit Dworkin's anti-pornography work. In fact, they alleged that *she* is a pornographer by quoting from her novel, *Ice and Fire*, out of context. The editors of *Penthouse* girded their loins with the flag, claiming that their reasons for publishing an interview with Dworkin "[went] to the heart of what our democracy is all about." Here's a sample of what *Penthouse* "democracy" is about:

> She's one of our most implacable enemies. A grotesque effigy of intellectual slime and hypocrisy. . .Dworkin is an inflexible, man-hating fanatic who cannot be taken seriously.. . .Let her speak and, if that voluminous girth permits, she will inevitably put her own big foot squarely into her own big mouth. (p. 8)

I wasn't surprised that *Penthouse* used Dworkin's fatness and the adjective "man-hating" to discredit her. But, how are we to rationalize Mayron's betrayal of Dworkin's trust? She gave *Penthouse* an opportunity to trash Dworkin that they couldn't have gotten any other way. Is this an isolated example? One that we shouldn't consider typical of women? Or is Mayron's betrayal only one well-publicized betrayal, one among many more that we don't know about?

That men might wish Feminism dead, because of the challenge it poses to their domination, is one thing. Unfortunately, my detective work suggests that women as well wish Radical Feminism and its political analysis of women's oppression *dead*. And that saddens me. As I pondered the significance of the examples I've mentioned, a friend brought me an issue of *The Harmonist*, a slick, New Age magazine, in which a piece by Alyse Fortier, entitled "Woman: Century 21," had been published. Fortier's thesis was stated beneath its title: "A new generation of Feminists is calling for a new look at some old strategies." What's "new" and what's "old"? Listen.

> Times have changed. As the baby boomers of the big chill generation become mothers and grandmothers, it has become clear that the old rhetoric will no longer do. Much has changed since the radical feminism of the sixties and seventies.. . .as it comes to grips with new problems, the women's movement is searching for new ways to raise its consciousness about the problems that face the wives and mothers of the 1980's. (p. 16)

What's "new" is focusing on the problems of "wives and mothers"; what's "old" is Radical Feminist analysis of how heteropatriarchal institutions, like marriage and motherhood, hold women subordinated to men. No need for me to analyze Fortier's language, because it came, virtually unchanged, from a book by Sylvia Ann Hewlett, one of the prophets of "post-Feminism," a woman with all the "right" credentials who produced the religious text of the right-wing and anti-Feminists, *A Lesser Life: The Myth of Women's Liberation in America* (1987).

Her title itself is ambiguous: one could read it as asserting that the achievement of women's liberation in America is a myth (with which I would agree), or that the movement to liberate women in America is a myth (which is the author's intended meaning). She doesn't use the phrase "post-Feminist" until it appears in the title of the final chapter of the book, "Epilogue: Voices from the Post-Feminist Generation." Hewlett's use of the label "post-Feminist" declares that Feminism, the Women's Liberation Movement, is over and done with. A woman has, again, done men's work for them, this time with a vengeance. Obtusely ignoring how dangerous the institution of marriage is to women, Hewlett informed us that Feminism is, once more, no longer alive and well in the U. S. Not, however, because of the semantic decay of the term in the popular media, but because, she claims, Feminists have attended to the "wrong" issues (such as economic equality, the ERA, the right to control our own bodies, rape, battering), and must now "move on" to "more important" issues, like supporting marriage, motherhood and making babies.

The books that Hewlett cited for her "evidence" made clear what she perceived to be Radical Feminist ideology: *Woman As Nigger, Marriage is Hell, The Baby Trap, The Female Eunuch, Sexual Politics,* and *Lesbian Nation* by Jill Johnston. Notice, please, that every single title in her list was published by a malestream publisher. Not a single title by a Feminist press is mentioned, nor is there any reference to Feminist or Lesbian-Feminist journals, such as *Sinister Wisdom, Trivia, Lesbian Ethics,* or *off our backs.* There's not even token acknowledgment of Mary Daly's work (for example, *The Church and the Second Sex* (1968; 1978), *Gyn/Ecology* (1978), and *Pure Lust* (1984)—all Radical Feminist texts). Even books that were published by malestream presses are ignored, such as Adrienne Rich's *Of Woman Born* (W. W. Norton, 1976). Her omissions reveal that Hewlett hadn't done her homework when she said: "It is easier to find Feminist positions on abortion, rape, the female orgasm, the rights of Lesbians, and genital mutilation in the Third World than to find out what Feminists think about motherhood" (189).

Ignoring the work of Adrienne Rich and Mary Daly, Hewlett used *Sisterhood is Powerful* to prove that Feminists don't care about motherhood, claiming that, out of seventy-four articles, "only one. . .has anything to do with motherhood" (189). But this assertion is false. In that anthology, no fewer than *twelve* essays and poems describe and analyze various aspects of what it means to be a mother in the U. S., and several more explicitly address the issues that concern Hewlett. Either Hewlett can't count, or her copy of the book was missing some pages. If one checks her footnote 32, it references *only* pages vii-xiii of Robin Morgan's Introduction to the book, but not a one of the articles she might have cited. Hewlett falsely dismissed a book she obviously hadn't read.

When I think about it, I am aghast at the implications of what this woman has done. "Post-Feminist era": The 'period that follows feminism', as though Feminism were already a historical period of yore instead of the political ideology that it is. Stranger, I've never heard anyone talking about living in a post-socialist era, a post-Marxist period, or a post-Christian age. (Of course, male ideologies have a longer shelf-life than women's.) Even the little word *era* erases the ideological substance of Feminist political analysis. Hewlett dismissed the entire analytical framework of Radical Feminism like so much froth on a beer, using tried and true methods: delusion, distortion, and deception. On the other hand, Hewlett must find Radical Feminists and Lesbians pretty scary if she felt justified in constructing such an elaborate hash of lies and omissions!

The Delusion

Hewlett began her book on a personal note: describing her own struggles to be a wife and mother, and to earn a Ph. D. in economics. So far, so good; Feminist analysis should be based on women's experiences. But by page 18, she was describing the origins of her delusion:

> *When the political activists of my generation* [my emphasis] told me that American women had never had it so good, I believed them; when they told me I could dictate my terms to life, I believed that, too.

Here, on the first page of her 400-pages-plus book, Hewlett made her first, and most serious error, attributing responsibility for her disillusionment to the "political activists of her generation," (read: Feminists), when, in fact, it was the *popular media* of this country that sold her that tripe. She bought the Madison Avenue package: the lie that women could, should, ought to be SuperWomen with a spotless home, healthy children, a contented hubby, and a successful career. She, like thousands of other women, has tried and failed to fulfill the demands of so many responsibilities. Hewlett is apparently ignorant of the fact that both the SuperWoman Syndrome and the Sexual "Revolution" were created by men, packaged by Madison Avenue, and bought by women who, like Hewlett, want society to subsidize her choices, even the bad ones. She's bitter, and she's angry. What she called her "double burden," as homemaker and wage-earner, provides the basis for her assertion that women's liberation in America is a myth. And she's right about that much: Women in the U. S. are a long way from liberation. If Feminists had achieved what we sought, we would have disbanded ourselves long ago, and Hewlett could have had a man *and* a career! As the accused agents of Hewlett's delusion, however, the Feminists she castigated in *A Lesser Life* were figments of her delusion.

The Distortion

Exactly what kind of "Feminism" did Hewlett pronounce "dead"? It's hard to say, because her understanding of feminism is so piecemeal and selective. First, she erroneously labeled every branch of U. S. Feminism "separatist." (I wish!) This description is simply false. Second, even though she devoted an entire chapter to the ideological split between Radical and Reform Feminists in the U. S., in other places she confused their very different politics, damning Reform Feminists for the ideas of Radical Feminists and vice versa. She was not aware, for example, that Radical Feminism isn't monolithic, but consists of at least seven or eight ideologically distinct factions. By pretending that she's knowledgeable about the various factions in U. S. Feminism and, simultaneously, conflating them, Hewlett made an inaccurate, disgusting mush of Feminism in general. (I'd be disillusioned, too!)

In her chapter on "Women's Liberation and Motherhood," Hewlett started out a long paragraph with Radical Feminism of the Redstocking variety, and ended up by merging Carolyn Heilbrun's androgynous model with the "Dress for Success" brand of Reform Feminism.

> . . .Men were enemy number one, but family, marriage, and children also came under direct attack because they were the mechanisms through which women's second-class status was perpetuated through time.. . .In the late sixties and early seventies significant numbers of young Feminists rejected the whole package—marriage, motherhood, and children—as a bad life choice for any woman. To be liberated came to mean wiping out all special female characteristics, leaving behind an androgenous shell of abstract personhood. *Stripped of their men and their children, these unfettered women could then join the mainstream and clone the male competitive model in the marketplace.* (p. 186; my emphasis)

Hewlett manages in this paragraph an amazing distortion: the "significant numbers of young Feminists" who rejected "marriage, motherhood, and children," are the same women "stripped of their men and their children" only a sentence later. How can a woman "be stripped" of that which she rejects as a "bad life choice"? Nor did she acknowledge that many of these same "significant numbers of young Feminists" identified themselves as Lesbians. *That* piece of information exposes how Hewlett distorted her presentation of Feminist analysis. The women she claims were "stripped" of their "special female characteristics" (men and babies), she turned into the "victims" of Feminism. To her credit, at least, even *she* knows that "marriage, motherhood, and children" are a "package."

The Deception

So it isn't any kind of Feminism familiar to me that Hewlett declared "dead," but a conglomeration of "mainstream" Feminism à la the original *Ms.* and the values, slogans, and images promulgated by commercial advertising. It's an unsavory mess of misinformation, distortion, and omission, which she presented to her, I imagine, already misinformed audience, as "American Feminism." It is this myth of her own creation which she then proposed to replace with a European import, called "Social Feminism." Using France, Sweden, and Italy as exemplars, "Social Feminism," she claimed, is the way to achieve what American Feminism refused to prioritize. As she said in the last sentence of her book: "We simply have to do much more to make American family life stronger and more secure" (417). Does that statement sound familiar? She adopted the right-wing agenda *in toto*.

Well, that was her plan, after all. Hewlett maintained throughout her book that American Feminists "failed" to pay attention to the "real concerns" of 90% of its potential constituency. "It is absurd," she said, "to expect to build a coherent Feminist movement, let alone a separatist Feminist movement, when you exclude and denigrate the *deepest emotion in women's lives*.. . .[I]t is impossible to build a mass women's movement on an anti-child, anti-mother platform" (188).

As she built her false case against Feminism in the U. S., Hewlett's strategy was clever and beguiling. On the one hand, she listed, and dismissed without rebutting, what she considered the "extraordinary slogans" of Feminism: "Marriage was hell, sex was political, coitus was killing, married women were prostitutes, babies were traps, intercourse was rape, love was slavery, families were prisons, and men were enemies" (185). At no point, however, did she offer any analysis or justifications for her own assumptions about the necessity for marriage, child-bearing, or motherhood. This tidy package, of course, presupposes heterosexuality. In fact, the idea of heterosexuality, on which her analysis depends, was so thoroughly assumed that the word *heterosexuality* doesn't even appear in the book's index! It's a given. What we do find are multiple listings in the index for "men" and "men and women." (Lesbians are mentioned three times.)

These entwined denials—her failure to address the Radical Feminist ideological framework and her refusal to question any of her own assumptions—underpin the apparently coherent and informed analysis Hewlett presents. One would have to be one of those villains, a Radical Feminist, to grasp the hidden thesis of *A Lesser Life*: Feminism in the U. S. can "survive" only if it becomes something else, what Hewlett calls "Social Feminism." This proposed transmogrification of Feminism is similar to taking a gourmet recipe that requires quality ingredients and substituting ingredients already on hand until the recipe, and the dish it will produce, no longer bear any resemblance to the original intent of the recipe. Hewlett's rather simple recipe for U. S. Feminism, obscured by numerous denials, distortions, falsehoods, and intellectual convolutions, can be stated rather simply: U. S. Feminism can "survive" only if we tell other women (and, by implication, men) what they want to hear.

What do these women want to hear? They want to be told that they can, in fact, "have it all," *without changing*. They want to be told that they can love men, have babies, enjoy the privileges, such as they are, meted out to heterosexual loyalists, and live interesting, productive, successful lives as career women. "Having *it* all" is a comforting idea, and it sells a lot of beer, but it's also a lie. What Hewlett failed to realize, because she blamed other women for failing her, is that she's pissed off because she, and all these other women, *have* been told these things were possible before, and within recent memory. Hewlett's angry because she was lied to and now she knows she was lied to, but she's misidentified who lied to her.

Her response is thus predictable. Had she been listening, she'd know that many Feminists have tried to warn her that the fable of SuperWoman was a baited trap; but she couldn't, or wouldn't, listen. What I wasn't prepared for was the viciousness of her anti-Feminist polemic. She blamed Feminists, not men, not capitalist economics, not, surely, her own assumptions about heterosexuality, marriage, and motherhood, not the patriarchal social structure and the institutions and assumptions that perpetuate it. It's no wonder that men raved about Hewlett's book: By ignoring other, contradictory statistics on male violence and, specifically, the varieties of male violence sheltered and nurtured by the nuclear family—wife battering, child battering, and incest, the incidence of all of which continues to rise—she exculpated the men who run this country, make the laws, and benefit directly from women's oppression within the institution of marriage.

Herein lies the crux of the contradiction that betrays Hewlett's misdirected anger: She ignored the very statistics she used to demonstrate the impoverishment of U. S. women. She said that (1) in the late '70s, 40-50% of the children born would "spend part of their youth in female-headed households" (109), and (2) "[t]wo-thirds of the women undergoing artificial insemination are single" (179), but her hidden agenda is "a thorough-going package of family supports" (415). She wasn't really interested in the problems of female-headed households, although she incorporated their statistics to make her case for marriage and family seem plausible. Her assumptions betrayed her. Right after she stated that two-thirds of the women being artificially inseminated are single, she concluded: "They want children but have failed to find Mr. Right" (179). Why did she think that any of those women were *looking* for "Mr. Right" in the first place? *Surely* she knew that many of the women having children via artificial insemination are Lesbians. Admitting it, however, would destroy the tidiness of her presentation.

In fact, people who live outside the institution of marriage are the *real* targets of her revisionism, and she makes this explicit on page 188: "The modern world is, after all, populated with divorcees, widows, gays, and singles, many of whom bear grudges against the male sex." Thus, the very groups one might expect to benefit most from Hewlett's program of Social Feminism, which includes federally-funded supports for working parents, are dismissed as man-haters.

Curiously, in a book that extolled breeding as a woman's "highest function" and that eulogized, once more, "the joys of motherhood," Hewlett referred over and over to the "burdens" of women. Are "burdens" "joys," or vice versa? If being wives, mothers, and wage-earners are "burdens," as Hewlett described them, why consent to these roles? What she called "burdens" I would call "potentials." The capability of breeding, for example, is a potential for many women. Born with functioning equipment, most women, like other animals, can produce offspring if they wish to. That potential, however, is not, as Hewlett seems to believe, an *imperative*, and to treat it as such is a particularly specious kind of reductionism, biological determinism.

In an Afterword, written in November, 1986, Hewlett articulated the determinism underlying her analysis: "Women can function successfully as male clones in the marketplace only if they never have children, and to demand this of most women is to *thwart their deepest biological need*" (412; my emphasis).

Hewlett accepted as given and unquestionable the male assumptions and institutions that continue to keep women subordinate and poor: marriage, the family, making babies, and heterosexuality, but then asserted that *Feminists* must assume responsibility for making it possible for women to be mothers, wives, and wage-earners, that *Feminists* must work to improve women's lives so that they can continue to believe that heterosexuality and the social institutions that support it are "natural."

We are to accomplish this, you understand, by scuttling the Feminist theoretical framework that defines Feminism as a gynecentric political analysis. This amounts to saying that Feminists have failed because we worked at the *causes* of women's oppression rather than the symptoms. Feminism, as Hewlett presented it, will be "meaningful" to other women only if we don't examine, analyze, or talk about the sources and methods that perpetuate our subjugation.

But women's poverty isn't accidental. It's not something isolated from other social policies or structures. It is part of the systematic, misogynistic ideology that feeds on women's subjugation, whether emotional or economic. Any analysis, like Hewlett's, that ignores the essential cause of women's oppression—men's hatred of women—can only propose band-aid solutions that cover the wounds without treating and eradicating the source of the infection. In order to push her political agenda, Hewlett didn't even listen to herself. While she devoted an entire chapter to how U. S. divorce laws impoverish women, and she accurately observed that "Too many married women are just a man away from poverty" (406), she failed to make the connection between coerced heterosexuality and women's poverty. And she failed to pay attention to what her informants told her.

> Cynthia Wall: "If my husband were ever to walk out I couldn't begin to support my kids; it worries me a lot."

> Jacquelyn Porter: "I was one of those foolish women who put all her faith and trust in the man of her dreams. He has already remarried."

> Donna Anderson: "Many of us are former wives of professional men who pleaded poverty when it came time to support us in our struggles to get back

on our feet; oftentimes they even refused to contribute to the education of their children."

No "thorough-going package of family supports" will help these women. It's the institutional lie of the "family" that has betrayed them.

By erasing Lesbians and keeping us marginal in her presentation, Hewlett herself couldn't perceive that she was perpetuating the lie that she believed. She was ignorant of how thoroughly she was limiting women's options. This narrow-mindedness was explicit in her unqualified acceptance of Charlotte Perkins Gilman's 1897 description of women's "choices":

> We have so arranged life, . . ., that a woman must 'choose'; she must either live alone, unloved, uncompanied, uncared for, homeless, childless, with her work in the world for sole consolation; or give up world service for the joys of love, motherhood, and domestic service. (p. 401)

Wryly, Hewlett comments, "Things have not changed very much." Maybe they haven't changed from her perspective, but Gilman's description is as flawed today as it was ninety years ago. I most assuredly rejected "motherhood" and "domestic service," but I am not "alone," "unloved," "homeless," etc., and, while I enjoy my "work in the world," it is not my "sole consolation." A woman doesn't have to be a Lesbian to live as I do, as many will attest, but ignoring the existence of Lesbians, an existence which exposes the false cause-effect structure of Gilman's description, was a glaring omission on Hewlett's part. Narrowing women's options in this way, failing to mention the many options we've created for ourselves, is a disservice no one should overlook.

Hewlett's program, ironically, cannot be achieved without the visibility of Radical Feminists as a potential threat to the men in power. It's in her own interest to keep us alive and visible, but she stubbornly alienates the one group that actually cares about the quality of women's lives. She seems unaware of this. The male powers-that-be, including even the liberal Democrats Hewlett was playing footsie with, will be more than happy to give Hewlett and her constituency everything they want in order to keep them breeding and nurturing and serving men—domesticated—and, at the same time, keep them working at underpaid jobs to maintain consumerism. If women want more than this domesticated servitude, they must be able to *convince male employers and legislators that they do have attractive options if their demands are refused.* Only Radical Feminists present and live these options. As long as men can comfortably believe that they have women right where they want them, underneath them, physically, emotionally, and economically, there's no compelling reason for them to offer women incentives to enter and remain in the workforce. If Hewlett had paid any attention to George Gilder (the "intellectual architect of Reaganomics"), she'd know that they want to remove women from the workforce to make room for men. (For an economist, Hewlett seemed purposely ignorant of the economic causes that have pushed married women out into the U. S. workforce.) Without Radical Feminism, Hewlett has no political leverage for making her program feasible; in fact, at no point did she offer a rationale for why married women should be working outside the home.

In spite of Hewlett's repeated allegation that Feminists *urged* other women to enter the workforce as though they were "male clones," Lesbians have known, and repeatedly said, that women aren't "like" men. Most men who embark on a career already have housekeepers who perform countless service functions for them: grocery-shopping, cooking, cleaning, errand-running, and washing clothes. Those who don't have a housekeeper at first pick one up along the way.

As a Lesbian academic, my life was divided into three major areas: my career, political activism, and maintenance shitwork, of the variety wives provide for men. Each area, in turn, consisted of numerous tasks or responsibilities, which required hours of work every week. My career, for example, involved some measure of performance in teaching, research, and service, and each of these had yet more detailed responsibilities. Teaching included office hours, advising, running the linguistics program, supervising theses for both graduates and undergraduates, and independent studies, as well as class preparation.

The men I was expected to equal or surpass in my performance, however, had *only* their academic careers to occupy their time and energies, yet most of them idled their time away baking breads, playing cribbage in the coffeeroom, and buying real estate. They had wives taking care of their day-to-day maintenance, and, because most of them were white, heterosexual males, they didn't have any "oppression" they were compelled to fight against in the political arena.

And this is the crucial point at which Hewlett's Social Feminism will most surely fail: If we ignore for a moment the speciousness of her supporting analysis, and accept, just for a moment, that the "double burden" she described is somehow inevitable, her stated advocacy of a program of political activism on behalf of married women who are also wage-earners is doomed to failure. If, as she asserted, the lives of such women are so difficult, where will they find the time and energy to mount a successful political movement on their own behalf? Political activism requires the commitment of a substantial quantity of time and energies if it is to succeed, and these women, already staggering under their "double burden," have little or nothing left to commit. Their time and their energies are consumed by caretaking their men and their children. Surely she doesn't expect us "singles" or Feminists, the two groups targeted by her analysis, to do this for her?

I won't make the mistake of some Feminists who have assumed that women like Hewlett are the unwitting dupes of patriarchal propaganda, unaware that they've been lied to. She isn't a stupid woman. She fabricated a persuasive, if cunningly selective, analysis. No. I think I'm finally prepared to buy the ridiculous idea that women purposely choose heterosexuality, choose men, choose the roles men have allotted them. I'm even willing to accept the proposition that they are heterosexuals because they *like* it. I don't understand, though, why those of us expunged from their "social" agenda—indeed, negated by it—are expected to sympathize with their situation and make their lives peachy-keen.

Because women like Hewlett willingly acknowledge me *only* if they think they can use me, I am as loath to financially subsidize heterosexuality as I am Reagan's "Star Wars" fantasies. But that's what Hewlett said she wants, and she has presented us with an appalling agenda of new "rights" including, but not limited to: "the right to have a child" (393) and "the [parents'] right to spend a few weeks with a new baby" (415). If, as Hewlett asserted, breeding is the "deepest biological need" of most women (412), how can it also be a "right" to be demanded in the political arena? If breeding is a "need" or an "instinct," which I doubt, since I don't have it, then women are going to breed with or without social supports. She cannot have it both ways, as determined as she seems to do so, and I'm unwilling to pay for it (but I do). Furthermore, implicit in these demands is rejection of the civil rights of the elderly (who are also impoverished), Lesbians and gays, anyone who is not a breeder. Is there any level of taxation that will create the funds necessary to take care of those of us who are already here and in need, like the elderly and the homeless, *and* finance the breeders? If heterosexuals are going to insist on their "right" to fuck and make babies, then I have to make explicit the conflict of interests that Hewlett failed to acknowledge.

Finally, underneath Hewlett's angry analysis lies a barely mentioned, unexamined, despair: She doesn't believe that men will change (she cites statistics to prove it), and she doesn't suggest that women's priorities might or should change. It is at this deepest level of unacknowledged despair that Hewlett's anti-Feminism is most virulent; she has abandoned the essential premise that change is necessary if women are to liberate themselves, and embraced the idea that change is *impossible*. Her program of "Social Feminism," and the analysis that makes it so appealing to her constituents, is a dreary acceptance of "things as they are."

Lessons from History

In the western version of patriarchy, ages and eras come and go according to some measure only men seem attuned to. What all of them have in common is that something or someone significant, *as perceived by men,* has to die or come to an end. When we ponder the systematic erasure of wimmin's political activism during the preceding centuries, there's a valuable lesson to be gleaned from patriarchal descriptions of the early twentieth century, the period immediately following passage of the constitutional amendment that "gave" U. S. women the vote. In patriarchal histories, this U. S. period is labeled the "Roaring Twenties." Interestingly enough, this "era" is also said to mark the end of the "first" wave of feminism (as though wimmin had never before noticed their own subjugation or tried to do anything about it). The patriarchal label fabricates the perceived "end" of more than a century of Feminist struggle for the rights of black people and white women, erases all preceding Feminist struggles, and redefines the very meaning of Feminist politics.

I've discussed the arguments presented in *A Lesser Life* because there's a lesson for us in Hewlett's book. Men are using exactly the same tactic to redefine the goals of Feminist politics in the latter part of the twentieth century, and there are women more than happy to aid and abet them. By the act of renaming the period of second-wave Feminism "post-Feminist," these people can control how a majority of people perceive contemporary events. Now, it's obvious to me why men would label as socially significant the cessation of Feminist political activism (if that's accepted as factual) and the beginning of what is usually described as a period of (relatively) less-inhibited activity for heterosexual women, thereby naming a period of time according to their own interests, and making more than one hundred years of Feminist activism *invisible*.

In the 1920s, men had just successfully defused and derailed a massive women's liberation movement. They had saved the patriarchal nuclear family for another century of violence and abuse, saved the patriarchal institution of marriage, put women back in their place—barefoot and pregnant—and, an added bonus, increased their access to women's bodies. It took them a while. And, along the way, it also took some scientific cunning to entice women back to men's dirty clothes and their beds.

Notice what is implicit here: the reassertion of men's "right" to the energy, support, and emotional dependence of women; the reassertion of the "naturalness" of heterosexuality; the denial, erasure, and obliteration of female bonding. Hewlett used exactly the same tactic.

Here's something else one can learn, if she wishes, from books like Hewlett's. When heterosexual Feminists start to talk about "respectability," "credibility," and "realism," they're politely dumping Lesbians from the women's liberation agenda. Just as fast as women set about living abanaclitically, 'without psychological dependence on male approval', there's always some woman willing to take us under by confabulation, 'replacing fact with fantasy in memory'. Just as fast as a bunch of Lesbians leaps up and says "Here we are," we're hustled back into our closets like so many disobedient children who shouldn't be seen *or* heard!

Let me return, for elucidation of this point, to the turn of the century. Again, naming was an important weapon in the patriarchal defense of male dominance and its corollary, female heterosexuality. At the end of the nineteenth century, as Feminism continued to gain strength, as wimmin grew in their certainty that they didn't *need* men to live productive, meaningful lives, men got desperate (necessity is the mother of invention, we're told), and invented two new labels for very old realities: "The Lesbian" and the "frigid woman."[1] These are semantically and socially reciprocal expressions. The one requires the other. You'll recall that good Queen Victoria made sure that Lesbians would remain beyond the barristers' reach by declaring that "Lesbians" didn't exist. Obviously, if something doesn't exist, one doesn't need laws forbidding it! But women have been loving each other since the first lizards discovered land. Who knows by what endearments they named themselves before the sexologists "discovered" that women could and did prefer women to men?

Prior to the sexologists' snooping, women-loving women were one of the best-kept secrets since the herbal remedies of the wicca. Is it any accident that the sexologists "dis-covered" and labeled *Lesbianism* as psychological pathology simultaneously with the "frigid woman" syndrome? The adjective *frigid*, when used as an attribute of women, means (as defined in the 1967 edition of *The Random House Dictionary*; the 1987 edition is less frank):

> a. indifferent or hostile to (hetero)sexual intercourse;
> b. unresponsive to (male) sexual advances or stimuli;
> c. not able to have an orgasm in (hetero)sexual intercourse.

As you may have guessed, I had to add the prefix *hetero-* to the word *sexual* and the adjective *male* to "sexual advances or stimuli," because these obvious elements were somehow omitted from the definition of *frigid*. (This oversight was not corrected in the 1987 edition.) The obvious goal of this linguistic "creativity" on the part of the sexologists was to establish heterosexuality as a "natural instinct" in women's collective psyche. Not coincidentally, a woman labeled "frigid" was also likely to be called a "latent" Lesbian. Notice that all three of the meanings of *frigid* assign responsibility, *agency*, to the woman so-named. *She* is "indifferent," "hostile," "unresponsive," and "not able to have an orgasm." *She* is at fault, hence culpable, blameworthy, and *guilty*. By accepting this male description of themselves, women accepted the idea that their natural feelings for other women were flawed, pathological.

Does anyone believe that the rise of "psychotherapy," Freud's election to "great thinker" status, and the fact that so many of his "patients" were women are historical coincidences? (I don't believe in "accidents.") Patriarchal labels require patriarchal definitions. Men create labels and definitions that legitimate and perpetuate male perceptions as "consensus reality." Men created the labels and the categories *Lesbian* and *frigid woman*, along with their alleged pathologies, as part of their war against the desire of nineteenth-century women to be free of male control, to live beyond the burden of male attention. Now, academic Feminists have "rediscovered" Freud, via Lacan. As a consequence, yet another generation of young women will struggle with their "pre-Oedipal" burden.

The names that survive, as well as those that are "lost," reveal the androcentrism of historical "significance": the Age of Industrialization, the Civil War Era, the Roaring Twenties, the Kennedy Era, the Viet Nam Era (or "Experience," as Jeanne Kirkpatrick once described it), the Computer Age, Information Age, and so on. One thing becomes immediately obvious when these "stages" are juxtaposed:

They all label arbitrary chunks of time according to male perceptions of which events, and which white men, are "historically" significant. These are the "Ages of Men." The process of describing history as a series of male deeds also successfully *erases* the historical significance of women (and blacks, and native Americans, and everybody but white men). Where, for example, is "Rosie the Riveter" in World War II descriptions? Patriarchal histories are fabulous reports of male undertakings; patriarchal historians are *undertakers* whose task it is to bury any evidence of women's activities and concerns. The history of men's "exploits," their "heroic deeds," is nothing but a lengthy enumeration of voracious exploitation. Men exploit the earth and its resources, including women, with apparent indifference to the consequences of their exploitation. Even eras labeled for male evil hide the exact nature of the evil-doing. The "McCarthy Era" is a meaningless label if one doesn't know what Joseph McCarthy did, and that descriptions of his undertakings focus on his anti-Communist hunts and ignore his equally vicious persecution of queers. I don't think I exaggerate when I say that patriarchal histories are elaborate *confabulations*, the process by which men 'replace fact with fantasy in memory', while they simultaneously *undertake* both the redescription of the meaning of women's lives and the erasure of women's work. Our lives disappear from memory, shoved aside by patriarchal necessity.

What is obvious is that it is Radical Feminists—and our discomforting analyses of women's oppression—whom women, as well as men, wish dead. Reform Feminism, renamed "Social Feminism," which accepts without question patriarchal descriptions of reality, is a caricature placed stage center, a hand puppet mouthing the words its master supplies. It is Reform Feminism, the assimilationist brand of Feminism, that is really dead, because it asks permission to live in the master's house as a *Penthouse* Pet. Reform Feminists have gotten what they wanted, and, having been welcomed into the bosom of patriarchy, they can revel in their latest Revlon masks.

I, for one, have no plans to pack up my Feminist politics and move into the refurbished patriarchal nest, no matter how much they redecorate it, no matter how bright and colorful the feathers are that line it. I believe all Feminists must resist again, and again, and yet again, all attempts to lure us back to the patriarchal roost, regardless of its apparent comfort and security. The family is not a "love-nest" in which women and children can safely snuggle.

Whatever the source of each attempt to domesticate us—whether it's the Darwinian, biological assertions of a Robin Fox or a George Gilder that women have some sex-specific "need" to continue our still-unsuccessful attempts to civilize men, or the equally deterministic assertion that women *qua* women are birthed carrying some genetic obligation to serve the male of the species—we must resist with all the strength, reason, and self-protection we can muster. Our efforts may fail, but we will certainly be suppressed if we remain silent or allow ourselves to be silenced.

I, for one, will *choose* the form my oppression takes. As a Lesbian, I have choices. I can elect to deny myself, deny my deep and lasting feelings for other women, and, yes, marry a man. I could choose that, and many Lesbians do, in fact, elect to live as though they were heterosexuals until the subterfuge and pretense is more painful than choosing themselves. They are as susceptible as any other woman to the lie that heterosexuality and marriage to a man are "safe." So they choose what they believe to be the "safe" way out of their dilemma. Their lives, such as they are, are one form of oppression.

Instead, I choose to enjoy and celebrate my Lesbian self—to live as an outcast without legal or civil rights, to live with scorn, denial, rejection and the threat of physical violence, to know that there is no place in this society where my stubbornness will be respected or rewarded. Either choice places Lesbians at the mercy of our oppressors, but my choice rejects the categories and assumptions of the "rightness"—righteousness—of my oppressors' justifications, and insures a living space more secure and safer than most heterosexual women can expect.

Epilogue

I was nauseated while I wrote this paper—queasy, sick to my stomach—but I didn't know why until I realized how precisely Hewlett's analysis of women's poverty, and the multitude of lies that supports it, replicated my own experience as an incest survivor.

I remember very clearly the day I decided to tell my mother that her new husband, my stepfather, had tried to rape me while she was hospitalized for a hysterectomy. It was a Sunday afternoon. The two of them were sitting on the couch, drinking. I stood in the hall doorway, on the opposite side of the living room. I tried to articulate what had occurred, fumbled for the words that would communicate to her my shock, betrayal, fear, and discomfort with this man she had brought into our lives.

As soon as he realized what I was trying to tell my mother, my stepfather arose and went off to the kitchen, where he hid while my mother silenced my pain by telling me that I'd "imagined" the whole thing, that I'd "misinterpreted" some innocent gesture on my stepfather's part, that, really, "nothing had happened."

Hewlett, in her role as "mother" and defender of the "family," has told Feminists that our perceptions are all wrong, mistaken, untrue. While the men she protects lurk out of sight, pretending innocence, she has done their dirty work for them, and her book is the weapon with which she attempted to dismember the integrity of women's liberation. But I survived the gaslighting of my perceptions, what I knew to be true, and most Feminists will survive Hewlett's destructive endeavors.

I know this because even mainstream Feminists have rejected Hewlett's analysis. It seems to me that we need to make explicit our choices, Lesbian choices, in the event that Hewlett's tide continues to roll her way. (I see many indications that it will.) Welcome to the "post-Feminist," "post-structuralist," "post-modern" age. Lesbians must see to our own self-interest, because that's what politics is all about: How do we identify what is in our own best interest?

Unfortunately, Lesbians seem unable to work coherently as a self-identified group on our own behalf, to mobilize ourselves in order to secure and defend even the most essential social guarantees. We have entered into coalitions with gaymen and hetero women, but have, so far, obtained little in return for our work on their behalf. Because we have yet to identify what might be our own self-interests, without the larger framework provided by Radical Feminist analysis—in which male violence, rape, incest, and women's right to control our bodies are identified as major issues—political Lesbians cannot stand alone.

Radical Feminism clearly serves *our* best interests. It affirms a gynecentric awareness, declares our right to autonomy from men and their self-interest, prioritizes Lesbians, and emphasizes the need for divesting our minds of the self-hatred taught to us by a male supremacist society. If what I believe is true, then Lesbians will have to be willing to take an even stronger stand on behalf of Radical Feminism than we might have in the past and work, in our own best interest, to derail this latest attempt to idealize and subsidize patriarchal definitions of what it means to be a woman. It's that, or pack our tents.

Endnote

1. For a detailed analysis of the connection between the labels *Lesbian* and *frigid* and how the sexologists of the late nineteenth- and early twentieth-centuries used them to suppress Lesbianism and coerce women into heterosexuality, see Sheila Jeffreys' *Anticlimax* (London: The Women's Press, 1990).

References

Adelman, Marcy. 1986. *Long Time Passing: Lives of Older Lesbians*. Boston: Alyson Publications.

Allen, Jeffner. 1990. *Lesbian Philosophies and Cultures*. Albany, New York: SUNY Press.

Anderson, Bonnie S., and Judith P. Zinsser. 1988. *A History of Their Own*, vol. 1. New York: Harper & Row.

Arnold, June. 1973. *The Cook and the Carpenter*. Plainfield, VT: Daughters, Inc.

Bev Jo, Linda Strega, and Ruston. 1990. *Dykes-Loving-Dykes*. Oakland, California: published by the authors.

Brody, Rachel. 1984. "Butch/Femme: Knowing Myself and Trusting in Desire," *Common Lives/Lesbian Lives* 11 (Spring), 56-60.

Brown, Jan. 1990. "Sex, Lies, and Penetration: A Butch Finally 'Fesses Up," *OutLook* 7 (Winter), 30-34.

Brossard, Nicole. 1986. *Lovhers*, trans. Barbara Godard. Montreal: Guernica.

Bulkin, Elly. 1980a. "An Old Dyke's Tale: An Interview with Doris Lunden," *Conditions* 6: 26-44.

_____. 1980b. "Racism and Writing: Some Implications for White Lesbian Critics," *Sinister Wisdom* 13 (Spring), 3-22.

_____. 1981. "Letter," *Sinister Wisdom* 16 (Spring), 94.

Califia, Pat. 1980. *Sapphistry: The Book of Lesbian Sexuality*. Tallahassee: Naiad Press.

Card, Claudia. 1989. "Defusing the Bomb: Lesbian Ethics and Horizontal Violence," *Lesbian Ethics* 3, 3 (Summer), 91-100.

Carr, Virginia Spencer. 1975. *The Lonely Hunter: A Biography of Carson McCullers*. New York: Doubleday/Anchor.

Cavin, Susan. 1985. *Lesbian Origins*. San Francisco: Ism Press.

Corinne, Tee. 1984. *Women Who Loved Women*. n.p.: Pearlchild.

Craigin, Elisabeth. 1937. *Either is Love*. New York: Harcourt, Brace.

Crane, Mary. 1986. Response to Linda Strega, in "Letters," *Lesbian Ethics* 2, 1 (Spring), 102-3.

Crompton, Louis. 1980/81. "The Myth of Lesbian Impunity: Capital Laws from 1270 to 1791," *Journal of Homosexuality* 6, 1/2 (Fall/Winter), 11-25.

Daly, Mary. [1968] 1978. *The Church and the Second Sex*. Boston: Beacon Press.

_____. 1978. *Gyn/Ecology: The Metaethics of Radical Feminism*. Boston: Beacon Press.

_____. 1984. *Pure Lust*. Boston: Beacon Press.

Delacoste, Fréderique, and Felice Newman. 1981. *Fight Back!: Feminist Resistance to Male Violence*. Minneapolis: Cleis Press.

Doughty, Frances. 1982. "Lesbian Biography, Biography of Lesbians," *Lesbian Studies: Present and Future*, ed. Margaret Cruikshank. Old Westbury, New York: The Feminist Press, 115-121.

Downing, Christine. 1991. *Myths and Mysteries of Same-Sex Love*. New York: Continuum.

Dreher, Sarah. 1991. "Behind the Scenes at the Lesbian/Gay Pride Marches," *Lesbian Outlook* 1 (August), 1-4.

Dworkin, Andrea. 1986. *Ice and Fire*. New York: Weidenfeld and Nicolson.

Echols, Alice. 1983. "The New Feminism of Yin and Yang," in *Powers of Desire: The Politics of Sexuality*, eds. Ann Snitow, Christine Stansell, and Sharon Thompson. Boston: Monthly Review Press, 438-59.

Ellis, Havelock. [1897] 1927. *Studies in the Psychology of Sex*, vol. 2 of *Sexual Inversion*. Philadelphia: F. A. Davis.

Engelbrecht, Penelope. 1990. "'Lifting Belly is a Language': The Postmodern Lesbian Subject," *Feminist Studies* 16, 1 (Spring), 85-114.

Faderman, Lillian. 1981. *Surpassing the Love of Men: Romantic Friendship and Love Between Women from the Renaissance to the Present*. New York: William Morrow.

_____. 1982. "Who Hid Lesbian History?," *Lesbian Studies: Present and Future*, ed. Margaret Cruikshank. Old Westbury: The Feminist Press, 115-121.

_____. 1991. *Odd Girls and Twilight Lovers: A History of Lesbian Life in Twentieth-Century America*. New York: Columbia UP.

_____, and Brigitte Ericksson. 1980. *Lesbian Feminism in Turn-of-the-Century Germany*. Tallahassee: Naiad Press.

Ferguson, Ann. 1982. "Patriarchy, Sexual Identity and the Sexual Revolution," *Feminist Theory: A Critique of Ideology*, eds. Nannerl O. Keohane, Michelle Z. Rosaldo, and Barbara C. Gelpi. Chicago: U. of Chicago Press, 147-161.

_____. 1990. "Is There a Lesbian Culture?," *Lesbian Philosophies and Cultures*, ed. Jeffner Allen. Albany: SUNY Press, 63-88.

Fortier, Alyse. 1987. "Woman: Century 21," *The Harmonist* 16-19; 40-41.

Foster, Jeannette. [1956] 1975. *Sex Variant Women in Literature*. Baltimore: Diana Press.

Foucault, Michel. 1978. *The History of Sexuality*, vol. 1, trans. Robert Hurley. New York: Vintage Books.

Frye, Marilyn. 1980. Review of *The Coming Out Stories, Sinister Wisdom* 14 (Summer), 97-98.

_____. 1983. "To Be and Be Seen: The Politics of Reality," *The Politics of Reality*. Freedom, California: The Crossing Press, 152-174.

_____. 1988. "Lesbian 'Sex'," *Sinister Wisdom* 35 (Summer/Fall), 46-54.

_____. 1990. "Do You Have to be a Lesbian to be a Feminist?" *off our backs* xx, 8 (August/September), 21-23.

Gaines, James R. 1987. "The Man Who Shot Lennon," *People* 27, 8 (February 23), 58-59; 65-73.

Grahn, Judy. 1971. *Edward the Dyke and Other Poems*. Oakland, California: The Women's Press Collective.

Grimard-Leduc, Micheline. 1988. "The Mind-Drifting Islands," in *For Lesbians Only*, eds. Sarah Lucia Hoagland and Julia Penelope. London: Onlywomen Press, 489-500.

Grumbach, Doris. 1984. *The Ladies*. New York: Ballantine.

Guide to Gracious Lesbian Living. 1989. Montreal: Lilith Publications,

van Gulik, Robert H. 1961. *Sexual Life in Ancient China*. Leiden: E. J. Brill.

Hall, Radclyffe. [1928] 1966. *The Well of Loneliness*. New York: Pocket Books.

Heilbrun, Carolyn. 1973. *Toward a Recognition of Androgyny*. New York: Alfred Knopf.

Herzer, Manfred. 1985. "Kertbeny and the Nameless Love," *Journal of Homosexuality* 12:1-26.

Hewlett, Sylvia Ann. 1986. *A Lesser Life: The Myth of Women's Liberation in America*. New York: Warner Books.

Hoagland, Sarah Lucia. 1988. *Lesbian Ethics: Toward New Value*. Palo Alto: Institute of Lesbian Studies.

Jay, Karla. 1975. "The Spirit Is Liberationist but the Flesh Is. . ., You Can't Always Get Into Bed With Your Dogma," in *After You're Out: Personal Experiences of Gay Men and Lesbian Women*, eds. Karla Jay and Allen Young. New York: Links Books, 211-14.

_____. 1988. *The Amazon and the Page: Natalie Clifford Barney and Renée Vivien*. Bloomington: Indiana UP.

_____, and Joanne Glasgow. 1990. *Lesbian Texts and Contexts*. New York: New York UP.

Jeffreys, Sheila. 1985. *The Spinster and Her Enemies: Feminism and Sexuality 1880-1930*. Oxon: Pandora.

_____. 1986. "Sado-Masochism: The Erotic Cult of Fascism," *Lesbian Ethics* 2, 1 (Spring), 65-82.

_____. 1990. *Anticlimax: A Feminist Perspective on the Sexual*

Revolution. London: The Women's Press.

_____. 1989. "Does It Matter if They Did It?," *Not a Passing Phase: Reclaiming Lesbians in History 1840-1985*. London: The Women's Press, 19-28.

Johnson, Sonia. 1989. *Wildfire: Igniting the She/volution*. Albuquerque, NM: Wildfire Books.

Kitzinger, Celia. 1987. *The Social Construction of Lesbianism*. London: Sage Publications.

Lakoff, G. and M. Johnson. *The Metaphors We Live By*. Chicago: U. of Chicago Press, 1980.

de Lauretis, Teresa. 1990. "Eccentric Subjects: Feminist Theory and Historical Consciousness," *Feminist Studies* 16, 1 (Spring), 115-150.

Lauritsen, John, and David Thorstad. 1974. *The Early Homosexual Rights Movement (1864-1935)*. New York: The Times Change Press.

Lesbian Connection 8, 2 (September/October, 1985).

Lesbian Connection 9, 1 (July/August, 1986), 17.

Lesbian Connection 13, 5 (March/April, 1991), 5.

Lesbian Connection 13, 6 (May/June, 1991), 12-13.

Lobel, Kerry, ed. 1986. *Naming the Violence: Speaking Out about Lesbian Battering*. Seattle: The Seal Press.

Lorde, Audre. 1978. *Uses of the Erotic: The Erotic as Power*. Brooklyn: Out & Out Books.

Loulan, JoAnn. 1984. *Lesbian Sex*. San Francisco: Spinsters Ink.

MacKinnon, Catharine A. 1989. *Toward a Feminist Theory of the State*. Cambridge, Massachusetts: Harvard UP.

Mariedaughter, Paula. 1986. "Too Butch for Straights, Too Femme for Dykes," *Lesbian Ethics* 2, 1 (Spring), 96-100.

Martin, Del, and Phyllis Lyon. 1972. *Lesbian/Woman*. New York: Bantam.

Mavor, Elizabeth. 1984. *A Year in the Life of the Ladies of Llangollen*. New York: Penguin.

Mayron, Michele. 1987. "Andrea Dworkin," *Penthouse* 18, 8 (April), 50-52; 56; 70; 72.

Moraga, Cherríe. and Amber Hollibaugh. 1983. "What We're Rollin Around in Bed With: Sexual Silences in Feminism," in *Powers of Desire: The Politics of Sexuality*, eds. Ann Snitow, Christine Stansell, and Sharon Thompson. Boston: Monthly Review Press.

Morgan, Robin. 1970. *Sisterhood is Powerful*. New York: Vintage.

Murphy, Marilyn. 1991. *Are You Girls Traveling Alone?: Adventures in Lesbianic Logic*. Los Angeles: Clothespin Fever Press.

Mushroom, Merril. 1983. "Confessions of a Butch Dyke," *Common Lives/Lesbian Lives* 9 (Fall), 39-45.

Neath, Jeanne F. 1987. "Let's Discuss Dyke S/M and Quit the Name Calling: A

Response to Sheila Jeffreys," *Lesbian Ethics* 2, 3 (Summer), 95-99.

Nestle, Joan. 1981. "Butch/Fem Relationships: Sexual Courage in the 1950s," *Heresies: The Sex Issue* 12, 3: 21-24.

_____. 1984. "The Fem Question," in *Pleasure and Danger: Exploring Female Sexuality*, ed. Carol Vance. Boston: Routledge and Kegan Paul.

_____. 1987. *A Restricted Country*. Ithaca, New York: Firebrand Books.

Penelope, Julia (Stanley). 1978. "Lesbian Separatism: The Linguistic and Social Sources of Separatist Politics," in *The Gay Academic*, ed. Louie Crew. Palm Spring, California: ETC Publications, 121-131.

_____. 1980a. "And now for the hard questions. . .," *Sinister Wisdom* 15 (Fall), 99-104.

_____. 1980b. "Mystery and Monster: The Lesbian in Heterosexual Fantasies," *Sinister Wisdom* 15 (Fall), 76-91.

_____. 1990. *Speaking Freely: Unlearning the Lies of the Fathers' Tongues*. Elmsford, New York: Pergamon Press.

_____, and Susan J. Wolfe. 1989. *The Original Coming Out Stories*, 2nd edition. Freedom, California: The Crossing Press. (Originally published as *The Coming Out Stories* by Persephone Press in 1980.)

Phelan, Shane. 1989. *Identity Politics: Lesbian Feminism and the Limits of Community*. Philadelphia: Temple UP.

Reddy, Michael. 1979. "The Conduit Metaphor—A Case of Frame Conflict," *Metaphor and Thought*, ed. Andrew Ortony. Cambridge: Cambridge UP, 284-324.

Rich, Adrienne. 1976. *Of Woman Born: Motherhood as Experience and Institution*. New York: W. W. Norton.

_____. 1980. "Response," *Sinister Wisdom* 14 (Summer), 104-105.

Roberts, JR. 1980. "'leude behauior each with other vpon a bed': The Case of Sarah Norman and Mary Hammond," *Sinister Wisdom* 14 (Summer), 57-62.

_____. 1982. "Black Lesbians Before 1970: A Bibliographical Essay," *Lesbian Studies: Present and Future*, ed. Margaret Cruikshank. Old Westbury, New York: The Feminist Press, 103-109.

Russ, Joanna. [1981] 1985. "Power and Helplessness in the Women's Movement," in *Magic Mommas and Trembling Sisters*. Trumansburg, New York: The Crossing Press, 43-54; originally published in *Sinister Wisdom* 18 (Fall), 49-56.

Samois. 1981. *Coming to Power*. Boston: Alyson Publications.

Schwarz, Judith. 1979. "*Yellow Clover*: Katharine Lee Bates and Katharine Coman," *Frontiers* IV, 1: 59-67.

_____. 1982. *Radical Feminists of Heterodoxy: Greenwich Village 1912-1940*. Lebanon, New Hampshire: New Victoria Publishers.

Sisley, Dr. Emily L., and Bertha Harris. 1977. *The Joy of Lesbian Sex*. New York: Simon and Schuster.

Sojourner, Sabrina. 1991. "Making Different Choices," *Sojourner* 16, 6 (February), 9.

Steakley, James D. 1975. *The Homosexual Emancipation Movement in Germany.* New York: Arno Press.

Stephenson, June. 1986. *Women's Roots, Status and Achievements in Western Civilization.* Napa, California: Diemer, Smith Publishing Co.

Strega, Linda. 1985. "The Big Sell-Out: Lesbian Femininity," *Lesbian Ethics* 1, 3 (Fall), 73-84.

Wittig, Monique. 1988. "One is Not Born a Woman," in *For Lesbians Only*, eds. Sarah Lucia Hoagland and Julia Penelope. London: Onlywomen Press, 439-48.

Woolston, Florence Guy. [1919] 1982. ". . .Marriage Customs and Taboo among the Early Heterodities. . .," Appendix B in *Radical Feminists of Heterodoxy, Greenwich Village 1912-1940* by Judith Schwarz. Lebanon, New Hampshire: New Victoria Publishers, 95-96.

Zimmerman, Bonnie. 1981. "What Has Never Been: An Overview of Lesbian Feminist Criticism," *Feminist Studies* 7, 3: 451-475.

_____. 1990. *The Safe Sea of Women.* Boston: Beacon Press.

Zita, Jacqueline. 1987. "'The Sex Question' and Socialist Feminism," *Sinister Wisdom* 31 (Winter), 120-127.